Gentle Leading and Neurodivergence

Moving beyond awareness campaigns, this book redefines leadership through emotional regulation, neuroscience, and radical inclusion, and offers a blueprint for creating psychologically safe environments where neurodivergent talent can thrive.

With growing calls for leadership that goes beyond inclusive to transformative, leaders are often expected to build psychological safety, support cognitive diversity, and regulate their own emotions—often without a roadmap. Now that roadmap is here, filled with practical tools to replace micromanagement with trust, build emotionally regulated communication systems, and leverage neurodivergent strengths in teams. The book includes real-world case studies, self-assessments, printable toolkits, the GENTLE™ Framework, and more, all designed to transform leadership from control to empowerment and burnout to resilience.

Suitable for corporate and startup leaders, Human Resources and Diversity, Equity, and Inclusion professionals, executive coaches, and neurodivergent entrepreneurs, this book is equally valuable for educators, organizational psychologists, and parents of neurodivergent adults entering the workforce.

Alexandra Robuste is the creator of Gentle Leading, a needs-based, emotionally intelligent leadership approach designed to replace micromanagement with empowerment and burnout with resilience. She is the founder of Apex Growth Academy and brings nearly 20 years of experience as a business growth architect across omnichannel sales and marketing to her consulting work.

Gentle Leading and Neurodivergence

Inclusive Leadership Strategies for Embracing Neurodiversity and Driving Workplace Innovation

Alexandra Robuste

Routledge
Taylor & Francis Group
NEW YORK AND LONDON

Designed cover image: Getty

First published 2026
by Routledge
605 Third Avenue, New York, NY 10158

and by Routledge
4 Park Square, Milton Park, Abingdon, Oxon, OX14 4RN

Routledge is an imprint of the Taylor & Francis Group, an informa business

ISBN: 9781041158547 (hbk)
ISBN: 9781041158530 (pbk)
ISBN: 9781003681540 (ebk)

DOI: 10.4324/9781003681540

Typeset in Sabon
by Deanta Global Publishing Services, Chennai, India

Contents

Figures

Tables

Acknowledgments and Intentions

This book wouldn't exist without the people who knowingly shaped, challenged, and propelled me into the leader—and the person—I am today.

To my sons, Yannick, Noah, and Luc—you handed me the ultimate crash course in leadership long before I even realized it. You taught me that leadership is about trust, emotional regulation, and truly understanding human needs. Without you, Gentle Leading would never have been born. To the mentors and misleaders alike—thank you for the blueprint and the warning signs. Some of the most enduring lessons come wrapped in tension. To the teams I've had the privilege to lead: your courage, resistance, and breakthroughs are written into these pages. Leadership is never a solo act. And to the person who gave me the space to turn post-its and patterns into paragraphs—thank you. Every sentence owes you quiet.

Introduction

Gentle Leading: The Neurodivergent Expansion

This book grew out of a deepening of the original inquiry—and from the undeniable need to expand the conversation.

It is structured in three parts, each building upon the last to translate lived experience into actionable leadership design.

Part I lays the conceptual groundwork. It introduces neurodivergence not as a deficit, but as a distinct cognitive dialect—one often misread, underrecognized, or forced into translation. This section explores how neurodivergent expression intersects with workplace systems, outlining why inclusion efforts often fall short when they fail to account for structural misunderstanding. It also delves into coping and masking—not just as personal strategies, but as systemic responses to unfit environments, and the cumulative toll they take on sustainability and psychological clarity.

Part II zooms in. It examines nine neurodivergent profiles with the greatest relevance in leadership contexts—from ADHD to Autism, Dyslexia to Giftedness—each explored through their patterns of expression, friction points, masking dynamics, and structural needs. This is followed by a brief but necessary overview of supplementary profiles like PTSD, bipolarity, NVLD, or auditory processing challenges—many of which fall through the cracks of traditional inclusion models but still shape leadership realities in profound ways.

Part III turns to application. It addresses how leaders can build and sustain neurodiverse teams—including what it means when neurodivergence is not just present within the team, but also within the leader themselves. Particular focus is given to mixed or opposing profiles (e.g., ADHD and High Sensitivity) and the unique negotiations that arise when divergent regulation patterns coexist. A dedicated section on nervous system stewardship underscores why sustainable leadership begins with regulation, not resilience—and why this matters for everyone, not just the neurodivergent. The final chapter explores neuroleadership through the lens of neurochemistry—examining how dopamine, serotonin, and other biochemical systems influence clarity, courage, motivation, and interpersonal coherence.

It became increasingly clear: needs-based leadership doesn't just reduce micromanagement. It improves retention, cultivates high-performing teams, and meaningfully reduces burnout and overfunctioning—especially for neurodivergent individuals. Why? Because it centers the regulation of the nervous system, not just organizational outcomes.

Neurodivergence was always part of the vision. Any leadership model that claims to be inclusive must reflect the full range of how people think, feel, and function. But truly serving the one in five people who are neurodivergent—and many more who remain undiagnosed—requires more than a chapter. It requires a shift. This is where needs-based leadership meets the lived experience of sensory overload, executive function challenges, masking, and invisible exhaustion. It's where psychological safety moves beyond theory and becomes a lifeline.

This book is written for two audiences—though they often overlap:

- Neurodivergent leaders who want to lead without masking, burning out, or contorting themselves into someone they're not.
- And those in leadership roles who want to meaningfully support neurodivergent team members—not just through policy, but through presence, structure, and everyday interaction.

Because when we build leadership around cognitive diversity, everyone benefits. Communication becomes clearer. Workflows more humane. Burnout less frequent. Innovation more natural. This is not a call for special treatment. It's a long-overdue call to treat difference as part of the design.

Welcome to the branch of Gentle Leading™ that dares to go deeper—into brains wired differently and workplaces built too narrowly. We're not adding complexity for its own sake. We're adding clarity where it's been missing. And in doing so, we're expanding what leadership can be—for all of us.

Let's begin.

Alexandra Robuste

Part I

Rethinking Leadership through a Neurodivergent Lens

Foundations for Understanding Divergence, Identity, and Structural Load

Chapter 1

Neurodivergence in Leadership

The Invisible Baseline and How Leadership Systems Undermine Neurodivergent Potential

1.1 The Invisible Baseline

How workplaces were built.

Standard indoor climate settings were calibrated in the 1960s to match the resting metabolic rate of a 40-year-old man—an assumption that still informs building codes and office environments today (Kingma & van Marken Lichtenbelt, 2015). This is one reason why many women—and others with lower baseline metabolic rates—report discomfort or persistent cold in shared workspaces.

Despite estimates that one in five people are neurodivergent (Maenner et al., 2020), most professional environments—from recruitment to leadership development—are still calibrated to neurotypical norms.

It challenges the idea that there is a normal way to think, learn, or behave.

These design choices may appear neutral, but they embed an unspoken norm. When foundational systems are built around a narrow standard, exclusion is not necessarily intentional—but it becomes structurally inevitable. And many of these defaults remain unchanged. Naming this difference is the first step toward addressing it.

When we don't question the invisible baseline, we risk mistaking exclusion for excellence—and calling neurotypicality a prerequisite for leadership. This book invites a different lens (Figure 1.1).

1.2 Defining Neurodivergence

From diagnostic labels to cognitive variation as a human constant.

Neurodivergence refers to naturally occurring variations in cognitive functioning. The term was coined by sociologist Judy Singer in the late 1990s to move beyond clinical deficit language and to frame cognitive diversity as a natural part of the human spectrum. According to the National Sym-

DOI: 10.4324/9781003681540-2

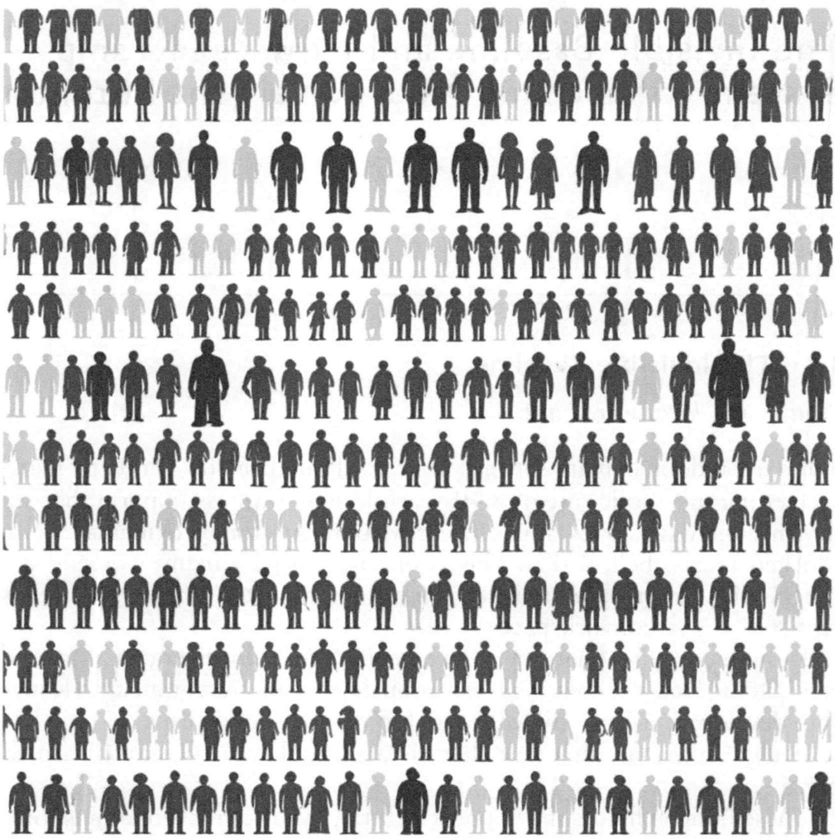

Figure 1.1 Estimated prevalence of neurodivergence. Approximately 15–20% of the global population is estimated to be neurodivergent (Baumer & Frueh, 2021; CDC, 2023).

posium on Neurodiversity (Syracuse University, 2011), neurodivergence describes "neurological variation that is recognized and respected as any other human variation."

Commonly recognized profiles include ADHD, autism, dyslexia, dyscalculia, dyspraxia, giftedness, high sensitivity (HSP), Tourette Syndrome, nonverbal learning disorder (NVLD), auditory processing disorder (APD), and, in some frameworks, obsessive-compulsive traits (OCD). Although traditionally classified as a clinical disorder, OCD traits—when not associated with distress—are increasingly understood as cognitive divergence (Walker, 2021).

Increasingly, this list is expanding to include profiles shaped by neurological variation or atypical cognitive pacing more broadly—such as epilepsy-related processing patterns, post-traumatic cognitive shifts (e.g., in complex PTSD), and mood-based divergence (e.g., bipolar spectrum conditions)—especially when these manifest as enduring differences in perception, regulation, or systemic sensemaking (Martínez-Arán et al., 2004).

While individual prevalence estimates—such as ~20% for high sensitivity (HSP), 5–8% for ADHD, or ~10% for dyslexia—are typically reported separately, they point to an important statistical reality: neurodivergent traits do not occur in isolation. Many individuals experience overlapping expressions—sometimes referred to as mixed or multiplex neurodivergence—involving sensory sensitivity, executive function variability, or divergent processing styles that span multiple profiles.

These overlaps complicate exact prevalence estimates. Yet, if we acknowledge that not all neurodivergent traits co-occur—and that some profiles affect distinct subgroups—then a purely overlapping model likely underestimates the actual reach of neurodivergence. Even without full additive calculation, the coexistence of multiple high-prevalence traits strongly suggests that the overall share of the population affected by neurodivergent cognition exceeds the commonly cited 15–20% range (Figure 1.2).

Thus, estimates from Baumer and Frueh (2021) and the CDC (2023) are best understood as conservative baselines—not accounting for subclinical expression, underdiagnosis, or cumulative patterns. This is not a niche.

Neurodivergent profiles also show notable familial clustering. Research across multiple conditions—including ADHD, autism, dyslexia, and Tourette Syndrome—indicates a strong heritable component, with first-degree relatives frequently exhibiting related traits or overlapping patterns of cognitive divergence (Faraone et al., 2005; Ronald et al., 2006). While genetic transmission does not follow a simple Mendelian pattern, familial prevalence data point to polygenic inheritance and shared environmental factors that influence expression. Many neurodivergent adults report recognizing similar traits in parents, siblings, or children—often retrospectively, once language or diagnostic access is available. This familial pattern underscores two key realities: first, that neurodivergence is rarely isolated to individuals; and second, that its recognition often emerges within intergenerational narratives, shaped as much by social framing and access to diagnosis as by biology itself.

1.3 Structural Misfit: When Systems Penalize Cognitive Difference

Neurodivergent underperformance is rarely about capacity—but about chronic misalignment with norm-based leadership environments.

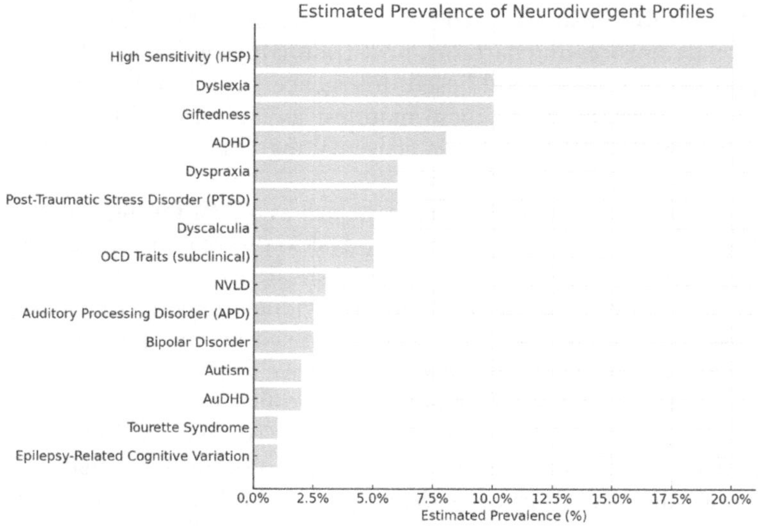

Figure 1.2 Epidemiological estimates of cognitive diversity. It presents estimated prevalence ranges for selected neurodivergent profiles, based on epidemiological and psychological research. While exact rates vary by region and criteria, the chart underscores the cognitive heterogeneity within modern workforces. Because many profiles co-occur, these figures are not additive—but collectively highlight how a substantial share of the population processes, relates, and leads differently. To avoid citation overload, one core source is referenced here (Gillberg, 2010); detailed references appear in the respective chapters.

Contemporary leadership structures are still largely shaped by implicit neurotypical norms—emphasizing linear problem-solving, real-time responsiveness, constant multitasking, and seamless social performance (Austin & Pisano, 2017). These environments often reward behavioral predictability over cognitive diversity, verbal fluency over reflective depth, and speed over strategic integration. For neurodivergent professionals, this can create a fundamental mismatch between institutional expectations and individual processing profiles—leading to frequent misinterpretation of capacity, communication, or intent.

Depending on one's position, this misalignment takes different forms. Neurodivergent leaders may expend invisible effort to adapt their leadership to dominant norms, while those managing neurodivergent team members must learn to recognize strength beyond conventional cues. Even among peers, collaboration across cognitive styles requires attunement to differing rhythms of expression, planning, and engagement.

If neurotypicality is the native cognitive language of the workplace, neurodivergent minds often operate in dialects that remain untranslated. The insights are present, the value real—but without systemic scaffolding, they are filtered out through noise, fatigue, or misinterpretation.

This mismatch is not limited to the workplace. It is reinforced through educational, social, and familial systems that reward norm conformity. Over time, these systems do not merely overlook neurodivergent potential—they suppress it by conflating difference with deficiency.

1.4 Intersectionality Matters: Neurodivergence Is Never Context-Free

Neurodivergence does not unfold uniformly—it is mediated by context, identity, and institutional response.

Cognitive traits are not interpreted in isolation. They are rendered meaningful—or problematic—through the lens of sociocultural norms. Diagnostic pathways, support systems, and leadership opportunities are all shaped by intersecting factors that position individuals differently within the same structures.

Gendered expectations also shape diagnostic and workplace outcomes. Neurodivergent men who express sensory sensitivity or emotional intensity often face dismissal or ridicule, as these traits conflict with dominant masculinity norms (Connell & Messerschmidt 2005). A man who requests reduced sensory input or time to decompress may be perceived as fragile or insufficiently resilient—traits rarely read as legitimate needs in male professionals.

Women with ADHD or autism, for example, are frequently underdiagnosed—not due to an absence of traits, but because these are masked through culturally reinforced behaviors such as compliance, empathy, or perfectionism (Haney, 2016; Kreiser & White, 2014).

A woman who struggles with attention or executive function may overcompensate through perfectionism or emotional labor—efforts often misread as competence rather than coping.

Racialized bias compounds disparities in the recognition and support of neurodivergence.

Studies show that Black, Brown, and Indigenous students who display neurodivergent traits are significantly more likely to be disciplined or pathologized than assessed or accommodated (Annamma et al., 2016). These early misreadings often carry into adulthood, limiting access to diagnosis, support, and leadership development.

Cultural stigma plays a critical role in how neurodivergent traits are perceived and addressed. In some communities, mental health remains a taboo subject; in others, diagnostic services may be inaccessible, under-resourced, or met with justified mistrust (Shim & Compton, 2018; Liao & Weng, 2018). These structural and cultural barriers contribute to delayed or missed diagnoses—particularly among women, BIPOC professionals, and immigrants. As a result, many receive diagnoses only after chronic workplace misalignment, burnout, or exclusion prompt deeper investigation into underlying cognitive differences (Kreiser & White, 2014; Ahmedani, 2011).

1.5 Toward Inclusive Leadership Architecture: Beyond Retrofitting Difference

What was designed can be redesigned.

Despite the increased visibility of DEI initiatives, neurodivergence remains conceptually marginalized and structurally underintegrated. It is too often framed narrowly—as a question of individual accommodation—rather than addressed as a core dimension of leadership design. This limited framing contributes to persistent misdiagnoses of disengagement, chronic overextension in coping strategies, and the erosion of both trust and talent across organizational levels.

The potential for transformation is substantial—especially when leadership frameworks are deliberately redesigned to reflect differences in regulation, processing, and relational rhythm. When inclusion is embedded not as a rhetorical gesture but as operational logic, it strengthens collective resilience, enhances decision-making, and fosters psychological safety.

Systemic incongruence often manifests not through overt dysfunction but through emotional volatility, executive fatigue, interpersonal friction, and attrition—patterns too often misread as personal inadequacy.

To meaningfully address this disconnect, it is essential not only to redesign leadership structures, but also to foster team-wide awareness and training around neurodivergent dynamics—transforming inclusion from an individual accommodation into a shared operational literacy.

A leadership model centered on clarity, autonomy, and needs-responsive design does not merely support neurodivergent individuals but strengthens entire teams. It prompts a reassessment of which behaviors are labeled functional, which capacities are valorized, and which patterns of engagement are resourced.

This chapter interrogates the limitations of conventional leadership paradigms and highlights leverage points for systemic redesign. The goal is not to normalize individual adaptation to narrow standards, but to reimagine leadership architectures that reflect the cognitive and affective diversity already present within today's workforce.

Where systems fail to accommodate divergence, the cost is cumulative and collective. Brilliance is reframed as resistance; burnout as apathy; adaptive masking as professionalism. Over time, these misreadings fracture psychological safety and undermine organizational sustainability.

1.6 The Mental Health Toll of Misrecognition

When systems align, inclusion becomes protection.

Burnout is not the only possible consequence of chronic masking and compensatory coping. Mounting evidence suggests that prolonged neurodivergence-incongruent environments can also lead to depression-like syndromes that stem not from serotonergic imbalance, but from sustained identity suppression, sensory overload, and social misalignment (Botha & Frost, 2020). These presentations may be misclassified as major depressive disorder, yet standard antidepressants often fail to address the root cause—or may even exacerbate emotional disconnection and masking-related dissociation (Gómez, 2021).

These complexities underscore the need for differential diagnostic protocols that explicitly assess for masking-related exhaustion and identity incongruence, particularly in cases of atypical depression or burnout resistant to standard interventions. Neurodivergence-informed assessment is not merely an accommodation—it is a prerequisite for effective and ethical care. As Moncrieff and Kirsch (2022) argue, meaningful support should move beyond the chemical imbalance paradigm and toward contextual, relational, and cognitive congruence.

The stakes of misrecognition extend far beyond disengagement or burnout. Emerging research indicates that neurodivergent individuals—particularly autistic adults, those with ADHD, or individuals with complex, late-identified profiles—face significantly elevated risks of suicidal ideation and suicide attempts (Cassidy et al., 2014) (Table 1.1). Crucially, this elevated risk is not intrinsically associated with the neurodivergent condition, but with prolonged exposure to environments that fail to provide adequate support, such as educational institutions, workplaces, and settings characterized by chronic masking, social isolation, and misdiagnosis (Botha, Dibb & Frost, 2020).

1.6.1 Comparative Suicide Risk in Neurodivergent Populations

These findings highlight an ethical opportunity: when leadership systems are thoughtfully adapted to reflect cognitive diversity, they not only enhance talent retention—they also support people on a deeply personal

Table 1.1 Summarizes suicide risk across neurodivergent groups, highlighting rates significantly above the global average. Elevated risk is linked not to neurodivergence itself, but to systemic exclusion, chronic masking, and unaccommodating environments.

Population	*Estimated suicide risk*	*Key sources*
General population	~9.3 per 100,000 annually (global average)	WHO (2023)
Autistic adults	Up to 9 × higher risk of suicide attempts	Cassidy et al. (2014)
Adults with ADHD	2–5 × higher risk of ideation and attempts	Impey and Heun (2012); Allely (2014)
Late-identified neurodivergent adults	Significantly elevated risk due to chronic masking and misfit	Botha, Dibb and Frost (2020)

level and foster environments that affirm psychological sustainability, resilience, and meaningful participation.

Cognitive diversity should not be treated as an afterthought. Leadership models gain clarity and effectiveness when they are designed to anticipate neurocognitive variation from the outset, rather than retrofitting inclusion into existing structures.

The Gentle Leading™ approach emerges from this recognition—offering a reorientation of leadership.

1.7 Introducing the Gentle Leading™ Approach

Neurodivergence is not a deficit, but a different way of structuring, leading, and transforming the world.

Gentle Leading™ was first introduced in a prior publication of the same title as a human-centered leadership philosophy rooted in psychological safety and relational intelligence.

At its core, Gentle Leading™ rests on three interdependent pillars:

- **Emotional regulation** as a prerequisite for clarity, responsiveness, and relational sustainability
- **A needs-based approach** that replaces assumptions and rigid standards with inquiry, flexibility, and fit
- **Autonomy as architecture**, not attitude—structurally embedded, not individually granted

While not developed exclusively for neurodivergent leadership contexts, the model aligns closely with neurodiversity-informed practice. It emphasizes systemic friction reduction, permission to diverge from linear norms, and the cultivation of safety across difference—through anticipatory design instead of exception management.

The Gentle Leading™ philosophy has conceptual parallels to the gentle parenting movement, particularly in its emphasis on co-regulation, clear boundaries without coercion, and attunement to individual nervous system needs. Yet it is critical to emphasize a central distinction:

Employees are not children, and leaders are not parental figures.

The relevance lies in translating principles instead of replicating roles—recognizing that sustainable leadership, like sustainable caregiving, depends on the capacity to hold complexity without defaulting to dominance.

Just as environmental systems once centered a single metabolic norm, traditional leadership models have long privileged a narrow cognitive and regulatory template. Reconfiguring those defaults is not about lowering standards, but about making excellence accessible across cognitive profiles.

1.8 Visualizing the Model: The G-E-N-T-L-E Framework

The six dimensions of the GENTLE Framework emerged from cross-analysis of three central domains: research on psychological safety and motivation (Deci & Ryan, 2000; Maslach & Leiter, 2016), leadership praxis in high-trust environments (Scott et al., 2019; Edmondson, 2018), and qualitative patterns observed in neurodivergent professional experience. Together, they constitute a leadership model in which clarity, regulation, and autonomy are embedded as foundational design elements for long-term viability.

G—**Grounded Clarity** counters ambiguity through clearly defined expectations and transparent communication.

E—**Empowerment over Control** replaces micromanagement with autonomy, trust, and distributed ownership.

N—**Needs-Based Flexibility** prioritizes adaptive responses to cognitive and sensory needs over rigid adherence to protocol. Supports neurodivergent inclusion by normalizing flexible pacing, task structure, and environmental conditions.

T—**Trust through Emotional Regulation** frames inner composure as the basis for relational clarity and leadership presence.

L—**Lead by Example** links behavioral modeling with accountability and psychological safety.

E—**Evolving Growth** embeds continuous feedback and adaptive learning into everyday team culture.

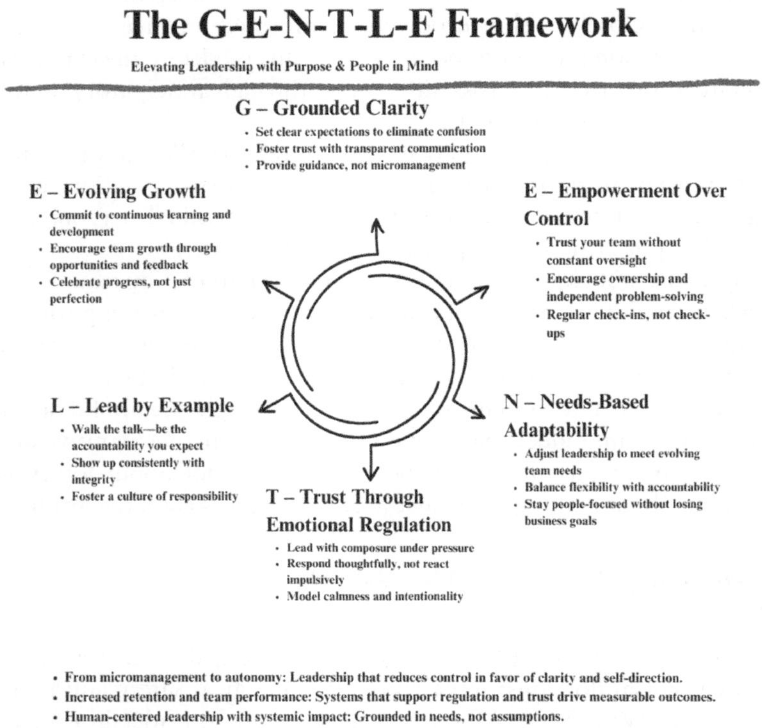

Figure 1.3 The GENTLE Framework: A needs-based, regulation-informed leadership model designed to foster clarity, autonomy, and sustainable team performance.

More than a mnemonic, the GENTLE Framework functions as a relational architecture for sustainable leadership. Practiced consistently, its principles are associated with increased psychological safety, reduced overfunctioning, and higher retention (Deci & Ryan, 2000; Scott et al., 2019; Miao et al., 2020). Rather than refining outdated norms, it offers a distinct trajectory—gentle, grounded, and growth-aligned (Figure 1.3).

1.9 Core Principles

Core conditions for leadership systems that enable regulation, autonomy, and sustainable engagement.

These principles form the foundation of Gentle Leading™. They articulate how leadership shifts when it is designed to respond to human regulation, autonomy, and relational clarity—rather than manage around their absence.

1.9.1 *Regulation before Reaction*

Leadership efficacy is contingent on a leader's capacity for self-regulation. Rather than beginning with action, effective leadership begins with physiological composure. Dysregulation—manifesting as hyperarousal, reactivity, or emotional withdrawal—compromises both interpersonal trust and strategic clarity. Sustainable leadership practice, therefore, must be rooted in nervous system awareness rather than retroactive communication strategies (Gross, 2013; Aldao et al., 2010).

1.9.2 *Clarity over Control*

Excessive control in leadership often reflects unacknowledged anxiety rather than functional rigor. While micromanagement may produce short-term compliance, it undermines autonomy and long-term engagement. *Gentle Leading*™ operationalizes clarity through co-constructed expectations, reliable workflow structures, and transparent communication—thereby fostering psychological safety and distributed ownership (Deci & Ryan, 2000; Scott et al., 2019).

1.9.3 *Empowerment through Needs-Based Design*

Optimal performance emerges not under pressure, but under conditions that meet individuals' core psychological needs. Autonomy, competence, safety, and rhythm are not discretionary enhancements—they are foundational for creativity, resilience, and adaptive problem-solving. *Gentle Leading*™ positions need-responsiveness not as accommodation, but as a strategic condition for collective effectiveness (Maslach & Leiter, 2016; Baumeister & Leary, 1995).

When clarity, autonomy, and regulation-informed leadership are absent, the cognitive and emotional burden on individuals increases—disproportionately so for neurodivergent professionals. In such contexts, masking becomes more than a social strategy; it becomes a structural necessity. The energy required to self-regulate, translate, and compensate is rarely visible, but its impact is cumulative. What appears as professionalism may, in fact, be adaptive overperformance sustained at personal cost.

1.10 The Masking Cost

Neurodivergence reflects not dysfunction, but an alternative cognitive architecture with strategic value.

Before attrition comes adaptation. In systems misaligned with cognitive diversity, neurodivergent professionals often rely on invisible survival strategies: scripting interactions, suppressing sensory responses, or mimicking normative behavior.

Masking refers to the suppression of one's natural patterns to avoid stigma or exclusion. While it may support short-term functioning, it incurs significant emotional and cognitive costs—often misread as competence, while signaling deep misfit.

Its full impact on leadership sustainability, psychological safety, and organizational misreading is explored in Chapter 3.

Persistent masking signals deeper structural disconnect rather than isolated coping. Effective inclusion is proactive by design, creating conditions in which diverse cognitive contributions can emerge without suppression or correction.

1.11 Inclusion as Strategy and Humanity

The tangible value of neurodivergent brains lies in their unmatched depth, pattern recognition, and principled insight.

Quantitative data underscores the case: Microsoft's Autism Hiring Program reported an approximately 90% three-year retention rate among neurodivergent hires—well above industry averages (Austin & Pisano, 2017). Beyond retention, measurable gains included up to a tenfold productivity increase in some teams, alongside improved process quality and efficiency. SAP's Autism at Work initiative likewise documented up to 30% productivity increases (Deloitte, 2025), paired with higher innovation metrics and employee engagement scores (Ernst & Young, 2025). These documented outcomes illustrate the strategic viability of inclusive design—they illustrate the strategic potential of inclusive design when properly implemented.

Yet the value of inclusive systems extends beyond neurodivergent professionals. When individuals are required to chronically adapt to rigid norms, entire systems incur the cost: psychological safety declines, trust deteriorates, and communication fractures. These effects manifest in elevated turnover, presenteeism, diminished innovation, and blind spots in strategic planning (Table 1.2).

1.12 Systemic Consequences of Exclusion

When systems misfit, talent disconnects.

The consistent need to suppress difference in order to belong reveals how organizational norms are shaped less by capacity than by conformity. The next section explores the role of ableism in codifying these expectations.

Table 1.2 Impacts are based on research findings related to neurodivergent experiences in organizational settings.

Systemic domain	*Impact of structural misfit*
Engagement	Disengagement emerges in the absence of psychological safety and structural support.
Collaboration	Misread communication and processing differences undermine cohesion and increase friction.
Talent retention	High-performing individuals leave when environments are cognitively unsustainable.
Leadership integrity	Leadership models lacking neuroinclusion remain incomplete and ethically insufficient.
Innovation capacity	Camouflage replaces contribution when neurodivergent thinking is not structurally welcomed.
Organizational intelligence	Ignoring cognitive variance limits collective insight and adaptive resilience.

Key sources include CIPD (2022), Scott et al. (2019), and Den Houting (2019); full citations appear in the reference list.

1.13 Ableism at Work

Bridging the gap between implicit bias and structural literacy to build systems that include by design, not by exception.

Discussions of neurodivergent leadership must engage with ableism in both its explicit manifestations and its implicit presence within normative organizational assumptions. At its core, ableism reflects the belief that certain cognitive or behavioral patterns are more legitimate, efficient, or professional than others. In many workplaces, this bias is not enacted interpersonally, but structurally (Brown, 2017; Scharff, 2018).

It becomes evident in (Table 1.3):

- Norms equating professionalism with eye contact, vocal consistency, or physical stillness.
- Evaluation criteria that privilege speed over depth, or constant availability over sustainable focus.
- Communication standards that marginalize nonverbal, asynchronous, or sensory-sensitive interaction.

A particularly problematic boundary is crossed when leaders assume the role of informal diagnosticians—assigning labels, speculating on conditions, or managing perceived difference without consent or expertise. This practice is neither ethical nor effective.

Table 1.3 What is perceived as neutral workplace behavior is often rooted in ableist assumptions—subtly privileging neurotypical modes of thinking, interacting, and regulating.

Common workplace standard	*Underlying ableist assumption*
Eye contact framed as a marker of professionalism	"Stillness and direct gaze signal competence."
Speed and visibility prioritized in performance reviews	"Faster means better; being visible means being valuable."
Verbal fluency equated with communication skills	"Only spoken clarity counts; verbal dominance signals leadership."
Stillness in meetings seen as attentiveness	"Physical calmness equals mental focus."
Leaders speculating on team members' neurotypes	"It's part of my role to assess how someone's brain works."
Self-regulation cues ignored or penalized	"Emotion signals instability; good regulation is invisible."

Clinical interpretation requires formal training; inclusive leadership requires structural literacy, psychological safety, and respect for disclosure boundaries (Burgstahler, 2015; McNaughton & Light, 2013).

1.14 From Awareness to Action

What inclusive leaders actually do.

In this context, inclusive leadership takes three interrelated forms:

- If you are neurodivergent, your task is not to contort yourself to fit a misaligned mold, but to shape workflows, boundaries, and environments that support regulation, rhythm, and long-term sustainability. Leading in alignment with your cognitive tempo—rather than in opposition to it—is not optional, but foundational.
- If you lead others, your role is not to "identify the neurodivergent," but to build systems that are cognitively inclusive by design—structured yet flexible enough to accommodate diverse needs, named or unnamed. Inclusive leadership does not require diagnostic certainty; it requires universal design, which benefits all.
- If you are both—neurodivergent and leading others with divergent profiles—your leadership becomes more layered. ADHD and high sensitivity, for example, can involve opposing regulation patterns: one seeks stimulation, the other protection from it. Here, inclusive leadership requires both self-awareness and system awareness—the ability to hold divergent needs, even when they diverge from your own. This

complexity is navigable through co-regulation, boundary clarity, and mutual respect.

Importantly, inclusive practice is not limited to formal leadership roles. Neuroinclusive action can—and must—emerge across all relational levels: among peers, across departments, and within collaborative constellations where leadership is distributed. Whether you are a team member, project lead, or organizational sponsor, your capacity to recognize and respond to neurocognitive variation meaningfully shapes the ecosystem in which others can thrive.

Inclusive leadership extends beyond attitudinal openness or intent. It demands a deeper understanding of the cognitive landscapes that shape attention, interaction, and decision-making in professional contexts. General principles are insufficient without specific insight into how neurodivergent patterns inform regulation, sensory processing, and communication.

The following chapter offers a conceptual and practical overview of key neurodivergent profiles—not as static diagnoses, but as dynamic cognitive dialects. By examining their distinct patterns and shared tensions, we lay the groundwork for equity-informed, system-aware leadership.

This understanding is not ancillary. It is essential for any organization committed to activating the full capacity of a cognitively diverse workforce.

References

Ahmedani, B. K. (2011). Mental health stigma: Society, individuals, and the profession. *Journal of Social Work Values and Ethics, 8*(2), 41–416.

Annamma, S. A., Connor, D., & Ferri, B. (2016). Dis/ability critical race studies (DisCrit): Theorizing at the intersections of race and dis/ability. *Race Ethnicity and Education, 19*(1), 1–19. https://doi.org/10.1080/13613324.2014.885422

Aldao, A., Nolen-Hoeksema, S., & Schweizer, S. (2010). Emotion-regulation strategies across psychopathology: A meta-analytic review. *Clinical Psychology Review*, 30(2), 217-237. https://doi.org/10.1016/j.cpr.2009.11.004

Allely, C. S. (2014). The link between ADHD and suicidality: Understanding the reasons and implications. *The Psychologist, 27*(6), 430–433.

Austin, R. D., & Pisano, G. P. (2017). Neurodiversity as a competitive advantage. *Harvard Business Review, 95*(3), 96–103. https://hbr.org/2017/05/neurodiversity-as-a-competitive-advantage

Baumeister, R. F., & Leary, M. R. (1995). The need to belong: Desire for interpersonal attachments as a fundamental human motivation. *Psychological Bulletin, 117*(3), 497–529. https://doi.org/10.1037/0033-2909.117.3.497

Baumer, N. T., & Frueh, S. (2021). *What is neurodiversity?* Harvard Health Publishing. https://www.health.harvard.edu/blog/what-is-neurodiversity-202111232645

Botha, M., & Frost, D. M. (2020). Extending the minority stress model to understand mental health experiences of autistic people. *Society and Mental Health, 10*(1), 1–34. https://doi.org/10.1177/2156869318804297

Botha, M., Dibb, B., & Frost, D. M. (2020). "Autism is me": An investigation of how autistic individuals make sense of autism and stigma. *Disability & Society, 35*(9), 1514–1537. https://doi.org/10.1080/09687599.2020.1822782

Brown, L. X. Z. (2017). *All the weight of our dreams: On living racialized autism.* Autistic Women and Nonbinary Network.

Burgstahler, S. (2015). *Universal design in higher education: From principles to practice* (2nd ed.). Harvard Education Press.

Cassidy, S., Bradley, L., Robinson, J., Allison, C., McHugh, M., & Baron-Cohen, S. (2014). Suicidal ideation and suicide plans or attempts in adults with Asperger's syndrome attending a specialist diagnostic clinic: A clinical cohort study. *The Lancet Psychiatry, 1*(2), 142–147. https://doi.org/10.1016/S2215-0366(14)70248-2

Centers for Disease Control and Prevention (CDC). (2023). *Data and statistics on autism spectrum disorder.* https://www.cdc.gov/ncbddd/autism/data.html

CIPD. (2022). *Neurodiversity at work: Guide for people professionals.* https://www.cipd.org/uk/knowledge/bitesize-research/neurodiverse-workforces/

Connell, R. W., & Messerschmidt, J. W. (2005). Hegemonic masculinity: Rethinking the concept. *Gender & Society, 19*(6), 829–859. https://doi.org/10.1177/0891243205278639

Deci, E. L., & Ryan, R. M. (2000). The "what" and "why" of goal pursuits: Human needs and the self-determination of behavior. *Psychological Inquiry, 11*(4), 227–268. https://doi.org/10.1207/S15327965PLI1104_01

Den Houting, J. (2019). Neurodiversity: An insider's perspective. *Autism, 23*(2), 271–273. https://doi.org/10.1177/1362361318820762

Deloitte. (2025). *Neurodiversity in the workplace: Unlocking the power of differences.* https://www.deloitte.com/us/en/insights/topics/talent/neurodiversity-in-the-workplace.html

Edmondson, A. C. (2018). *The fearless organization: Creating psychological safety in the workplace for learning, innovation, and growth.* Wiley.

Ernst & Young. (2025). *EY global neuroinclusion at work study 2025.* https://www.ey.com/content/dam/ey-unified-site/ey-com/en-gl/services/consulting/documents/ey-global-neuroinclusion-at-work-study-07-2025.pdf

Faraone, S. V., Perlis, R. H., Doyle, A. E., Smoller, J. W., Goralnick, J. J., Holmgren, M. A., & Sklar, P. (2005). Molecular genetics of attention-deficit/hyperactivity disorder. *Biological Psychiatry, 57*(11), 1313–1323. https://doi.org/10.1016/j.biopsych.2004.11.024

Gillberg, C. (2010). The ESSENCE in child psychiatry: Early symptomatic syndromes eliciting neurodevelopmental clinical examinations. *Research in Developmental Disabilities, 31*(6), 1543–1551. https://doi.org/10.1016/j.ridd.2010.06.002

Gómez, L. (2021). *The psychotherapy of dissociation: Theory, research and practice.* Routledge.

Gross, J. J. (2013). Emotion regulation: Taking stock and moving forward. *Emotion, 13*(3), 359–365. https://doi.org/10.1037/a0032135

Haney, J. L. (2016). Autism, females, and the DSM-5: Gender bias in autism diagnosis. *Social Work in Mental Health, 14*(4), 396–407. https://doi.org/10.1080/15332985.2015.1031858

Impey, M., & Heun, R. (2012). Completed suicide, ideation and attempt in attention deficit hyperactivity disorder. *Acta Psychiatrica Scandinavica, 125*(2), 93–102. https://doi.org/10.1111/j.1600-0447.2011.01798.x

Kingma, B., & van Marken Lichtenbelt, W. D. (2015). Energy consumption in buildings and female thermal demand. *Nature Climate Change*, *5*, 1054–1056. https://doi.org/10.1038/nclimate2741

Kreiser, N. L., & White, S. W. (2014). ASD in females: Are we overstating the gender gap in diagnosis? *Clinical Child and Family Psychology Review, 17*, 67–84. https://doi.org/10.1007/s10567-013-0148-9

Liao, K. Y.-H., & Weng, C.-Y. (2018). Mental health literacy in Asian American communities: Considerations for intervention. *Asian American Journal of Psychology, 9*(3), 211–219. https://doi.org/10.1037/aap0000123

Maenner, M. J., Shaw, K. A., Bakian, A. V., et al. (2020). Prevalence of autism spectrum disorder among children aged 8 years — Autism and Developmental Disabilities Monitoring Network, 11 sites, United States, 2016. *Morbidity and Mortality Weekly Report (MMWR), 69*(SS-4), 1–12. https://doi.org/10.15585/mmwr.ss6904a1

Martínez-Arán, A., Vieta, E., Reinares, M., Colom, F., Torrent, C., Sánchez-Moreno, J., … & Salamero, M. (2004). Cognitive function across manic or hypomanic and depressive episodes in bipolar disorder. *Archives of General Psychiatry, 61*(2), 239–247. https://doi.org/10.1176/appi.ajp.161.2.262

Maslach, C., & Leiter, M. P. (2016). *Burnout: A multidimensional perspective.* Psychology Press.

McNaughton, D., & Light, J. (2013). The iPad and mobile technology revolution: Benefits and challenges for individuals who require augmentative and alternative communication. *Augmentative and Alternative Communication, 29*(2), 107–116. https://doi.org/10.3109/07434618.2013.784930

Miao, Q., Newman, A., Schwarz, G., & Cooper, B. (2020). How leadership and commitment influence public service employees' burnout and engagement: The role of psychological safety. *Public Management Review, 22*(5), 704–729. https://doi.org/10.1080/14719037.2019.1599059

Moncrieff, J., & Kirsch, I. (2022). Deluded by the brain chemical imbalance theory: Why antidepressants do not work as claimed. *Molecular Psychiatry*, *27*, 293–299. https://doi.org/10.1038/s41380-022-01661-0

Ronald, A., Happé, F., & Plomin, R. (2006). The genetic relationship between individual differences in social and nonsocial behaviours characteristic of autism. *Developmental Science*, *9*(5), 474–482. https://doi.org/10.1111/j.1467-7687.2006.00508.x

Scharff, C. (2018). *Gender, subjectivity, and cultural work: The classical music profession*. Routledge.

Scott, C., Colquitt, J. A., Paddock, E. L., & Judge, T. A. (2019). A meta-analytic review of the antecedents, correlates, and consequences of organizational trust. *Journal of Applied Psychology, 104*(8), 1003–1034. https://doi.org/10.1037/apl0000383

Shim, R. S., & Compton, M. T. (2018). Addressing the social determinants of mental health: If not now, when? *Psychiatric Services, 69*(8), 844–846. https://doi.org/10.1176/appi.ps.201800060

Syracuse University. (2011). *National symposium on neurodiversity*. https://news.syr.edu/blog/2011/10/03/symposium-to-focus-on-neurodiversity

Walker, J. J. (2021). OCD traits as cognitive divergence: A dimensional view. *Journal of Obsessive-Compulsive and Related Disorders, 27*, 100–112. https://doi.org/10.1016/j.jocrd.2020.100612

WHO. (2023). *Suicide worldwide in 2019: Global health estimates.* World Health Organization. https://www.who.int/publications/i/item/9789240026643

Chapter 2

The Dialects of Divergence

An Overview of Neurodivergent Profiles in Leadership Contexts

2.1 Difference ≠ Deficit

Understanding cognitive wiring and leadership potential.

If the human cognitive landscape has a dominant language, then neurodivergent ways of thinking are its dialects—distinct, precise, and essential to the full conversation and each with its own structure, rhythm, and nuance. We have not yet learned these dialects, and in doing so, leadership systems overlook the depth and precision they contain (Fletcher-Watson et al., 2021). Yet in many organizations, these dialects remain unknown, and it's time that we start learning them.

Effective leadership in a cognitively diverse world requires more than behavioral observation—it calls for an understanding of the neurological structures that shape how individuals process, prioritize, and respond to their environments. As outlined earlier, neurodivergence does not signal deficiency—it reflects a difference in cognitive wiring: a brain that operates outside dominant norms, yet remains fully capable, complex, and valid (Singer, 1999; Armstrong, 2010; Kapp, 2020).

These differences may be invisible, but their impacts are not (Walker, 2021). When neurodivergent processing patterns are misinterpreted through normative expectations, they are often pathologized—seen not as legitimate variations, but as shortcomings or deficits (Baumer & Frueh, 2021).

Inclusive leadership begins with perception. Neurodivergence is not a deviation to be corrected, but a set of cognitive orientations that challenge linear models of behavior, interaction, and performance. It is not a monolith, but a spectrum—often misread, seldom designed for, and rarely named in leadership discourse. What is still labeled "outlier behavior" is, in reality, part of the shared neurocognitive architecture through which teams think, relate, and innovate.

DOI: 10.4324/9781003681540-3

This chapter lays the conceptual groundwork for understanding how divergent minds interact with organizational systems—not through diagnostic classification, but through patterns of regulation, responsiveness, and relational fit. It examines how self-regulatory behaviors are often dismissed as habits, how co-occurring traits complicate linear expectations, and how structural norms continue to obscure cognitive difference under the guise of professionalism (Pellicano, den Houting et al., 2022). To further situate these dynamics, the sections that follow analyze three interrelated foundations: first, the widespread misconceptions that distort how neurodivergent traits are perceived; second, the cognitive dialects through which divergence is expressed in leadership contexts; and third, the complexity of mixed profiles, which challenge fixed trait assumptions and reveal the dualities many leaders must navigate in practice.

To reimagine the value of neurodivergent cognition, it helps to envision leadership shaped by the explicit valuation of cognitive difference—rather than its mere tolerance. One such vision comes from neurodivergent advocate Nina Roosen:

> *ADHD would be my motivator and the engine of innovation, always sparking new ideas.*
>
> *Autism would be my strategist and analyst, offering precision and focus to guide our path.*
>
> *Dyscalculia would be my creative thinker and designer, bringing unique solutions and a fresh perspective.*
>
> *Dyslexia would be my communicator and inspiring storyteller, connecting us with powerful narratives.*
>
> *Giftedness would be my visionary, charting bold new futures for the tribe.*
>
> *High sensitivity would be my empathetic mediator and healer, nurturing harmony and understanding.*
>
> *Together, this team would make us unbeatable in survival and innovation.*
>
> *Nina Roosen, If I would be leading a tribe*

This vision is not utopian. It is entirely achievable and grounded in the lived realities and systemic contributions of divergent individuals. Realizing it in practice depends on addressing the perceptual and structural barriers that still render cognitive difference in leadership invisible.

Such understanding is not a matter of inclusion alone; it is central to intelligent team architecture, energy-sensitive collaboration, and sustainable innovation in cognitively diverse environments.

Yet despite growing awareness, core misconceptions persist, and they are not benign. They perpetuate systemic misrecognition by conflating cognitive variation with dysfunction, thereby reinforcing ableist norms in organizational life. Traits such as divergent executive functioning, social patterning, or sensory regulation are too often misread as deficiencies, rather than as indicators of environmental misalignment. This misframing not only displaces responsibility for inclusion onto individuals, but also undermines the legitimacy of neurodivergent leadership itself.

As Campbell (2009) notes, "Ableism is not simply about the overt exclusion of disabled people; it is the deep-seated belief that some bodies and minds are inherently more valuable, capable, or 'normal' than others" (p. 5). Such beliefs, even when implicit, shape what is considered professional, promotable, or "leadership material" in ways that routinely marginalize neurodivergent professionals.

2.2 The Invisible Effect of Divergence

True inclusion begins when we move from implicit bias to structural literacy.

Neurodivergent expression is sometimes invisible, but continuously active—shaping how individuals process, relate, regulate, and recover. In neurotypical systems, these patterns are frequently misinterpreted as behavioral flaws or professional shortcomings (Walker, 2021; Baumer & Frueh, 2021). Tools such as the Systemic NeuroCognitive Indexing Protocol™ (SNIP) make these invisible patterns visible in a neutral, non-diagnostic way, mapping how cognitive variations present across domains and providing a foundation for targeted, needs-informed leadership strategies.

The next section introduces fifteen core domains of neurodivergent expression—patterns that carry tangible implications for team dynamics, regulation, and inclusive system design (Table 2.1).

2.2.1 Sensory and Emotional Processing

This domain refers to how individuals perceive, filter, and respond to both environmental stimuli and emotional cues. In neurodivergent profiles, this processing often occurs with heightened intensity or reactivity—resulting in deeper affective resonance, but also increased vulnerability to overstimulation, misreading, or emotional exhaustion in conventional work settings.

- **Sensory Sensitivity** (heightened reactivity to sound, scents, light, texture, or temperature)
- Sensory overload can trigger avoidance, fidgeting, or shutdown—frequently misread as anxiety or defiance (Robertson & Simmons, 2015).
- **Emotional Intensity** (deep or rapid-onset emotional responses)
- Individuals may express strong empathy and passion, yet be misjudged as "too reactive" in emotionally neutral or affect-suppressive cultures (Díaz-Román et al., 2016).
- **Rejection Sensitivity** (heightened sensitivity to perceived criticism or exclusion, often linked to trauma or ADHD)
- May result in overaccommodation, masking, or social withdrawal. Particularly prevalent in autistic and ADHD adults (Dodson, 2025; Asherson et al., 2016).

2.2.2 *Cognitive and Temporal Regulation*

This area involves the regulation of attention, memory, and time orientation—core functions that shape how individuals process information and sequence action. In neurodivergent profiles, divergence in these areas can result in pacing mismatches, planning difficulties, or variable responsiveness—often misinterpreted as disorganization, inefficiency, or disengagement.

- **Time Perception Differences** (difficulty estimating, sensing, or tracking time)
- Known as "time blindness," this impairs transitions, deadline planning, and task pacing (Barkley et al., 2001).
- **Attention Regulation** (alternation between distraction and hyperfocus)
- Often mistaken for inconsistency or lack of discipline, this reflects dopamine-based attention variance (Hupfeld et al., 2019).
- **Processing Speed Variation** (unusually fast or slow cognitive processing)
- Can lead to delayed responses or overwhelm in fast-paced discussions—frequently misread as confusion or low competence (Wechsler, 2014).
- **Working Memory Challenges** (difficulty holding and manipulating information in real time)
- Affects planning and verbal fluency; often interpreted as inattentiveness or poor preparation (Gathercole et al., 2008).

2.2.3 *Motor and Energy Rhythms*

This domain encompasses variation in motor coordination, movement regulation, and energy distribution over time. Neurodivergent individuals—especially those with dyspraxia, autism, or ADHD—may exhibit kinetic adaptations. These are often strategies of self-regulation rather than signs of impairment, yet are frequently pathologized in systems that equate stillness with focus and consistency with competence.

- **Motor Regulation Differences** (fidgeting, stimming, dyspraxic movement patterns)
- Often misinterpreted as distractibility or immaturity, these behaviors serve as regulatory mechanisms for sensory and emotional balance (Lingam et al., 2009).
- **Energy Pattern Divergence** (nonlinear or situationally dependent energy levels)
- Includes phenomena such as "spoon theory," boom-bust energy cycles, and context-based fatigue patterns common in autistic and ADHD profiles (Raymaker et al., 2020).

2.2.4 *Social and Communication Styles*

This domain encompasses the diverse ways in which individuals express themselves, engage relationally, and interpret social cues. Neurodivergent communication may differ from dominant norms in rhythm, framing, or interactional conventions—often reflecting adaptive strategies rather than deficits. Yet when filtered through neurotypical expectations, these differences are easily misunderstood, leading to misattribution, underrecognition, or exclusion from key relational and leadership dynamics.

- **Language and Expression Divergence** (use of scripting, metaphor, delayed speech, or atypical pacing)
- Often perceived as evasive, robotic, or overly formal, these expression styles reflect alternative cognitive processing rather than a lack of authenticity or engagement.
- **Social Cognition Variability** (differences in interpreting social cues, tone, hierarchy, or sarcasm)
- Can lead to miscommunication or exclusion in informal networks and impact perceived leadership visibility or team integration (Begeer et al., 2010).
- **Context Sensitivity** (performance fluctuates based on trust, predictability, or sensory environment)
- Commonly misinterpreted as inconsistency or fragility, this pattern reflects systemic attunement rather than a personal deficit (Botha & Frost, 2020).

Table 2.1 Outlines key domains in which neurodivergent traits commonly manifest in leadership and professional settings. While not diagnostic, these dimensions influence regulation, trust, and team dynamics—and are often misunderstood or overlooked despite their tangible impact on engagement and performance.

Dimension	*Impact on leadership*
Sensory sensitivity	Reactions to stimuli require adaptive space and interaction pacing.
Emotional intensity	Strong affect may be misread as volatility but reflects depth and conviction.
Rejection sensitivity	Fear of criticism can prompt masking or withdrawal without safety.
Time perception	Temporal variance disrupts planning; benefits from external anchors.
Attention regulation	Shifting focus patterns require autonomy and pacing flexibility.
Attention regulation	Atypical speed affects dialogue flow; async formats improve participation.
Working memory	Sequencing challenges impact planning; visual cues aid retention.
Motor regulation	Movement-based coping may be misread as inattentive behavior.
Energy rhythms	Fluctuating energy requires recovery-integrated scheduling.
Expression style	Atypical tone or pacing reflects internal structuring, not deficit.
Social cognition	Cue interpretation gaps can affect trust and informal rapport.
Context sensitivity	Performance shifts with safety and predictability; design must account for it.
Executive functioning	Task management improves with clarity and autonomy.
Cognitive style	Nonlinear, integrative thinking drives innovation but may clash with linear norms.
Regulatory load	Hidden effort to self-manage can lead to fatigue and attrition.

Note: Beyond recognized patterns of neurodivergent expression, many individuals engage in subtle, often overlooked forms of sensory or emotional regulation. These include actions such as hair twirling, nail nibbling, cheek chewing, or selective disengagement—such as difficulty recalling names—as a way to manage input load.

Misophonia, the heightened emotional reactivity to specific sounds (e.g., chewing, pen clicking, throat clearing), may similarly reflect auditory sensory defensiveness rather than irritability or lack of emotional control.

Interpreting these micro-patterns through a neuroinclusive lens allows for more accurate recognition and reduces the tendency to frame regulation as dysfunction, resistance, or disengagement.

2.2.5 Executive Function and Systems Thinking

This domain encompasses the capacities involved in organizing action, sequencing thought, and navigating complexity—ranging from task management to abstract pattern integration. While neurodivergent individuals may experience friction with conventional expectations around task initiation, prioritization, or switching, they frequently bring systems-level insight, innovative logic, and conceptual fluency that remain underrecognized in rigid performance structures.

- **Executive Functioning Differences** (planning, prioritizing, initiating, and switching tasks)
  Often referred to as the "CEO of the brain," executive functioning enables leaders to manage cognitive load under pressure. Divergence in this area can affect follow-through or pacing, especially in overstimulating or multitasking environments (Barkley, 2011; Dawson & Guare, 2018).
- **Cognitive Style Divergence** (systems thinking, divergent ideation, nonlinear logic)
  Characterized by pattern detection, strategic abstraction, and lateral insight, these strengths are particularly valuable in ambiguity-rich or innovation-driven contexts—but frequently undervalued in systems that privilege procedural thinking or linear execution (Armstrong, 2010; Dijkstra & van Dijk, 2017).

2.3 From Dimensions to Profiles: A Comparative Map

Understanding divergence through functional dialects.

The subtle regulatory patterns discussed above illustrate how neurocognitive variation is enacted in everyday professional life. Beneath these microbehaviors lie distinct functional dialects—coherent configurations of perception, processing, and regulation that shape how individuals engage with complexity, decision-making, and relational environments.

The following profiles are explored in dedicated chapters due to their systemic relevance in leadership contexts (Table 2.2). Each reflects a recognizable pattern of cognitive rhythm, regulatory need, and interpersonal engagement that interacts meaningfully with organizational structures.

Profiles were selected based on two inclusion criteria:

1. **Prevalence or growing recognition** within professional settings;
2. **Systemic impact**, including influence on task execution, relational dynamics, leadership styles, and structural friction (APA, 2013).

The comparative overview below introduces each core profile with a focus on its leadership-relevant cognitive strengths and regulatory tensions.

2.4 Core Cognitive Dialects Profiles: Explored in Full Chapters

Table 2.2 This table presents core profiles discussed in depth throughout the volume. While most reflect clinical categories (e.g., ADHD, Autism), profiles like Giftedness and High Sensitivity (HSP) are also included due to their distinct neurocognitive traits and leadership implications.

Neurodivergence	*Core strength*	*How it shows up in leadership*
ADHD	Innovation, urgency-driven ideation	• Energized by challenge and speed • May struggle with follow-through or detail fatigue
AuDHD	Visionary disruption with systemic logic	• Oscillates between hyperfocus and shutdown • Integrates divergent patterns at pace
Autism	Precision, deep systems thinking	• Builds structured, principled solutions • May resist ambiguity or sensory overload
Dyslexia	Narrative insight, strategic abstraction	• Leads through metaphor and vision • May find conventional formats cognitively costly
Dyscalculia	Relational creativity, intuitive judgment	• Strong emotional attunement in leadership • May struggle in metrics- or time-heavy domains
Dyspraxia	Adaptive problem-solving, persistence	• Effective in abstract strategy and improvisation • Coordination demands may cause fatigue
Giftedness	Complexity mastery, rapid cognition	• Excels in visionary leadership and deep synthesis • May clash with slow or rigid systems
HSP	Emotional depth, sensory discernment	• Creates calm, ethically attuned workspaces • Sensitive to intensity, pace, or relational tension
Tourette Syndrome	Expressive resilience, authenticity	• Leads with candor and emotional visibility • May face bias due to involuntary expressions

Note: Giftedness is not formally classified as neurodivergence but entails cognitive intensities that intersect with regulation demands. HSP, a temperament trait, is included for its prevalence (15–20%) and its relevance to sensory-emotional processing in leadership contexts.

2.5 Supplementary Profiles: Additional Forms of Cognitive and Emotional Divergence in Leadership

Highlighting distinct constellations beyond the core profiles.

The following profiles are referenced across integrative sections due to their increasing visibility in neurodiversity-informed leadership design

Table 2.3 NVLD and APD—Profiles like Nonverbal Learning Disorder (NVLD) and Auditory Processing Disorder (APD) are not DSM-5 neurodevelopmental conditions, yet show consistent patterns requiring adaptation in leadership contexts.

Profile	*Definition/core feature*	*Relevance to leadership*
Nonverbal Learning Disorder (NVLD)	Discrepancy between strong verbal skills and weak spatial/contextual reasoning	• Affects spatial planning, contextual interpretation, and fluid collaboration • May lead to social misreads or coordination strain in fast-changing settings (Cornoldi et al., 2016)
Auditory Processing Disorder (APD)	Difficulty decoding verbal input, especially in noisy or rapid environments	• Influences verbal clarity, multi-speaker engagement, and auditory task processing • Benefits from visual communication and pacing support (Moore, 2018; Dillon & Cameron, 2021)

(Table 2.3). To reflect their origin and function, they are organized into three thematic clusters:

2.5.1 Functional Divergence Profiles

Functionally neurodivergent, though not formally classified as clinical ND.

These profiles exhibit stable cognitive variation that influences communication, learning, and leadership—but are often overlooked due to lack of diagnostic clarity.

2.5.2 Psychiatric and Neurological Divergence

Conditions reframed within the expanded neurodiversity discourse.

This cluster reflects a broader paradigm shift: acknowledging psychiatric and neurological conditions as forms of sustained cognitive-emotional divergence, particularly when they affect leadership rhythm, regulation, and social integration (Table 2.4).

2.5.3 Structurally Excluded Neurodevelopmental Profiles

Formally neurodevelopmental, yet marginalized in ND discourse (Table 2.5).

Table 2.4 Bipolar, OCD, PTSD, Epilepsy.

Profile	*Definition/core feature*	*Relevance to leadership*
Nonverbal Learning Disorder (NVLD)	Verbal reasoning strength paired with spatial and nonverbal processing challenges.	• Strong verbal clarity and logic • May struggle with spatial reasoning or ambiguity in fast-changing settings
Auditory Processing Disorder (APD)	Difficulty decoding auditory input despite normal hearing acuity.	• Excels with visual input and structured information • May need support in fast, noisy, or auditory-dominant contexts
Obsessive-Compulsive Traits (OCD)	Trait-level need for control, order, and error-avoidance.	• Enhances reliability and quality standards • May reduce flexibility, delegation, or adaptivity under stress
Bipolar Disorder	Oscillating access to energy, drive, and executive function.	• May bring urgency, bold vision, and rapid ideation • Requires rhythm-based adaptation to support sustainability
Post-Traumatic Stress Disorder (PTSD)	Altered affect regulation, threat perception, and relational safety mechanisms.	• Heightened attention to risk, trust, and justice dynamics • Benefits from trauma-informed leadership environments
Epilepsy-Related Cognitive Variation	Episodic executive strain, postictal fatigue, and sensory sensitivity.	• Requires flexible pacing and episodic design • Can contribute deep pattern sensitivity and crisis durability

These profiles are included for their relevance to pacing, system interaction, and leadership sustainability—even if traditionally pathologized.

At the same time, many professionals experience overlapping traits—such as sensory sensitivity alongside executive function variability, or the cognitive speed of giftedness paired with the emotional regulation demands of ADHD. These mixed profiles generate paradoxical needs and complex internal negotiations that do not map neatly onto single-diagnosis models. Instead, they reveal the necessity of more fluid, responsive leadership environments—ones that honor cognitive duality, allow for oscillation, and support integration over correction.

Table 2.5 Formally Neurodevelopmental, Structurally Excluded-Intellectual Disability (ID) is included in DSM-5's neurodevelopmental category (APA, 2013), yet often omitted from workplace neurodiversity conversations—due to historic emphasis on "high-functioning" profiles.

Profile	*Definition*	*Leadership relevance*
Intellectual Disability (ID)	Global developmental delay affecting intellectual and adaptive functioning.	Often overlooked in leadership contexts; offers groundedness, consistency, and procedural integrity when supported (Schalock et al., 2010).

2.6 The Relevance of Mixed Profiles

Why Binary Thinking Fails in Neurodivergent Realities.

Neurodivergence rarely presents as a single, isolated profile. Many individuals meet diagnostic criteria for more than one neurodivergent condition—such as autism co-occurring with ADHD (often referred to as AuDHD), or dyslexia appearing alongside anxiety or dyspraxia (Antshel et al., 2013).

Coexisting traits often produce paradoxical demands: a need for structure coupled with a craving for novelty, verbal fluency paired with auditory processing challenges, or deep emotional attunement alongside difficulty decoding real-time social cues (Table 2.6). Some constellations remain subtle; others—particularly when underdiagnosed or combined with high environmental load—create chronic friction.

What may seem inconsistent from the outside often reflects an internal negotiation between competing processing modes. A leader may speak with eloquence yet struggle to follow spoken directions. A systems thinker may anticipate future patterns while overlooking immediate tasks. Hyperfocus may alternate with task paralysis—misread as unreliability rather than the consequence of bandwidth overload.

Conventional leadership cultures that valorize consistency and linear performance often misinterpret such variability as dysfunction (Russell et al., 2019; den Houting, 2019). Even well-intentioned supports can fall short when they isolate traits without addressing their interaction.

True inclusion requires infrastructures that embrace oscillation, permit self-authored regulation, and normalize dynamic functioning. What appears contradictory is often a coherent dialect—one that reveals the intelligence embedded in paradox.

"Paradox is not dysfunction—it's duality."

2.7 Coexisting Needs in Mixed Neurocognitive Profiles

Table 2.6 This table illustrates common dualities found in mixed neurodivergent profiles. It highlights how strengths often coexist with contrasting challenges, leading to frequent misinterpretation in professional settings. Understanding these dialectical patterns enables more accurate support and systemic design.

Observable trait or strength	*Often coexists with…*	*Leadership misread*	*Systemic insight*
High verbal fluency	Low auditory processing	"Excellent communicator"	Needs written or asynchronous input to fully process information
Strategic foresight	Working memory limitations	"Big picture, but scattered"	Requires scaffolding to sustain and implement vision
Hyperfocus on meaningful tasks	Executive paralysis on routine tasks	"Inconsistent"	Activation depends on novelty, meaning, and interest
Need for clarity and structure	Craving for spontaneity and ideation	"Contradictory"	Needs structured freedom: stability in form, flexibility in flow
Detail sensitivity (e.g. dyscalculia)	Global reasoning or pattern insight	"Strong thinker, but sloppy"	Not sloppiness—divergent processing mode
Eloquence in writing	Delayed verbal response or social fatigue	"Withdrawn in meetings"	Writing as primary or preferred communication channel

2.8 Neurodivergence and Functional Limitation

How environments define (dis)ability.

While many forms of neurodivergence can be effectively supported through thoughtful design and adaptive leadership structures, it is essential to distinguish between neurodivergence as cognitive difference and disability as functional limitation. Not all neurodivergent profiles automatically constitute a disability in legal or practical terms. Rather, disability status depends on the extent to which cognitive traits substantially impair participation in major life or work activities—a threshold defined by frameworks such as the Americans with Disabilities Act (ADA, 1990) or the WHO's International Classification of Functioning (ICF, WHO, 2022).

From a conceptual standpoint, this distinction reflects two competing models: the *medical model*, which locates disability in the individual, and the *social model*, which views it as the result of environmental barriers and systemic inflexibility. A neurodivergent individual may function with full agency in a contextually attuned environment but become disabled in a setting that demands constant masking, sensory tolerance, or neurotypical executive functioning (Oliver, 1996; Shakespeare, 2006).

Profiles such as Level 3 autism, severe Tourette Syndrome, or chronically unregulated ADHD may entail persistent functional limitations—not solely due to intrinsic impairment, but because existing professional infrastructures often lack the adaptability to meet such substantial support needs. In some contexts, meaningful inclusion is not a matter of will or awareness alone, but constrained by operational, sensory, or relational demands that exceed current capacity for adaptation. Even where legal recognition is in place, implementation remains inconsistent—especially in high-demand environments where unspoken norms of masking and overcompensation continue to shape perceptions of competence (Barkley, 2011; Volkow et al., 2009).

As we turn toward the mechanisms individuals use to navigate these gaps—particularly masking and coping—we shift from system design to lived adaptation. These strategies emerge as intelligent responses to environmental friction, enabling participation in spaces that may not yet be fully inclusive. Understanding these adaptive patterns is essential for designing leadership systems that minimize concealment and foster authentic engagement.

References

ADA. (1990). *Americans with Disabilities Act of 1990, as amended.* https://www.ada.gov/law-and-regs/ada/

American Psychiatric Association. (2013). *Diagnostic and statistical manual of mental disorders* (5th ed.). https://doi.org/10.1176/appi.books.9780890425596

Antshel, K. M., Zhang-James, Y., & Faraone, S. V. (2013). The comorbidity of ADHD and autism spectrum disorder. *Expert Review of Neurotherapeutics, 13*(10), 1117–1128. https://doi.org/10.1586/14737175.2013.840417

Armstrong, T. (2010). *The power of neurodiversity: Unleashing the advantages of your differently wired brain.* DaCapo Lifelong Books.

Asherson, P., Buitelaar, J., Faraone, S. V., & Rohde, L. A. (2016). Adult attention-deficit hyperactivity disorder: Key conceptual issues. *The Lancet Psychiatry, 3*(6), 568–578. https://doi.org/10.1016/S2215-0366(16)30032-3

Barkley, R. A. (2001). The executive functions and self-regulation: An evolutionary neuropsychological perspective. *Neuropsychology Review, 11*(1), 1–29. https://doi.org/10.1023/A:1009085417776

Barkley, R. A. (2011). *Executive functions: What they are, how they work, and why they evolved.* Guilford Press.

Baumer, N., & Frueh, J. (2021). What is neurodiversity? *AMA Journal of Ethics, 23*(6), E519–E525. https://doi.org/10.1001/amajethics.2021.519

Begeer, S., Malle, B. F., Nieuwland, M. S., & Keysar, B. (2010). Using theory of mind to represent and take part in social interactions: Comparing individuals with high-functioning autism and typically developing controls. *European Journal of Developmental Psychology, 7*(1), 104–122. https://doi.org/10.1080/17405620903024263

Botha, M., & Frost, D. M. (2020). Extending the minority stress model to understand mental health problems experienced by autistic people. *Society and Mental Health*, *10*(1), 20–34. https://doi.org/10.1177/2156869318804297
Campbell, F. K. (2009). *Contours of ableism: The production of disability and abledness*. Palgrave Macmillan.
Cornoldi, C., Mammarella, I. C., & Fine, J. G. (2016). Nonverbal learning disabilities: Diagnosis and treatment. New York, NY: Guilford Press.
Dawson, P., & Guare, R. (2018). *Smart but scattered: The revolutionary "executive skills" approach to helping kids reach their potential*. Guilford Publications.
den Houting, J. (2019). Neurodiversity: An insider's perspective. *Autism*, *23*(2), 271–273. https://doi.org/10.1177/1362361318820762
Díaz-Román, A., Díaz-Román, A., & Escribano, B. (2016). Emotional dysregulation in adults with ADHD: The role of personality traits. *Journal of Attention Disorders*, *24*(6), 865–875.
Dijkstra, A. F. J., & van Dijk, F. (2017). Nonlinear thinking and the neurodivergent advantage. *Systems Research and Behavioral Science*, *34*(2), 131–144. https://doi.org/10.1002/sres.2414
Dillon, H., & Cameron, S. (2021). Separating the causes of listening difficulties in children. *Ear and Hearing*, *42*(5), 1097–1108. https://doi.org/10.1097/AUD.0000000000001069
Dodson, W. (2025, May 9). *New insights into rejection sensitive dysphoria*. ADDitude. https://www.additudemag.com/rejection-sensitive-dysphoria-and-adhd/
Fletcher-Watson, S., Bölte, S., Crompton, C.J., Jones, D., Lai, M.-C., Mandy, W., Pellicano, L., Stahmer, A., Taylor, J., & Mandell, D. (2021). Publishing standards for promoting excellence in autism research. *Autism, 25*(6), 1501–1504. https://doi.org/10.1177/13623613211019830
Gathercole, S. E., Dunning, D. L., Holmes, J., & Norris, D. (2008). Working memory training and generalization. *Applied Cognitive Psychology*, *25*(6), 812–824. https://doi.org/10.1002/acp.1775
Hupfeld, K. E., Abagis, T. R., & Shah, P. (2019). Living "in the zone": Hyperfocus in adult ADHD. *ADHD Attention Deficit and Hyperactivity Disorders*, *11*, 191–208. https://doi.org/10.1007/s12402-018-0272-y
Kapp, S. K. (2020). *Autistic community and the neurodiversity movement: Stories from the frontline*. Palgrave Macmillan. https://doi.org/10.1007/978-981-13-8437-0
Lingam, R., Hunt, L., Golding, J., Jongmans, M. J., & Emond, A. (2009). Prevalence of developmental coordination disorder using DSM-IV at 7 years of age: A UK population-based study. *Pediatrics*, *123*(4), e693–e700. https://doi.org/10.1542/peds.2008-1770
Moore, D. R. (2018). Auditory processing disorder (APD). *Ear and Hearing*, *39*(4), 617–620. https://doi.org/10.1097/AUD.0000000000000536
Oliver, M. (1996). *Understanding disability: From theory to practice*. Macmillan.
Pellicano, E., & den Houting, J. (2022). Annual research review: shifting from 'normal science' to neurodiversity in autism science. *Journal of Child Psychology and Psychiatry*, *63*(4), 381–396. https://doi.org/10.1111/jcpp.13534
Raymaker, D. M., Teo, A. R., Steckler, N. A., Lentz, B., Scharer, M., Delos Santos, A., ... & Nicolaidis, C. (2020). "Having all of your internal resources exhausted beyond measure and being left with no clean-up crew": Defining autistic burnout. *Autism in Adulthood*, *2*(2), 132–143. https://doi.org/10.1089/aut.2019.0079

Robertson, A. E., & Simmons, D. R. (2015). The sensory experiences of adults with autism spectrum disorder: A qualitative analysis. *Perception*, *44*(5), 569–586. https://doi.org/10.1068/p7833

Russell, G., Mandy, W., Elliott, D., White, R., Pittwood, T., & Ford, T. (2019). Selection bias on intellectual ability in autism research: A cross-sectional review and meta-analysis. *Molecular Autism*, *10*(1), 9. https://doi.org/10.1186/s13229-019-0260-x

Schalock, R. L., Borthwick-Duffy, S. A., Bradley, V. J., Buntinx, W. H. E., Coulter, D. L., Craig, E. M., Gómez, S. C., Lachapelle, Y., Luckasson, R. A., Reeve, A., Shogren, K. A., Snell, M. E., Spreat, S., Tassé, M. J., Thompson, J. R., Verdugo, M. A., Wehmeyer, M. L., & Yeager, M. H. (2010). *Intellectual disability: Definition, classification, and systems of supports* (11th ed.). American Association on Intellectual and Developmental Disabilities.

Shakespeare, T. (2006). *Disability rights and wrongs*. Routledge.

Singer, J. (1999). *Why can't you be normal for once in your life?* In M. Corker & S. French (Eds.), *Disability discourse* (pp. 59–67). Open University Press.

Volkow, N. D., Wang, G. J., Kollins, S. H., Wigal, T. L., Newcorn, J. H., Telang, F., ... & Swanson, J. M. (2009). Evaluating dopamine reward pathway in ADHD: Clinical implications. *JAMA*, *302*(10), 1084–1091. https://doi.org/10.1001/jama.2009.1308

Walker, N. (2021). *Neuroqueer heresies: Notes on the neurodiversity paradigm, autistic empowerment, and postnormal possibilities*. Autonomous Press.

Wechsler, D. (2014). *Wechsler Intelligence Scale for Children – Fifth Edition (WISC-V)*. Pearson.

WHO. (2022). *International Classification of Functioning, Disability and Health (ICF)*. https://www.who.int/standards/classifications/international-classification-of-functioning-disability-and-health

Chapter 3

The Hidden Load—Coping, Masking, and the Cost of Adaptation

Why Adaptive Effort Is a Leadership Concern

3.1 Beneath the Surface: Why Adaptive Effort Is a Leadership Concern

The invisible labor of fitting in—and the structural cost of overlooking it.

Inclusive leadership requires more than acknowledging visible diversity; it demands recognition of the unseen cognitive and emotional labor many neurodivergent professionals perform daily. Often, the most taxing aspect of work is not the task itself, but the sustained effort required to navigate environments designed around neurotypical norms.

These adaptive efforts—ranging from mental scripting and sensory regulation to emotional self-monitoring—are frequently habitual, invisible, and identity-relevant. Though often framed as coping strategies, they come at a cumulative cost: burnout and anxiety, diminished authenticity, and the erosion of psychological safety (Cage & Troxell-Whitman, 2019; Raymaker et al., 2020).

Such labor is not inherently pathological; rather, it reflects resilience in the face of systemic misfit. But resilience should not be a prerequisite for basic participation. For organizations committed to genuine inclusion, recognizing and reducing the need for chronic adaptation should become a leadership imperative.

While professional development often centers on observable traits, it frequently overlooks the internal mechanisms individuals engage to remain legible and functional within neurotypical systems. Rather than interchangeable constructs, these are differentiated forms of response shaped by context, intent, and systemic demand. For example, masking and compensatory coping represent distinct adaptive strategies, each with different implications for performance, well-being, and retention (Livingston et al., 2019a; Cage et al., 2018; Botha & Frost, 2020). Outward markers such as punctuality or composure can therefore mask deeper strain—fatigue, sensory overload, fear of exposure, or emotional withdrawal—illustrating the disconnect between external functionality and hidden effort (Figure 3.1).

DOI: 10.4324/9781003681540-4

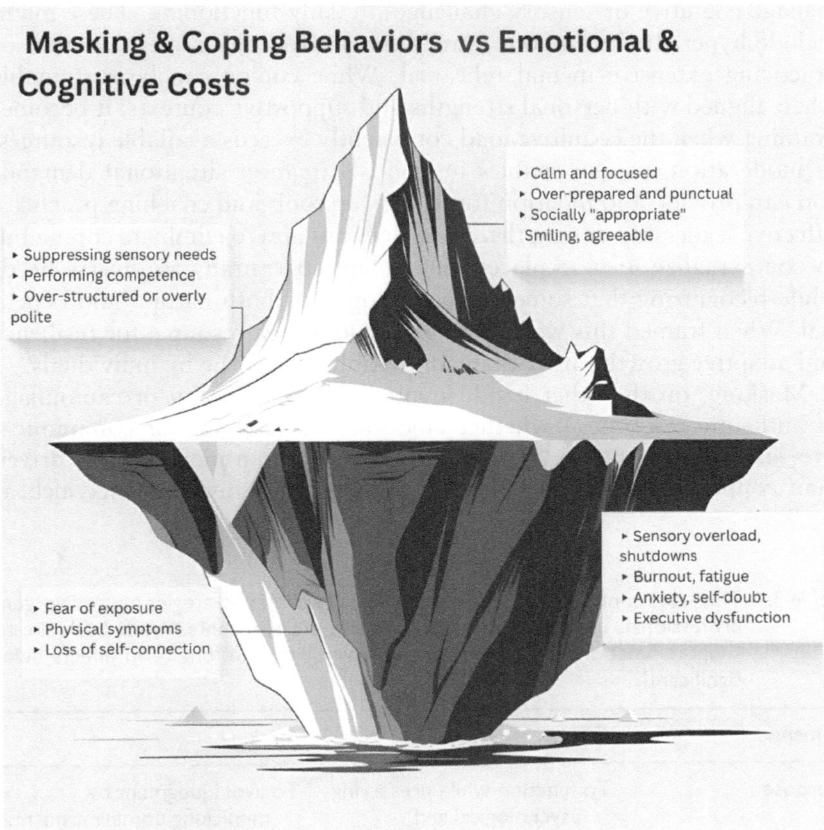

Figure 3.1 Iceberg model contrasting visible coping and masking behaviors (above the surface) with the hidden emotional and cognitive load (below the surface). Outward traits such as calmness or punctuality may conceal internal strain—sensory overload, fatigue, or fear of exposure—illustrating the disconnect between external functionality and unrecognized effort.

3.2 Coping and Masking—Dual Modalities of Adaptation

Divergent strategies of adaptation in non-inclusive systems.

Not all adaptation looks the same. In fact, it comes in two flavors: coping and masking—both of which are widespread among neurodivergent professionals navigating systems not built for their wiring (Table 3.1).

Coping refers to the set of conscious or semi-conscious strategies used to manage cognitive or sensory challenges in daily functioning. These might include hyper-structuring one's environment, relying on memory aids, or practicing extensive mental rehearsal. While coping can be sustainable when aligned with personal strengths and supportive contexts, it becomes draining when the cognitive load consistently exceeds available resources. In moderation, coping enables individuals to meet situational demands and can provide a foundation for leadership tools and coaching practices. Effective leadership design, therefore, does not aim to eliminate coping but to contextualize it: workplaces must adapt structurally to diverse needs while recognizing that some degree of coping is both natural and beneficial. When framed this way, coping functions as a resource for resilience and adaptive growth rather than an invisible cost borne by individuals.

Masking, on the other hand, involves the suppression or camouflage of authentic responses—whether emotional, behavioral, or communicative—in order to appear "typical." Masking is often more socially driven than coping and tends to intensify in high-stakes environments such as

Table 3.1 This table contrasts coping and masking as two core strategies neurodivergent professionals use to navigate non-inclusive environments. While both aim to support functioning, their motivations, visibility, and long-term effects differ significantly.

Dimension	*Coping*	*Masking*
Purpose	To function while preserving psychological and physiological integrity	To avoid judgment by mimicking dominant norms
Sustainability	Often sustainable with support and autonomy	Typically unsustainable; leads to burnout and disconnection
Visibility	Sometimes observable through strategies (e.g., structure, tools)	Often invisible; perceived as "normal" or "competent"
Emotional and Cognitive Cost	Sometimes observable through strategies (e.g., structure, tools)	Undermines authenticity; increases stress and mental fatigue
Risk to Organizations	Low—can strengthen resilience when supported	High—burnout and attrition often remain hidden until too late
Common Expressions	Headphones, mental rehearsal, sensory regulation	Forced eye contact, mirroring tone, suppressing stimming
Systemic Implication	Informs inclusive design and flexible leadership	Reinforces superficial inclusion and erodes psychological safety

leadership roles, client-facing situations, or unaccommodating team cultures (Hull et al., 2017; Livingston et al., 2019b).

3.2.1 *Coping vs. Masking: A Comparative Overview*

While Coping serves to function; masking serves to belong—yet often at a profound personal cost. Research increasingly links chronic masking to heightened rates of anxiety, identity diffusion, and burnout, particularly in individuals with ADHD and autism (Botha & Frost, 2020; Cage & Troxell-Whitman, 2019). Importantly, masking is not deception.

3.2.2 *Coping and Masking: Distinct Mechanisms, Shared Burden*

Adaptive strategies may differ in form, but both carry cognitive and emotional costs—especially when invisibility is mistaken for ease.

Many neurodivergent professionals engage in both coping and masking simultaneously. One may prepare extensively for meetings (coping), while suppressing stimming, delayed responses, or clarification needs (masking). The result is an appearance of competence that often conceals substantial internal strain.

Consider the dyslexic founder who avoids whiteboards—not for lack of insight, but due to the stress of real-time spelling under social scrutiny (Bigozzi et al., 2017). Or the executive with ADHD managing a complex system of productivity tools, yet unable to access them efficiently due to working memory limitations (Barkley, 2011).

This reflects adaptations to systems that prioritize normative behavior over cognitive inclusion. They underscore the hidden labor involved in "passing" and the performance cost of invisibility.

This volume frames coping and masking not merely as individual strategies but as structural responses—shaped by environmental design, institutional norms, and unspoken professional expectations. Reframing the question from "Why is this person struggling?" to "What are they managing that remains unseen?" shifts the analytical lens from deficit to context.

Coping, when voluntary and supported, may foster resilience. Chronic masking, especially when socially mandated, is linked to identity erosion and its cost (Figure 3.2).

> While coping supports neurodivergent sustainability through alignment, masking demands conformity at the cost of authenticity. Misrecognizing one for the other can compromise both inclusion efforts and leadership trust.
>
> Adapted from Botha & Frost (2020), Raymaker et al. (2020)

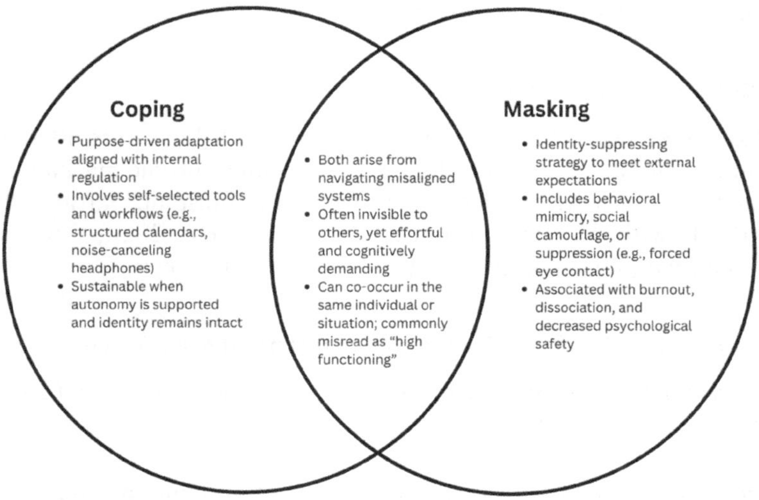

Figure 3.2 Coping and masking as overlapping strategies of neurodivergent adaptation—distinguishing supportive versus suppressive mechanisms in response to non-inclusive environments.

High performance can conceal high cost. In neurodivergent professionals, what appears as consistency often reflects sustained adaptation—masking, coping, or both (Table 3.2). Recognizing these invisible efforts is key to building systems that support sustainability over surface reliability.

3.2.3 *Adaptive Behaviors and Leadership Misreads*

While adaptive strategies enable short-term participation in non-inclusive systems, their cumulative toll cannot be overlooked. Prolonged adaptation under conditions of misfit increases the likelihood of emotional exhaustion and burnout—often long before outward signs of disengagement become visible.

> When a person is forced to adapt to a system not built for them, that adaptation is misread as dysfunction. But what if the dysfunction lies in the system itself?
>
> Nick Walker, *Neuroqueer Heresies*

Yet not all forms of depletion stem from overload. In high-capacity minds, sustained underchallenge can produce a parallel form of attrition: psychological exhaustion rooted not in excessive demand, but in chronic

Table 3.2 This table illustrates how neurodivergent self-regulation strategies—such as sensory coping, scripting, or pacing adjustments—are frequently misinterpreted in professional settings. Common leadership misreads include assumptions of disengagement, defiance, or inconsistency.

Behavior observed	*Common misread*	*What might be happening*
Always prepared	High performer	Masking perfectionism to avoid judgment
Quiet in meetings	Disengaged	Overstimulated, scripting, or masking confusion
Avoiding group whiteboards	Not contributing	Dyslexic or anxious under real-time public pressure
Turns off camera often	Unprofessional	Sensory regulation, autistic burnout, or self-preservation
Rapid-fire speech	Dominating or erratic	ADHD urgency or time anxiety
Appears withdrawn post-project	Not a team player	Burnout or masking collapse after sustained high output

Note: These are not diagnostic categories, but interpretive prompts to build systemic awareness in leadership contexts (Walker, 2021; Botha & Gillespie-Lynch, 2022).

stagnation. The following section introduces *boreout*—a phenomenon particularly relevant for individuals whose cognitive drive is met with monotony rather than complexity.

3.2.4 *Stagnation as Stressor: Recognizing Boreout in High-Capacity Minds*

Underwhelmed, undervalued, unseen: The cost of understimulation.

While burnout has received increasing organizational attention, its counterpart—boreout—remains markedly underrecognized, particularly among gifted, autistic, and ADHD professionals with high cognitive drive and sensitivity to novelty. Boreout describes a state of psychological exhaustion caused not by excessive demand, but by persistent understimulation, lack of challenge, and experiential monotony (Stock, 2015; Rothlin & Werder, 2009). In neurodivergent professionals, this disconnect between internal capacity and external task structure may result in disengagement, low mood, and quiet attrition—frequently misinterpreted as apathy or performance decline.

In leadership contexts, boreout may manifest as silent withdrawal, reduced initiative, or masked compliance—easily mistaken for low motivation. Yet in reality, it reflects structural underutilization and a chronic mismatch between cognitive capacity and role demands (Rothlin & Werder, 2009).

To counteract this, evidence-based strategies emphasize participatory redesign. Rothlin and Werder (2009) recommend fostering task enrichment by aligning job scope with employee input and creating space for competence-driven stretch zones. For instance, leaders can initiate collaborative "task calibration" dialogues, where employees identify one area for increased autonomy, problem-solving, or innovation. In one-on-one conversations, team members might be invited to formulate and present a personal "stretch goal" they would find intrinsically meaningful.

Importantly, boreout is often masked—especially in high-capacity professionals socialized to appear engaged. Underchallenge may be concealed through overpreparation, feigned busyness, or emotional distancing, making it harder to detect and easier to misread as satisfaction or lack of ambition.

3.3 From Awareness to Adaptation Design

Insight without redesign sustains exclusion.

Identifying masking and coping is not the endpoint of inclusive leadership—it is the beginning of structural redesign. Without corresponding adaptation, awareness risks becoming observation without intervention.

Leadership must move beyond behavior interpretation to environmental configuration. The presence of invisible labor—strategic masking, emotional filtering, sensory buffering—requires more than empathy. It requires infrastructure.

Too often, organizations host diagnosis-aware dialogues while leaving institutional systems untouched. But meaningful change occurs when performance expectations, communication protocols, and leadership development pathways are reimagined to support cognitive plurality—not merely accommodate it.

As den Houting (2019) notes, distress is often less about neurodivergent traits and more about the environments in which they are expressed. Leadership that aims for sustainability must shift from decoding behavior to reshaping context—reducing the need for camouflage rather than rewarding its success.

> Masking isn't lying. It's a survival skill.
>
> Adapted from Hull et al. (2017)

Structural generosity in practice is not about solving every divergence with a workaround. It is about building systems that can flex. Inclusion begins where design assumes variation—not exception.

The following chapters unfold in two key directions.

Chapters 4 to 12 explore distinct neurodivergent profiles in leadership, each with its own cognitive architecture, strengths, and friction points. Later chapters turn inward—examining the neurobiological foundations of regulation, decision-making, and connection. Together, these perspectives invite a more layered, inclusive, and ethically grounded understanding of what it means to lead in cognitively diverse environments.

References

Barkley, R. A. (2011). *Executive functions: What they are, how they work, and why they evolved*. Guilford Press.

Bigozzi, L., Tarchi, C., Vagnoli, L., Valente, E., & Pinto, G. (2017). Reading fluency as a predictor of school outcomes across grades. *Frontiers in Psychology, 8*, 200.

Botha, M., & Frost, D. M. (2020). Extending the minority stress model to understand mental health problems experienced by autistic people. *Society and Mental Health, 10*(1), 20–34. https://doi.org/10.1177/2156869318804297

Botha, M., & Gillespie-Lynch, K. (2022). Come as you are: Examining autistic identity development and the neurodiversity movement through an intersectional lens. *Human Development*, *66*(2), 93–112. https://doi.org/10.1159/000524123

Cage, E., & Troxell-Whitman, Z. (2019). Understanding the reasons, contexts and costs of camouflaging for autistic adults. *Journal of Autism and Developmental Disorders, 49*, 1899–1911. https://doi.org/10.1007/s10803-018-03878-x

Cage, E., Di Monaco, J., & Newell, V. (2018). Experiences of autism acceptance and mental health in autistic adults. *Journal of Autism and Developmental Disorders, 48*, 473–484. https://doi.org/10.1007/s10803-017-3342-7

den Houting, J. (2019). Neurodiversity: An insider's perspective. *Autism, 23*(2), 271–273. https://doi.org/10.1177/1362361318820762

Hull, L., Mandy, W., & Petrides, K. V. (2017). Behavioural and cognitive sex/gender differences in autism spectrum condition and typically developing males and females. *Autism, 21*(6), 706–727. https://doi.org/10.1177/1362361316669087

Livingston, L. A., Colvert, E., Social Relationships Study Team, Bolton, P., & Happé, F. (2019a). Good social skills despite poor theory of mind: Exploring compensation in autism spectrum disorder. *Journal of Child Psychology and Psychiatry, 60*(1), 102–110. https://doi.org/10.1111/jcpp.12886

Livingston, L. A., Shah, P., & Happé, F. (2019b). Compensatory strategies below the surface in autism: A qualitative study. *The Lancet Psychiatry, 6*(9), 766–777.

Raymaker, D. M., Teo, A. R., Steckler, N. A., Lentz, B., Scharer, M., Delos Santos, A., ... & Nicolaidis, C. (2020). "Having all of your internal resources exhausted beyond measure and being left with no clean-up crew": Defining autistic burnout. *Autism in Adulthood, 2*(2), 132–143. https://doi.org/10.1089/aut.2019.0079

Rothlin, P., & Werder, P. (2009). *Boreout: Overcoming workplace demotivation*. Kogan Page.

Stock, R. M. (2015). Is boreout a threat to frontline employees' innovative work behavior? *Journal of Managerial Psychology, 30*(3), 284–299. https://doi.org/10.1108/JMP-07-2013-0222

Walker, N. (2021). *Neuroqueer heresies: Notes on the neurodiversity paradigm, autistic empowerment, and postnormal possibilities*. Autonomous Press.

Part II

Neurodivergent Profiles in Leadership Contexts

Chapter 4

ADHD

Fast Brains, Dynamic Drive: Leadership on a Nonlinear Timeline

4.1 The ADHD Spectrum and Its Strategic Relevance in Leadership

Attention by relevance, action by urgency: ADHD as a nonlinear executive profile.

This chapter examines the leadership implications of ADHD across several domains: attention regulation, time perception, divergent thinking, emotional modulation, sensory processing, interest-driven motivation, and environmental fit.

ADHD—Attention Deficit Hyperactivity Disorder—is both one of the most studied and one of the most misunderstood neurodevelopmental conditions. Increasingly, it is recognized not as a singular disorder, but as a spectrum of cognitive regulation differences that affect how individuals attend to information, manage impulses, modulate emotion, and respond to environmental stimulation (Barkley, 2015; Thomas et al., 2015).

Rather than signifying an absence of attention, ADHD involves inconsistent attention allocation—often governed by novelty, urgency, or emotional salience. As a dysregulation of core neurochemical systems that govern attention, motivation, and impulse control. Specifically, ADHD is associated with functional differences in the dopaminergic and noradrenergic pathways of the brain—networks responsible for reward anticipation, task salience, and cognitive persistence (Volkow et al., 2007; Arnsten & Rubia, 2012).

These neurotransmitter imbalances affect the prefrontal cortex, which plays a central role in executive functions such as planning, inhibition, and emotional regulation. Dopamine modulates the brain's ability to prioritize information, while norepinephrine supports alertness and working memory. When these systems are underactive or inconsistently activated, the result is not an absence of focus—but a context-contingent attentional pattern: individuals with ADHD often focus intensely on intrinsically

DOI: 10.4324/9781003681540-6

rewarding tasks while struggling to sustain attention on low-stimulation or externally imposed demands (Dodson, 2025).

Thus, ADHD reflects not a global dysfunction, but a regulation spectrum—shaped by neurobiological sensitivity to novelty, urgency, and reward anticipation. Rather than a fixed trait or static impairment, ADHD manifests as a dynamic interaction between nervous system responsiveness and environmental fit.

ADHD is commonly classified into three presentations:

- **Primarily Inattentive Type** (formerly called ADD): Characterized by distractibility, internal drift, forgetfulness, and difficulty initiating or completing routine tasks. It is frequently underdiagnosed in adults, especially women and individuals who internalize symptoms.
- **Primarily Hyperactive-Impulsive Type**: Marked by motor restlessness, impulsivity, verbal interruptions, and challenges with inhibitory control. This subtype is more often diagnosed in childhood due to its externalized symptoms.
- **Combined Type**: Involves clinically significant traits of both inattention and hyperactivity/impulsivity. It is the most common subtype in adult populations (Figure 4.1).

Importantly, ADHD does not present uniformly. A critical distinction exists between **regulated** and **unregulated ADHD** in leadership settings:

- **Regulated ADHD** refers to individuals who, through environmental alignment, medication, coaching, or adaptive strategy use, have developed systems to support executive functioning and reduce volatility. These leaders often leverage traits like creativity, spontaneity, and high responsiveness as strengths.
- **Unregulated ADHD**, in contrast, describes scenarios where the individual faces chronic misfit with their environment—leading to time blindness, emotional dysregulation, overstimulation, and performance inconsistency. Without structural support, this often results in burnout, misinterpretation of potential, or role mismatch.

Understanding ADHD as a regulation spectrum rather than a binary condition allows leadership development frameworks to better accommodate fluctuating needs, nonlinear strengths, and context-contingent challenges. When strategically supported, ADHD can fuel innovative thinking, rapid problem-solving, and empathic leadership—especially in fast-paced, dynamic, or vision-driven environments.

As noted in Chapter 1, ADHD often goes undiagnosed into adulthood—particularly in women and high-performing individuals—due to camouflaging strategies and contextual fit. This section focuses on how

ADHD in Leadership • Spectrum Traits and Impact

Inattentive	Hyperactive-Impulsive	Combined

Key Traits • Distractibility • Disorganization • Difficulty sustaining focus	**Key Traits** • High energy • Restlessness • Impulsivity	**Traits from both types** • Traits from both types
Leadership Strengths • Strong listening skills • See context creatively • Analytical problem-solving	**Leadership Strengths** • Decisiveness • Enthusiastic drive • Improvisation ability	**Leadership Strengths** • Strategic vision • Energetic communication • Intuitive pattern-spotting
Strain Points • Inconsistent follow-through • Mind-wandering • Engagement slumps	**Strain Points** • Impatience with processes • Talking over others • Regulating emotions	**Strain Points** • Inconsistency • Time blindness • Emotional swings

Figure 4.1 ADHD subtypes with leadership traits and friction points. This figure outlines the three ADHD subtypes—Inattentive, Hyperactive-Impulsive, and Combined—and links them to common leadership strengths and challenges. It highlights how subtype-specific traits (e.g., distractibility, impulsivity) can manifest as both assets and strain points in leadership roles, depending on regulation and context.

Adapted from Barkley (2015) and DSM-5 (APA, 2013).

such late recognition intersects with leadership roles and systemic misreading (Simon et al., 2009).

Recent research suggests a notable overrepresentation of ADHD traits in leadership and entrepreneurial contexts (Wiklund et al., 2017). Attributes such as intuitive pattern recognition, nonlinear problem-solving, and rapid decision-making—often penalized in educational systems—may become competitive advantages in volatile, high-stakes environments.

Yet these cognitive strengths carry significant regulatory demands.

The same neurobiological mechanisms that support rapid ideation, high-pressure responsiveness, and intuitive problem-solving can also increase vulnerability to emotional lability, attentional depletion, and executive dysfunction. ADHD is not inherently deadline-driven but interest-driven—resulting in fluctuating engagement, nonlinear energy rhythms, and an elevated risk of burnout, especially in leadership contexts characterized by sustained ambiguity, multitasking, or stimulus imbalance.

While this chapter focuses on ADHD-specific regulation patterns, it is worth noting that nervous system regulation is a universal leadership function—not limited to neurodivergent individuals. The ability to modulate emotional states, maintain strategic clarity, and recover from overstimulation is foundational to sustainable leadership practice. Part III of this book explores this in depth, offering system-wide approaches to somatic regulation, stress calibration, and leadership resilience across cognitive profiles.

Rather than reflecting a lack of focus, the ADHD profile invites a reframing of executive function as situationally responsive rather than chronically disordered. The following patterns illustrate how this non-linear attentional style—when understood structurally—can shape both strengths and sustainability in leadership roles.

4.2 ADHD in Leadership: Patterns of Expression—Strength Zones and Strain Points

Leadership on fast-forward: navigating intensity, insight, and instability.

4.2.1 *Hyperfocus*

Spectrum Role: Laser-Focused Visionary
Type: Strength—with regulatory caution

Hyperfocus is a core, though often misunderstood, feature of ADHD. Contrary to the stereotype of distractibility, many ADHD individuals do not lack attention—they struggle to regulate it. Hyperfocus describes a state of intense, immersive concentration where attention locks onto a task so completely that external cues, physical needs, and the passage of time may vanish from awareness (Hupfeld, Abagis, & Shah, 2019). These episodes are frequently triggered by novelty, emotional salience, or intrinsic interest, creating a powerful loop of cognitive reward.

In leadership contexts, hyperfocus can generate remarkable output. Whether crafting a launch strategy, building a complex model, or solving a high-stakes problem, the ADHD brain in a flow state is capable of extraordinary depth, precision, and creative synthesis. Work completed during these phases often exceeds typical performance benchmarks—not through discipline, but through full-body cognitive immersion.

Nonetheless, this strength carries regulatory risks. Individuals may struggle to exit the focus state, missing deadlines, social cues, or critical shifts in team dynamics. What appears from the outside as "inflexibility" or "tunnel vision" may in fact be task inertia—a neurobiological difficulty in switching attention once the brain is fully engaged. Post-hyperfocus crashes are common, marked by fatigue, disorientation, or emotional depletion.

Many people with ADHD mask these dynamics by minimizing their intensity—downplaying the hours spent in a single task or overcompensating through multitasking in meetings. Some pre-schedule deliverables to disguise variability, while others joke about being "obsessed" to preempt judgment.

Sustainable leadership begins with honoring, rather than pathologizing, these focus rhythms. Teams should co-design transition protocols that support gentle re-entry from deep work—such as buffer time between focused tasks and meetings, asynchronous check-ins, or visual scheduling tools. Assignments aligned with interest zones not only optimize performance but also reduce cognitive friction.

For leaders who have ADHD themselves, self-regulation requires conscious choreography around hyperfocus cycles. Recovery time is essential—what feels like peak flow is also neurochemical expenditure. You might experiment with integrating decompression elements into your routine, such as hydration, movement, sensory resets, or intentional disengagement. Developing awareness of the transition from productive cognitive immersion to diminishing returns is critical for sustaining performance.

When time dissolves, attention doesn't disappear—it scatters. What looks like disorganization is often temporal dissonance: a mismatch between internal pacing and external demands. Unlike hyperfocus, which stretches time inward, time blindness collapses it—making it hard to start, stop, or *feel* time passing. For ADHD leaders, this isn't a flaw in discipline, but a difference in time perception and dopamine regulation (Barkley, 1997; Toplak et al., 2006). Leadership here means learning to *interface* with time, not just track it.

4.2.2 *Time Blindness and Temporal Dissonance*

Spectrum Role: Timeless Improviser
Type: Potential Hurdle—with high adaptability

For many individuals with ADHD, time is not an internal compass but a conceptual abstraction—experienced more through urgency and emotion than through clocks or calendars. This phenomenon, often termed *time blindness*, disrupts one's ability to accurately perceive duration, anticipate deadlines, or intuitively estimate how long tasks will take (Barkley, Murphy, & Fischer, 2008). The result is a nonlinear experience of time that can oscillate between total immersion in a task and sudden panic when deadlines appear unexpectedly close.

Rather than indicating irresponsibility, this temporal dissonance often reflects an alternate form of attentional rhythm. Leaders with this pattern may spend hours perfecting a single task without noticing time has passed, or underestimate project timelines—only to compensate with bursts of adrenaline-fueled productivity under pressure. This capacity for real-time improvisation becomes a strength in fast-moving or high-stakes environments, where quick pivots and decisive action are valued.

That said, in settings that rely heavily on structured planning and time tracking, these individuals may face recurring hurdles: missed transitions, double-booked calendars, and last-minute rushes. Without scaffolding, time can feel like a fluid, unreliable variable—prompting cycles of procrastination, shame, and overcorrection. To cope and mask these difficulties, many ADHD professionals create rigid external systems: detailed color-coded schedule. Others rely on emotion-driven urgency—using social pressure, guilt, or fear as a last-resort motivator.

Sustainable leadership requires reframing time support as a systems issue. Rather than penalizing lateness or inconsistency, teams can co-create external temporal anchors—visual progress boards, shared milestone check-ins, or clear phase delineations within projects. Normalizing recalibration conversations allows for course correction before collapse. Adaptive support mechanisms allow temporal divergence to coexist with strategic accountability (Doyle & McDowell, 2015).

From a self-regulation perspective, ADHD professionals benefit from tools that translate abstract time into tangible cues: visual timers, countdown clocks, or real-time productivity dashboards. Protecting transition space is equally essential—brief rituals such as walking resets, sound cues, or shifting physical location can help the brain release one mode and enter another. In an ADHD-informed leadership model, time is navigated through precision, pacing, and creative externalization.

People with ADHD benefit from designing environments that externalize time, protect transition space, and normalize nonlinear pacing. By openly naming their time strategies (e.g., "I work in visual blocks, not hourly increments"), they reduce misinterpretation and invite collaborative support.

When time loses its grip, attention doesn't vanish—it fragments. What follows is not stillness, but a surge of cognitive activity: racing thoughts, idea storms, and erratic momentum that can feel energizing or overwhelming, depending on context and containment.

4.2.3 Racing Mind and Creative Surges

Spectrum Role: Divergent Thinker
Type: Strength—with directional challenges

The ADHD cognitive profile is often characterized by dynamic, nonlinear processing—marked by rapid ideation, intuitive pattern recognition, and bursts of creative intensity. What may appear externally as scattered thinking is, in fact, an accelerated form of synthesis: a fast-moving internal dialogue that constantly reframes, reimagines, and connects. Leaders with this style often excel in ambiguity-rich environments, innovation sprints, and early-phase strategy. They energize teams with imaginative thinking, adaptive reframing, and a bold willingness to explore beyond convention.

Yet this generativity unfolds in rhythms—not as a steady flow. Moments of deep engagement may alternate with attentional drift, especially when tasks shift from visioning to maintenance, or from novelty to routine. This fluctuation is often misunderstood as inconsistency. In reality, it reflects a physiological interplay between interest-based attention, dopamine regulation, and task salience (Barkley, 2011; Kooij et al., 2010).

In the workplace, these dynamics may manifest as strong starts followed by waning focus, intense bursts of creativity during ideational surges, or frequent context-switching between topics. Colleagues may misread these patterns as distractibility or impulsiveness. Leaders themselves may begin to internalize such misinterpretations—experiencing shame around unfinished work or difficulty sustaining momentum across the project lifecycle.

Systemically, organizations can support divergent thinkers by moving away from uniform productivity models. This includes embedding idea repositories, building in collaborative handoff structures, and decoupling task value from visibility or linearity. Teams benefit when creative drive is channeled through shared prioritization rituals, rotating innovation sprints, or designated spaces for asynchronous ideation.

Just as creativity can arrive in nonlinear bursts, so too can communication—fluid in one context, faltering in another. The ADHD mind often moves between verbal brilliance and sudden blankness, not from inconsistency but from regulation load.

4.2.4 Verbal and Social Expression Variability

Spectrum Role: Expressive Instinctive
Type: Strength—with communication risk zones

Among individuals with ADHD, verbal and social expression fluctuates with shifts in focus, energy, and emotional regulation. Rather than presenting as a stable trait, communicative output mirrors real-time cognitive and sensory states. In high-stimulation contexts, speech may be rapid, associative, and animated; under stress or overload, it may fragment or fall silent.

These patterns reflect neurobiological variability in attention, arousal, and impulse regulation (Barkley, 2011; Brown, 2020). Rapid tangents or hesitations are less about inconsistency than adaptive response. In writing, the gap between ideation speed and structural formulation often generates friction—particularly in tasks demanding clarity, polish, or linear logic.

In leadership, this expressive range can energize or confuse. A leader may appear articulate and visionary in one setting, then quiet or nonlinear in another. When fluency is equated with competence, such shifts may be misinterpreted—impacting credibility, trust, and team dynamics.

Misreading silence as disinterest or intensity as volatility undermines psychological safety and distorts relational cues. Inclusion efforts must move beyond stylistic expectations toward structural accommodation: multimodal formats (e.g., voice notes, diagrams, or concise bullet points) support communicative clarity without penalizing expressive variation.

When verbal expression stumbles or intensifies, it often mirrors a deeper internal state. Behind the surface of social fluidity or withdrawal lies an emotional regulation system working overtime—especially under sensory or relational strain.

4.2.5 Emotional Regulation and Sensory Sensitivity

Spectrum Role: Deep Reactor
Type: Strain Point—with transformative strength potential

Emotional reactivity and sensory sensitivity are core neurophysiological dimensions of the ADHD profile—central traits, not peripheral effects. The ADHD nervous system registers emotional and sensory input with heightened immediacy and intensity, a dynamic often described as "quick ignition" (Shaw et al., 2014). This amplified responsivity shapes how individuals perceive stress, navigate relationships, and engage with complex environments.

In daily settings, this may manifest as abrupt withdrawal, irritability, or difficulty concentrating—particularly in overstimulating contexts such as open-plan offices, extended meetings, or emotionally charged interactions. These responses are often misread as unprofessional or impulsive, when they in fact reflect a nervous system attempting to restore internal balance amid insufficient emotional or sensory regulation.

In leadership roles, the same sensitivity may enable deep attunement, relational intelligence, and value-driven decision-making. Yet without supportive structures, sustained exposure to high emotional or sensory load can result in exhaustion, fluctuating presence, or dysregulated behavior under pressure. Sharp tonal shifts, disengagement, or sensory shutdowns are frequently misinterpreted as volatility—when they more accurately signal overload.

Systemically, these traits serve as early indicators of environmental or relational misfit. Rather than framing them as weaknesses, organizations can respond by normalizing sensory variation and emotional recalibration. Design features such as predictable scheduling, low-stimulation spaces, recovery zones, and emotional decompression protocols help sustain function without pathologizing difference.

The interplay between emotional arousal and sensory sensitivity lays the groundwork for one of the most complex executive challenges: initiating and sustaining action. This shift brings us to the role of interest-based motivation and its paradoxes in ADHD leadership behavior.

4.2.6 *Interest-Based Drive and Procrastination Dynamics*

Spectrum Role: Deadline Sprinter
Type: Strain Point—with adaptive power under pressure

The ADHD nervous system responds less to obligation than to stimulation. Motivation typically arises from novelty, emotional salience, or urgency—an interest-based activation pattern that diverges from task models rooted in sequential planning or importance (Volkow et al., 2007). This creates a regulatory paradox: while deadline proximity can trigger intense productivity, low-stimulation tasks often elicit disengagement or delay.

In team settings, this may manifest as uneven task initiation, pacing variability, or last-minute surges that mask underlying engagement challenges. For leaders, similar dynamics are often reframed as intuitive triage or visionary timing—yet the internal experience frequently involves fluctuating executive access and significant physiological cost.

This pattern overlaps with—but is distinct from—hyperfocus. While hyperfocus emerges from internal immersion, deadline surges are reactive, driven by external urgency and dopaminergic sensitivity. Both reflect the same neurobiological substrate and often alternate within daily workflows. Recognizing this shared circuitry reframes behavior not as inconsistency, but as functional adaptation to shifting regulatory states.

The same urgency-driven engagement that fuels crisis response can produce exceptional output—provided systems are aligned with attentional rhythms rather than working against them. Many ADHD professionals develop coping mechanisms such as manufactured urgency, pressure stacking, or oscillation between intensity and inertia. Though effective in the short term, these patterns often obscure underlying depletion and normalize unsustainable pacing.

From an inclusion standpoint, procrastination should be reframed as a regulatory threshold—not a failure of willpower. Task initiation improves when environments emphasize structured autonomy, curiosity-driven framing, and collaborative momentum. Practical scaffolds—such as adaptive timeboxing, novelty-sequenced workflows, or activation rituals—can improve engagement without enforcing linear consistency.

The challenge is not simply to "overcome" procrastination, but to design environments that align with the underlying motivational architecture

Regulatory State	Typical Interpretation	Inclusive Design Response	Physical Impact
1. Low stimulation (under activation, low dopamine)	"Laziness" "Avoidance" "Lack of motivation"	Introduce novelty, sensory engagement, micro-deadlines	Cognitive fatigue, anticipatory stress
2. Urgency trigger (Dopamine urge)	"Last-minute rush"	Support structured urgency through adaptive timeboxing and pacing	Adrenaline spike, narrowed focus
3. Deadline Sprint (Hyperfocus under pressure)	"Overdrive mode" "Chaotic intensity"	Rrequires recovery structures and regulated closure rituals	Short-term output, post-task crash
4. Depletion / Recovery (Post-sprint dysregulation)	"Inconsistency" "Burnout"	Needs restorative pacing, systemic recovery cues and co-regulation	Executive depletion, exhaustion

Figure 4.2 **From Procrastination to Regulation – Adaptive Design Framework.** This visual maps four regulatory states shaping motivation and task engagement. Each phase links typical misinterpretations with inclusive design responses and physical impact, illustrating how structured novelty, adapting pacing, and recovery cues support sustainable performance.

of ADHD. When cognitive pacing is supported rather than suppressed, urgency dependence gives way to sustainable performance—and deadline sprints become just one mode among many, not the only path to delivery.

4.2.7 *Environmental Alignment as Structural Leverage*

Cognitive potential is conditional on structural alignment.

Many patterns explored in the preceding sections—such as hyperfocus, procrastination dynamics, emotional volatility, or masking—share a common denominator: they are not static traits, but context-contingent expressions of a sensitive regulatory system. In ADHD, performance is rarely governed by capacity alone, but by the degree of environmental resonance with attentional architecture (Brown, 2020; Dodson, 2020).

When systems are overstimulating, overly rigid, or misaligned with intrinsic motivation, individuals with ADHD—whether in leadership or team roles—may exhibit distractibility, avoidance, or erratic output. Conversely, autonomy-supportive, meaningful, and well-paced environments can unlock disproportionately high engagement and innovation.

Rather than treating environmental adaptations as exceptional accommodations, organizations should reframe them as **core design levers** that enable sustainable cognitive access. Structural fit is not a luxury—it is the infrastructure through which neurodivergent strengths become usable, scalable, and enduring.

To operationalize this alignment, the following tools translate internal variability into functional scaffolds for sustainable performance.

4.3 Optional Tools to Try—ADHD in Leadership Context

These optional strategies support ADHD-related regulation by externalizing executive functions, stabilizing momentum, and reducing the hidden cognitive load associated with attentional fluctuation in leadership contexts.

Rather than enforcing compliance with neurotypical norms, these strategies aim to create functional alignment between individual activation patterns and leadership demands. Their role is not to normalize, but to sustain: enabling performance without exhaustion, and responsiveness without masking. When embedded transparently, such tools also model inclusive leadership practice—showing that adaptation is not a deficit, but a form of strategic self-leadership.

1. Anchored Time Cues

Use external markers like visual timers, music playlists, or ambient light changes to signal the passage of time. This helps orient attention, especially during hyperfocus or time blindness.

→ Supports multisensory scaffolding and executive function regulation (Gawrilow et al., 2014; Miyake et al., 2000).

Application: Especially helpful for ADHD and AuDHD traits involving time blindness or hyperfocus; builds temporal orientation and supports smoother transitions.

2. Timeboxing with Recovery Blocks

Structure work into intentional deep-focus sessions (e.g., 90 minutes), followed by non-negotiable recovery breaks (e.g., 15–30 minutes) to prevent dopamine crashes and cognitive fatigue.

→ Based on the Pomodoro technique and fatigue recovery research (Meijman & Mulder, 1998; Csikszentmihalyi, 1990).

Application: Supports ADHD, autistic, and gifted profiles with intensity-driven cognition—mitigates overstimulation and executive depletion.

3. Transition Scripts and Rituals

Use small, repeated behaviors (like closing tabs, walking, or switching music) to signal that a task has ended and prevent cognitive inertia.

→ Supports task-switching and executive segmentation (Miyake et al., 2000).

Application: Helps autistic, ADHD, and dyspraxic individuals manage transitions and prevent residual cognitive load after task shifts.

4. Temporal Landmarks

Organize the day by reference points (e.g., "after lunch" or "before the team check-in") instead of clock time to give abstract time a tangible structure.

→ Aligned with embodied cognition and temporal mapping (Núñez & Cooperrider, 2013).

Application: Especially useful for AuDHD and NVLD traits that struggle with abstract time concepts or standard scheduling formats.

5. Forward-Planning Prompts

Use reflective questions like "What will I need in 2 hours?" or "What would success look like by 3 PM?" to stimulate future-oriented thinking.

→ Drawn from prospective memory and time-projection research (Barkley et al., 2001).

Application: Builds temporal scaffolding for ADHD and gifted profiles with fluctuating executive foresight, task ignition, and time-related motivation.

6. Calendar Buffering with "Bleed Space"

Schedule tasks in blocks with buffer zones between them to allow for overruns, transitions, or activation delays.

→ Time-contingent planning research supports this for ADHD (Kerns et al., 2001).

Application: Prevents executive overload in ADHD and autistic profiles; supports pacing for dyspraxic and PTSD-affected individuals with variable activation timing.

7. Delayed Gratification Visualizers

Use visible rewards, progress bars, or "streak tracking" to make long-term goals emotionally engaging.

→ Based on delay aversion in ADHD (Sonuga-Barke, 2002).

Application: Motivates sustained effort in ADHD and AuDHD professionals who struggle with reward delay and task persistence in low-stimulation phases.

8. Landing Zones for Recovery

After high-output activity (e.g., presentations, negotiations), allow decompression time—via nature, silence, movement, or music—to transition out of activation.

→ Polyvagal-informed self-regulation technique (Porges, 2011).

Application: Regulates the nervous system in autism, HSP, ADHD, and PTSD traits prone to post-stimulation shutdown or adrenal fatigue.

9. Interoceptive Reminders (Hydration, Snacks, Posture)

Use scheduled nudges or alarms to check in with the body, preventing neglect of physical needs during hyperfocus.

→ Improves interoceptive awareness (Craig, 2002).

Application: Especially beneficial for autistic, AuDHD, and gifted professionals with diminished interoceptive tracking during cognitive immersion.

10. Decentralized Idea Capture Systems

Keep a "drop zone" for spontaneous ideas (Post-its, Notion board, voice memos), enabling mental offloading without task switching.

→ Supports dual-processing and cognitive load reduction (Evans & Stanovich, 2013).

Application: Protects working memory in ADHD, gifted, and dyslexic minds prone to nonlinear ideation or thought stacking.

11. Communicated Focus Windows

Share designated "deep work" times with your team to reduce unnecessary interruptions.

→ Builds autonomy, predictability, and respect for neurodivergent pacing (Deci & Ryan, 2000).

Application: Helps ADHD, autism, and HSP profiles establish boundaries around concentration—reducing context-switching strain and masking pressure.

12. Transparent Time Strategy Communication

Name your time-management approach openly (e.g., "I plan in visual blocks"). This sets expectations and promotes shared understanding.

→ Enhances inclusion and neurodivergent visibility (Doyle & McDowall, 2015).

Application: Fosters psychological safety for individuals with dyslexia, dyspraxia, ADHD, or executive function disorders who rely on atypical structures.

The tools above offer structural support; real-world examples help illustrate how ADHD-informed leadership can translate cognitive difference into systemic innovation.

4.4 Restless Vision, Systemic Reinvention—ADHD Leadership as a Catalyst for Scalable Innovation

When structure fails, ingenuity designs its own system.

ADHD-Inspired Business Ingenuity.

Ingvar Kamprad, the founder of IKEA, is frequently cited as a business leader whose behavioral and cognitive patterns align with ADHD traits. His hallmark restlessness, low tolerance for inefficiency, and bias for action became the driving forces behind a global retail revolution. Rather than conforming to established models of furniture retail—often slow, expensive, and service-heavy—Kamprad designed a system that mirrored his cognitive strengths: intuitive navigation, flat-pack modularity, and frictionless scalability.

His difficulty with traditional bureaucracy translated into a business architecture grounded in simplicity, autonomy, and user-driven design—an approach that disrupted not just how people buy furniture, but how they engage with space. In this sense, his leadership exemplifies a core ADHD pattern: turning internal urgency and frustration with constraint into visionary systemic redesign.

Kamprad's model became more than a commercial success—it became a structural metaphor for ADHD-informed leadership: fast iteration, customer-centered modularity, and scalable systems that do not penalize cognitive divergence, but build with it.

While ADHD alone reshapes how time, focus, and motivation are experienced, the co-occurrence of autistic traits introduces a second axis of neurocognitive difference. In AuDHD, the dance between impulsivity and rigidity, between cognitive speed and sensory depth, creates a unique leadership signature—often misunderstood through either lens in isolation. To understand this blend, we must examine where ADHD's momentum meets autism's patterning.

References

American Psychiatric Association. (2013). *Diagnostic and statistical manual of mental disorders* (5th ed.). https://doi.org/10.1176/appi.books.9780890425596

Arnsten, A. F. T., & Rubia, K. (2012). Neurobiological circuits regulating attention, cognitive control, motivation, and emotion: Disruptions in neurodevelopmental psychiatric disorders. *Journal of the American Academy of Child and Adolescent Psychiatry*, *51*(4), 356–367. https://doi.org/10.1016/j.jaac.2012.06.015

Barkley, R. A. (1997). Behavioral inhibition, sustained attention, and executive functions: Constructing a unifying theory of ADHD. *Psychological Bulletin*, *121*(1), 65–94. https://doi.org/10.1037/0033-2909.121.1.65

Barkley, R. A. (2011). *Executive functions: What they are, how they work, and why they evolved*. Guilford Press.

Barkley, R. A. (2015). *Attention-deficit hyperactivity disorder: A handbook for diagnosis and treatment* (4th ed.). Guilford Press.

Barkley, R. A., Edwards, G., Laneri, M., Fletcher, K., & Metevia, L. (2001). Executive functioning, temporal discounting, and self-directedness in adolescents with attention-deficit/hyperactivity disorder (ADHD). *Journal of Abnormal Child Psychology*, *29*(6), 541–556. https://doi.org/10.1023/a:1012233310098

Barkley, R. A., Murphy, K. R., & Fischer, M. (2008). *ADHD in adults: What the science says*. Guilford Press.

Brown, T. E. (2020). *A new understanding of ADHD in children and adults: Executive function impairments*. Routledge.

Craig, A. D. (2002). How do you feel? Interoception: The sense of the physiological condition of the body. *Nature Reviews Neuroscience*, *3*(8), 655–666. https://doi.org/10.1038/35094500

Csikszentmihalyi, M. (1990). *Flow: The psychology of optimal experience*. Harper & Row.

Deci, E. L., & Ryan, R. M. (2000). The "what" and "why" of goal pursuits: Human needs and the self-determination of behavior. *American Psychologist*, *55*(1), 68–78. https://doi.org/10.1037/0003-066X.55.1.68

Dodson, W. (2025). *New insights into rejection sensitive dysphoria*. ADDitude. https://www.additudemag.com/rejection-sensitive-dysphoria-and-adhd/

Doyle, N., & McDowall, A. (2015). Is coaching an effective adjustment for dyslexic adults? *Coaching: An International Journal of Theory, Research and Practice*, *8*(2), 154–168. https://doi.org/10.1080/17521882.2015.1065894

Evans, J. St. B. T., & Stanovich, K. E. (2013). Dual-process theories of higher cognition: Advancing the debate. *Perspectives on Psychological Science*, *8*(3), 223–241. https://doi.org/10.1016/j.tics.2013.03.002

Gawrilow, C., Gollwitzer, P. M., & Oettingen, G. (2014). If–then plans benefit executive functions in children with ADHD. *Journal of Experimental Child Psychology*, *125*, 63–73. https://doi.org/10.1016/j.jecp.2013.09.009
Hupfeld, K. E., Abagis, T. R., & Shah, P. (2019). Correction to: Living "in the zone": hyperfocus in adult ADHD. *Child Indicators Research*, *12*(3), 1043. https://doi.org/10.1007/s12402-019-00296-6
Kerns, K. A., & Price, K. J. (2001). An investigation of prospective memory in children with ADHD. *Child Neuropsychology*, 7(3), 162–171. https://doi.org/10.1076/chin.7.3.162.8744
Kooij, S. J. J., Bejerot, S., Blackwell, A., Caci, H., Casas-Brugué, M., Carpentier, P. J., ... Asherson, P. (2010). European consensus statement on diagnosis and treatment of adult ADHD: The European Network Adult ADHD. BMC Psychiatry, 10(67). https://doi.org/10.1186/1471-244X-10-67
Meijman, T. F., & Mulder, G. (1998). Psychological aspects of workload. In P. J. D. Drenth, H. Thierry, & C. J. de Wolff (Eds.), *Handbook of work and organizational psychology: Vol. 2. Work psychology* (pp. 5–33). Psychology Press.
Miyake, A., Friedman, N. P., Emerson, M. J., Witzki, A. H., Howerter, A., & Wager, T. D. (2000). The unity and diversity of executive functions and their contributions to complex "frontal lobe" tasks: A latent variable analysis. *Cognitive Psychology*, *41*(1), 49–100. https://doi.org/10.1006/cogp.1999.0734
Núñez, R., & Cooperrider, K. (2013). The tangle of space and time in human cognition. *Trends in Cognitive Sciences*, *17*(5), 220–229. https://doi.org/10.1016/j.tics.2013.10.008
Porges, S. W. (2011). *The polyvagal theory: Neurophysiological foundations of emotions, attachment, communication, and self-regulation*. W. W. Norton & Company.
Shaw, P., Stringaris, A., Nigg, J., & Leibenluft, E. (2014). Emotion dysregulation in attention deficit hyperactivity disorder. *American Journal of Psychiatry*, *171*(3), 276–293. https://doi.org/10.1176/appi.ajp.2013.13070966
Simon, V., Czobor, P., Bálint, S., Mészáros, Á., & Bitter, I. (2009). Prevalence and correlates of adult attention-deficit hyperactivity disorder: Meta-analysis. *British Journal of Psychiatry*, *194*(3), 204–211. https://doi.org/10.1192/bjp.bp.107.048827
Sonuga-Barke, E. J. S. (2002). Psychological heterogeneity in ADHD: A dual pathway model of behaviour and cognition. *Behavioural Brain Research*, *130*(1–2), 29–36. https://doi.org/10.1016/S0166-4328(01)00432-6
Thomas, R., Sanders, S., Doust, J., Beller, E., & Glasziou, P. (2015). Prevalence of attention-deficit/hyperactivity disorder: A systematic review and meta-analysis. *Pediatrics*, *135*(4), e994–e1001. https://doi.org/10.1542/peds.2014-3482
Toplak, M. E., Dockstader, C., & Tannock, R. (2006). Temporal information processing in ADHD: Findings to date and new methods. *Journal of Neuroscience Methods*, *151*(1), 15–29. https://doi.org/10.1016/j.jneumeth.2005.09.018
Volkow, N. D., Wang, G.-J., Kollins, S. H., Wigal, T. L., Newcorn, J. H., Telang, F., ... Swanson, J. M. (2007). Evaluating dopamine reward pathway in ADHD: Clinical implications. *JAMA*, *64*(8), 932–940. https://doi.org/10.1001/archpsyc.64.8.932
Wiklund, J., Yu, W., Tucker, R., & Marino, L. D. (2017). ADHD, impulsivity and entrepreneurship. *Journal of Business Venturing*, *32*(6), 627–656. https://doi.org/10.1016/j.jbusvent.2017.01.002

Chapter 5

Autism

Pattern, Integrity, and the Architecture of Thought

5.1 Understanding Autism: From Cognitive Difference to Strategic Depth

Sensory logic, systemic vision: the autistic leadership spectrum.

This chapter explores the leadership dimensions of autism through five core domains: social communication differences, sensory processing patterns, focused interests and deep expertise, emotional integrity and moral reasoning, and distinct cognitive-executive functioning profiles.

Autism is a neurodevelopmental condition that reflects a qualitatively distinct way of processing sensory, cognitive, and social information. It is not a deficit of intelligence or ability, but a divergent cognitive architecture marked by monotropic attention (deep focus on selected topics), heightened perceptual sensitivity, and a preference for clarity, coherence, and predictability in both thought and communication.

Rather than a single fixed profile, autism exists on a broad spectrum. Individuals may differ significantly in sensory thresholds, language style, executive function, and social presentation. Some show high verbal fluency with strong analytical skills—historically classified under "Asperger's Syndrome," a term no longer used diagnostically but still descriptively relevant for many adults. Others may present with minimal verbal language but display advanced system reasoning, pattern recognition, or ethical clarity.

Understanding autism as a spectrum helps reframe perceived inconsistencies: an individual may demonstrate exceptional competence in one domain while requiring accommodations in another. This heterogeneity is not a flaw—it is a signature of autistic cognition.

DOI: 10.4324/9781003681540-7

5.2 From Cognitive Divergence to Strategic Contribution

Reframing traits as strategic leadership capacities.

Autistic traits often deviate from dominant leadership norms, yet they carry substantial value—particularly in environments where clarity, systems integrity, and depth matter more than social performance (Nonaka & Takeuchi, 1995).

Key cognitive traits include:

- **Monotropic focus**—deep, sustained attention on areas of interest, fostering expertise and innovation (Murray, 2020)
- **Sensory sensitivity**—heightened awareness of sensory input, which can lead to overload in unmodulated environments
- **Literal and direct communication**—often misread as blunt, but rooted in sincerity, precision, and efficiency
- **Reduced social mimicry**—less concern with unspoken norms, paired with a high drive for fairness, consistency, and logic

These characteristics, while frequently misinterpreted, reveal their strategic value when reframed through leadership design and contextual support (Figure 5.1).

5.3 Dual-Lens Infographic

Reframing autistic communication in leadership contexts.

Reframing autism as a differentiated cognitive design reveals its strategic value across roles—not only in leadership, but wherever systems rely on substance over display, and precision over performativity (Milton, 2012) (Figure 5.1).

5.4 Autistic Leadership: Clarity beyond Convention

Seeing structure differently.

Before we can explore how autism shapes leadership, we must first reconsider the cultural narratives that frame it. Public perception of autism remains influenced by outdated archetypes—such as the stereotype of isolated brilliance or social incompetence—which obscure the diverse realities of autistic adults in professional life.

Behaviors like avoiding eye contact or using highly precise language are often misinterpreted as evasive or cold. In reality, they may reflect sensory regulation, directness, or a preference for cognitive clarity over social

Reframing Autistic Communication

Common Misinterpretation	Autistic Communication Reality	Strategic Value Realized
Avoids eye contact → "evasive," "untrustworthy	Reduces visual input to conserve sensory energy or enhance verbal focus	Enables deep presence and focused listening
Speaks slowly or precisely → "cold"	Prioritizes clarity and accuracy over social performativity	Builds trust through verbal integrity and precision
Doesn't join small talk → "disengaged"	Minimizes non-essential interaction to preserve cognitive resources	Delivers focused, high-value contributions
Corrects errors → "pedantic"	Demonstrates commitment to detail and factual accuracy	Safeguards quality and mitigates long-term risk
Intense focus on one topic → "rigid"	Shows deep expertise and sustained cognitive engagement	Fuels innovation through specialization and domain mastery

Figure 5.1 Contrasts common misinterpretations of autistic communication with their functional basis and professional contribution. When viewed through a neurodivergent-informed lens, behaviors often seen as deficits reveal strengths in focus, integrity, and cognitive depth.

performance. These misreadings can contribute to underrecognition, misalignment, or exclusion in leadership development.

Autistic cognition brings a distinctive kind of leadership strength: pattern recognition that bypasses noise, principled thinking that resists superficial consensus, and a capacity for sustained attention that drives deep innovation. In contrast to leadership norms that prize charisma, rapid exchange, and social fluency, autistic leaders often lead through systems thinking, integrity, and structural clarity.

Understanding autism in this light reframes it—not as a leadership limitation, but as a differentiated cognitive design with unique strategic value. Particularly in complex environments, these capacities are not marginal—they are essential:

- **Structural foresight**: anticipating consequences before they unfold
- **Integrity under pressure**: resisting conformity when systems drift into ethical gray zones

- **Sustained expertise**: building deep knowledge through intense, long-term focus
- **Transparent communication**: fostering trust through clarity and consistency

According to the CDC (2023), about 1 in 36 children in the United States is identified as being on the autism spectrum. The European Commission estimates that 7–10 million people in the EU are autistic—yet many adults remain undiagnosed due to outdated diagnostic criteria and gendered bias (Lai et al., 2015; Loomes et al., 2017). This duality creates unique tensions and synergies that resist linear categorization.

The following patterns explore how autistic traits manifest in leadership settings not as dysfunctions, but as cognitive architectures shaped for depth, precision, and ethical constancy. To access their full contribution, systems must differentiate interpersonal comfort from conceptual clarity—and recognize principled cognition as a leadership asset.

5.5 Autism in Leadership: Patterns of Expression—Strength Zones and Strain Points

Structured vision, quiet influence—autistic leadership through systems thinking and purposeful design.

5.5.1 *Social Communication Differences*

Spectrum Role: Intentional Communicator
Type: Strength—with context-dependent barriers

Social communication differences in autistic leadership are often misinterpreted through a neurotypical lens. Traits such as directness, literal language processing, reduced use of eye contact, and a preference for substantive over phatic exchange are not indicators of social deficit, but of alternative communicative logic (Milton, 2012; Hellendoorn et al., 2015). These patterns reflect a strong orientation toward clarity, authenticity, and cognitive efficiency—especially in task-focused or high-integrity environments.

Challenges arise when these modes of interaction collide with high-context cultures that rely on indirect cues, emotional subtext, or performative rapport. What is intended as respectful precision may be perceived as aloofness or inflexibility. The burden of adaptation often falls on autistic professionals, who mask by scripting conversation, mimicking affect, or tolerating ambiguity—all of which deplete executive resources and compromise authenticity.

Yet these same individuals often excel at offering unambiguous feedback, articulating expectations, and identifying inconsistencies in logic or group process. Their communication style is well-suited to environments that value transparency, ethical alignment, and strategic coherence.

Supporting social communication differences in neurodivergent leadership does not require wholesale cultural overhaul, but targeted systemic recalibrations. These include offering multimodal contribution formats (e.g., written summaries, visual inputs, asynchronous dialogue), structuring interactions for clarity, and decoupling social fluency from assumptions of competence. For autistic leaders, this means being empowered to communicate in ways that preserve strategic clarity and cognitive energy. For team members, it means having access to collaborative formats that do not penalize literalness, directness, or processing latency.

Beneath verbal expression lies a subtler and often more influential factor: sensory processing. While language may draw attention, it is the environment—what is sensed, not said—that most directly governs availability, regulation, and long-term participation. Understanding how autistic professionals sustain leadership presence requires shifting the lens: from expression to perception, and from output to input.

5.5.2 Sensory Processing Differences

Spectrum Role: Sensory Strategist
Type: Regulation Challenge—with adaptive potential

Sensory processing differences are among the most consistent yet often misunderstood dimensions of autistic cognition. These differences can manifest as hypersensitivity, hyposensitivity, or context-dependent fluctuation—shaped by both neurobiological variation and environmental factors (Robertson & Baron-Cohen, 2017). While typically invisible, they significantly influence focus and energy regulation.

Autistic professionals may experience standard work environments—such as bright lighting, background noise, or open-plan layouts—as overwhelming rather than neutral. These are not preferences, ratherinvoluntary neurological responses. When sensory systems are overstimulated, the result may be cognitive shutdown, withdrawal, or exhaustion—often misread as disinterest or avoidance. Over time, repeated sensory strain without opportunities for regulation can accumulate into chronic stress, heightening vulnerability to burnout and reducing long-term engagement (Jordan, I. 2020).

Nonetheless, when environments are modulated to support sensory regulation, these sensitivities can become assets. Many autistic leaders exhibit heightened attunement to spatial, aesthetic, or emotional cues, which enhances decision-making in domains such as UX design, branding, and interpersonal dynamics. Sensory intuition can function as a form of anticipatory intelligence—surfacing concerns or opportunities others overlook.

For autistic leaders, this means advocating for settings that support regulation before performance: structured solitude before visibility, low-stimulation preparation before high-stakes delivery. For team members, it means being able to choose engagement modes that align with their regulatory needs without penalty or pathologization. Both benefit from a culture where retreat is understood not as avoidance, but as recalibration.

Sensory regulation determines what gets through. But once external noise is filtered, a different kind of signal emerges: focused attention. In autistic cognition, that focus often coalesces into sustained, self-directed inquiry—what's commonly referred to as "special interests." Far from narrow, these domains of deep expertise represent engines of innovation, resilience, and identity.

5.5.3 *Focused Interests and Deep Expertise*

Spectrum Role: Specialist
Type: Strength—with contextual friction

Autistic professionals frequently demonstrate exceptional expertise rooted in sustained, immersive engagement with specific domains of interest. These focused pursuits—often referred to as "special interests"—are not peripheral hobbies but core cognitive structures that provide coherence, motivation, and direction across time. Far from indicating rigidity, they frequently generate high-impact insights, interdisciplinary synthesis, and innovative system interventions (Mottron, 2011; Baron-Cohen et al., 2009).

Rather than following traditional curricular or career paths, many autistic leaders cultivate autodidactic learning trajectories that exceed formal expectations. Their work is often marked by deep pattern recognition, conceptual precision, and strategic foresight—particularly when interests align with organizational relevance. Despite this, such forms of expertise are still frequently misread as eccentricity, narrowing access to leadership roles that reward generalism over mastery.

In many professional environments, autistic strengths generate friction due to a mismatch between deep-focus cognition and prevailing performance expectations—less because of what is contributed than how it diverges from normative interaction rhythms. Demands to multitask, quickly shift topics, or dilute intensity often undermine the very contributions organizations most need. Both autistic leaders and team members frequently feel pressure to mask their depth—adopting superficial range over true relevance, or softening clarity to conform to performative norms.

Organizations can amplify this strength by anchoring roles in expertise rather than extroversion, allowing leaders to shape strategy through substance, not performance. Structured autonomy, deep-work cycles, and alignment with values-based missions create the conditions where sustained focus becomes a catalytic force—for innovation, integrity, and long-term vision.

Focused minds don't just organize information—they organize meaning. For many autistic leaders, that meaning is anchored in values. Precision of thought often goes hand in hand with precision of conscience. The same integrity that drives deep work also underpins ethical decision-making, moral clarity, and a deep discomfort with performative compromise.

5.5.4 Emotional Integrity and Moral Reasoning

Spectrum Role: Principled Anchor
Type: Strength—with relational complexity

Rather than calibrating decisions to external expectations, many autistic professionals operate from an internally anchored moral framework—one that prioritizes congruence between values, intentions, and action. This principled orientation is often misread as inflexibility or a lack of political tact, yet it reflects a commitment to systemic trustworthiness and psychological safety (Davidson & Henderson, 2010; Raymaker et al., 2020).

Organizational environments that tolerate inconsistency, performative behavior, or unethical compromise can elicit acute distress in autistic professionals. Violations of fairness—whether subtle or overt—are rarely shrugged off as inconsequential. While responses may not be outwardly expressed in the moment, the emotional and cognitive impact is significant. Left unacknowledged, this dissonance can lead to moral injury, withdrawal, or attrition from roles that require constant ethical suppression.

Sustainable leadership environments benefit from explicitly integrating ethical clarity into decision-making frameworks. For autistic leaders, principled dissent is not an act of defiance—it is an act of alignment. Their resistance to ethical ambiguity does not stem from rigidity, but from a deep internal coherence that prioritizes systems integrity over short-term compromise. In moments of organizational drift, such leaders often function as moral barometers, voicing what others may sense but hesitate to articulate.

For autistic team members, ethical discomfort may be expressed less overtly: through disengagement, heightened emotional reactivity, or sudden withdrawal from tasks that feel misaligned. These responses are frequently misread as inflexibility or overreaction, when in fact they signal a deeper misfit between core values and contextual expectations. Rather than pathologizing such signals, it is more generative to ask: Which value is being activated?

Values create clarity—but they don't always simplify action. Even with strong ethical alignment, many autistic professionals experience friction when initiating, sequencing, or adapting tasks. This isn't a gap in competence—it's a difference in cognitive rhythm. And in systems built for speed over depth, that rhythm is often out of sync with organizational tempo.

5.5.5 Cognitive and Executive Functioning Patterns

Spectrum Role: Deep Diver
Type: Strength—with systemic friction

Autistic cognition is often characterized by monotropism—an attentional style in which mental resources converge deeply on one topic or domain at a time (Murray et al., 2005). This mode of focus enables original frameworks, analytical precision, and high-fidelity outcomes when environmental conditions allow for clarity, autonomy, and minimal switching. Yet within systems calibrated for speed, multitasking, or verbal spontaneity, these patterns can be misread as inflexibility or disengagement.

Executive functioning differences do not reflect lower intelligence. They are a signal distinct modes of initiation, sequencing, and cognitive transition. These capacities are sensitive to internal states—such as fatigue or sensory input—and external structures like ambiguity, noise, or task switching. What often appears as silence, delay, or perfectionism may, in fact, be the consolidation phase of layered, nonlinear processing.

To navigate neurotypical expectations, many autistic professionals—both leaders and team members—develop sophisticated compensatory strategies: scripting interactions in advance, rigidly structuring workflows, or simulating multitasking while internally shielding focus. These adaptations, though often effective on the surface, are cognitively and emotionally costly. Because the external result may appear seamless, the internal effort remains invisible—leading to chronic overload, misrecognition, or lack of appropriate support.

Sustainable leadership systems require more than informal tolerance—they require structural accommodations that legitimize neurodivergent modalities as part of organizational design intelligence. This includes asynchronous contribution formats, visual task mapping, flexible transition pacing, and decoupling presence from constant visibility.

To operationalize the cognitive profiles outlined above, the following tools offer practical strategies that align with autistic processing styles. Designed to reduce cognitive friction and minimize the need for masking, these supports enable sustained performance and authentic engagement—whether in leadership roles or team-based collaboration.

5.6 Optional Tools to Try—Autism in Leadership Context

These optional strategies support autistic leadership by externalizing social expectations, modulating sensory input, and reducing the hidden cognitive load associated with nonlinear processing, monotropic focus, and masking.

Rather than enforcing neurotypical communication or work styles, these strategies aim to create **functional coherence between autistic cognitive traits and leadership demands**. Their goal is not to normalize but to enable: sustaining clarity without depletion, participation without camouflage. When implemented transparently, these tools also model inclusive systems thinking—demonstrating that adaptation is not a concession, but a strategic design principle.

1. Visual Agendas and Structured Meetings

Use visual or written agendas to reduce ambiguity and preview interaction flow.

→ Supports social predictability and low-context processing (Livingston & Happé, 2017).

Application: Supports autistic and AuDHD leaders by reducing ambiguity and offsetting challenges with low-context or fast-paced verbal input.

2. Asynchronous Communication Channels

Enable formats like shared documents, voice notes, or delayed-response platforms to reduce real-time pressure.

→ Reduces masking and supports reflection-based engagement (Milton, 2012).

Application: Enables autistic, ADHD, and dyslexic individuals to engage without time pressure, mitigating verbal processing latency and working memory strain.

3. Sensory Load Mapping

Audit environments for potential sensory triggers—noise, fluorescent lights, clutter—and adjust accordingly.

→ Supports sensory modulation and environmental fit (Robertson & Baron-Cohen, 2017).

Application: Regulates sensory defensiveness in autism, HSP, and PTSD profiles, reducing the risk of shutdown or fight/flight reactions in overstimulating settings.

4. Recovery Rituals

Establish grounding routines after high-demand tasks (e.g., deep pressure, silence, walking).

→ Informed by Polyvagal Theory and autistic nervous system research (Porges, 2011).

Application: Helps restore nervous system balance after hyperarousal in ADHD, autism, giftedness, and trauma-related profiles; supports post-task decompression.

5. Deep-Dive Knowledge Channels

Provide opt-in spaces for interest-based, detail-rich contributions (e.g., documentation hubs, deep-dive briefings).

→ Leverages monotropic attention and expertise (Murray, 2020).

Application: Harnesses monotropic focus in autism, hyperfocus tendencies in ADHD, and abstraction strength in giftedness without social derailment.

6. Ethical Anchoring Tools

Use value grids, boundary scripts, or visual decision trees for moral clarity in ambiguous situations.

→ Supports principled cognition and integrity-based decision-making (Hull et al., 2017).

Application: Anchors ethical reasoning in autism, OCD traits, and gifted profiles who may experience heightened moral intensity or decision paralysis in gray zones.

7. Processing Time Buffers

Build in silent reflection periods after meetings or emotionally charged discussions.

→ Protects integration time and reduces cognitive fatigue (Boucher, 2007).

Application: Supports delayed processing and emotional integration for HSPs, autistic thinkers, and dyspraxic leaders prone to timing lag or response latency.

8. Parallel Thinking Boards

Use visual maps to separate ideation from execution (e.g., whiteboards, digital mind maps).

→ Supports cognitive offloading and sequencing (Evans & Stanovich, 2013).

Application: Helps ADHD, dyslexic, and AuDHD professionals externalize complex ideas, balance divergent thinking with execution, and reduce executive overload.

The strategies above offer structural support for common autistic leadership needs; they gain full meaning when applied in context. The following real-world example illustrates how these tools can be embedded into practice as conscious adaptations that transform cognitive difference into systems-level clarity and ethical impact.

5.7 Structured Expression, Ethical Depth—Autistic Leadership through Narrative Architecture and Emotional Integrity

Precision, purpose, and internal authorship.

Sir Anthony Hopkins has spoken openly about being diagnosed late in life with autism (in his case formerly Asperger's), reflecting on how it clarified patterns of lifelong difference rather than pathologizing them. In interviews, he has rejected reductive labeling, stating: "*We're all on the spectrum somewhere... Labels just get in the way*." Rather than conforming to social expectations of emotional expressiveness or interpersonal style, Hopkins channels emotional depth through precise structure, rehearsal, and internal discipline—hallmarks of autistic cognition when applied through intentional design.

His leadership influence in creative environments emerges not through traditional relational performance, but through coherence, consistency, and mastery of craft. On film sets and in rehearsal processes, he is known for extraordinary preparation—often learning entire scripts before production begins—and for requiring clarity, order, and discipline in collaborative environments. His presence commands trust, not through emotional display, but through reliability, deep focus, and respect for process.

His influence extends beyond acting. As a composer, he wrote the orchestral suite And the Waltz Goes On, which was premiered decades after its completion. The work reflects his long engagement with internal structure, musical architecture, and aesthetic intentionality—hallmarks of autistic creative leadership grounded in delayed expression, not diminished insight.

Hopkins also models one of the core tenets of sustainable autistic leadership: the ability to maintain boundaries without compromising presence. He selectively engages with publicity, avoids overstimulation, and designs his professional life to preserve autonomy and creative control. This self-structuring is not a retreat from leadership, but a condition for maintaining clarity, emotional steadiness, and creative excellence over time.

His leadership illustrates that influence does not require extroversion or immediacy. Instead, it can be built through principled authorship, focused execution, and a deep fidelity to one's internal standards—qualities often undervalued in conventional models, but essential to neurodivergent leadership at scale.

While autism often reshapes interaction, perception, and systems engagement, dyslexia reminds us that cognition itself is not linear. Both profiles challenge conventional educational assumptions, but where autism highlights depth in structure and routine, dyslexia brings forth strengths in visual thinking, spatial reasoning, and nonlinear problem-solving. Here, we move from sensory-cognitive processing to language-based divergence.

References

Baron-Cohen, S., Ashwin, E., Ashwin, C., Tavassoli, T., & Chakrabarti, B. (2009). Talent in autism: Hyper-systemizing, hyper-attention to detail and sensory hypersensitivity. *Philosophical Transactions of the Royal Society B: Biological Sciences*, *364*(1522), 1377–1383. https://doi.org/10.1098/rstb.2008.0337

Boucher, J. (2007). Memory and generativity in very high functioning autism: A firsthand account and an interpretation. *Autism*, *11*(3), 255–264. https://doi.org/10.1177/1362361307076863

Centers for Disease Control and Prevention. (2023). *Data & statistics on autism spectrum disorder*. https://www.cdc.gov/autism/data-research/

Davidson, J., & Henderson, V. L. (2010). "Coming out" on the spectrum: Autism, identity and disclosure. *Social & Cultural Geography*, *11*(2), 155–170. https://doi.org/10.1080/14649360903525240

Evans, J. St. B. T., & Stanovich, K. E. (2013). Dual-process theories of higher cognition: Advancing the debate. *Perspectives on Psychological Science*, *8*(3), 223–241. https://doi.org/10.1177/1745691612460685

Hellendoorn, A., Wijnroks, L., & Leseman, P. (2015). Autism and the mirror neuron system: An explorative review of current literature. *Developmental Disabilities Research Reviews*, *15*(3), 146–160. https://doi.org/10.1002/ddrr.66

Hull, L., Mandy, W., Lai, M.-C., Baron-Cohen, S., Allison, C., Smith, P., & Petrides, K. V. (2017). Development and validation of the camouflaging autistic traits questionnaire (CAT-Q). *Journal of Autism and Developmental Disorders*, *49*(3), 819–833. https://doi.org/10.1007/s10803-018-3792-6

Jordan, I. (2020). *Ethical dissonance: How leadership misalignment fuels burnout in value-driven roles*. Leadership Studies Quarterly.

Lai, M.-C., Lombardo, M. V., Auyeung, B., Chakrabarti, B., & Baron-Cohen, S. (2015). Sex/gender differences and autism: Setting the scene for future research. *Journal of the American Academy of Child and Adolescent Psychiatry*, *54*(1), 11–24. https://doi.org/10.1016/j.jaac.2014.10.003

Livingston, L. A., & Happé, F. (2017). Conceptualising compensation in neurodevelopmental disorders: Reflections from autism spectrum disorder. *Neuroscience & Biobehavioral Reviews*, *80*, 729–742. https://doi.org/10.1016/j.neubiorev.2017.06.005

Loomes, R., Hull, L., & Mandy, W. P. L. (2017). What is the male-to-female ratio in autism spectrum disorder? A systematic review and meta-analysis. *Journal of the American Academy of Child and Adolescent Psychiatry*, *56*(6), 466–474. https://doi.org/10.1016/j.jaac.2017.03.013

Milton, D. E. M. (2012). On the ontological status of autism: The "double empathy problem". *Disability & Society*, *27*(6), 883–887. https://doi.org/10.1080/09687599.2012.710008

Mottron, L. (2011). Changing perceptions: The power of autism. *Nature*, *479*(7371), 33–35. https://doi.org/10.1038/479033a

Murray, D. (2020). Monotropism: An interest-based account of autism. *Autistic Spectrum Quarterly*, *1*(1), 5–12. https://www.researchgate.net/publication/338127881_Monotropism_-_An_Interest_Based_Account_of_Autism

Murray, D., Lesser, M., & Lawson, W. (2005). Attention, monotropism and the diagnostic criteria for autism. *Autism*, *9*(2), 139–156. https://doi.org/10.1177/1362361305051398

Nonaka, I., & Takeuchi, H. (1995). *The knowledge-creating company: How Japanese companies create the dynamics of innovation*. Oxford University Press.

Porges, S. W. (2011). *The polyvagal theory: Neurophysiological foundations of emotions, attachment, communication, and self-regulation*. W. W. Norton & Company.

Raymaker, D. M., Teo, A. R., Steckler, N. A., Lentz, B., Scharer, M., Delos Santos, A., Arnold, S. R., & Kapp, S. K. (2020). "Having all of your internal resources exhausted beyond measure and being left with no clean-up crew": Defining autistic burnout. *Autism in Adulthood*, *2*(2), 132–143. https://doi.org/10.1089/aut.2019.0079

Robertson, C. E., & Baron-Cohen, S. (2017). Sensory perception in autism. *Nature Reviews Neuroscience*, *18*(11), 671–684 https://doi.org/10.1038/nrn.2017.112

Chapter 6

AuDHD

At the Intersection of Urgency and Structure

6.1 The Overlap of ADHD and Autism in Leadership (AuDHD)

Understanding why paradoxical needs require precision in leadership environments.

This section maps the leadership dynamics of AuDHD as a dual-expression profile, marked by the interplay of autistic and ADHD traits.

Through four core paradoxes—Structure vs. Novelty, Verbal Fluency vs. Processing Latency, Hyperfocus vs. Sensory Overload, and Social Mirroring vs. Social Fatigue—it traces how internal divergence intersects with external demands, revealing adaptive intelligence that calls for systemic flexibility.

Recent studies estimate that between 30% and 80% of individuals diagnosed with autism also meet criteria for ADHD, and vice versa (Leitner, 2014; Antshel et al., 2016). This co-occurring profile—commonly referred to as AuDHD—represents more than the sum of two diagnoses: it constitutes a distinct neurocognitive constellation with its own regulatory patterns, leadership expressions, and systemic needs.

Individuals with AuDHD may simultaneously crave predictability and novelty, seek stimulation while requiring solitude, speak with fluency yet need time to integrate. These paradoxes are not situational—they are embedded in the cognitive architecture. Four tension fields emerge repeatedly in leadership contexts: (1) a cognitive split between structure-seeking and stimulus-driven modes, (2) a disconnect between verbal agility and processing latency, (3) performance peaks that rely on fragile sensory balance, and (4) social adaptability that masks deep needs for clarity and identity coherence (Table 6.1).

DOI: 10.4324/9781003681540-8

Table 6.1 The AuDHD Paradox Grid maps four core domains where ADHD and autistic traits co-express in leadership. Each axis reflects dual traits that can create inner tension and external misreading. With intentional design—through modular workflows, decompression tools, and neurodivergent-aware communication—these tensions can become drivers of creative and sustainable leadership.

Core trait axis	*ADHD expression*	*Autistic expression*	*Leadership tension*	*Strategic design need*
Structure ↔ Novelty	Seeks stimulation, improvises	Needs predictability, routines	Rigidity vs. chaos	Modular systems with flexible execution
Verbal Fluency ↔ Processing Time	Speaks fast, engages in dynamic dialogue	Needs reflection, delayed integration	Eloquence ≠ readiness	Built-in pause and follow-up structures
Hyperfocus ↔ Sensory Overload	Deep immersion in tasks	High sensory sensitivity	Productivity collapse under sensory load	Sensory-buffered environments, decompression phases
Social Adaptation ↔ Social Fatigue	Charming, mirroring, social intuition	Exhaustion, masking, withdrawal	Misread as disengaged or inconsistent	Normalize social pacing, bandwidth check-ins

6.2 The AuDHD Paradox Grid: Navigating Dual Traits in Leadership

Where dual traits collide, leadership tension becomes potential.

This duality creates unique tensions and synergies that resist linear categorization. What follows is a profile of expression marked by oscillation: between structure and novelty, verbal fluency and cognitive latency, clarity and overwhelm. These patterns reflect not contradiction, but a composite form of executive function forged at the intersection of divergent processing logics.

6.3 AuDHD in Leadership: Patterns of Expression—Strength Zones and Strain Points

Harnessing divergent energy and deep focus to lead across complexity.

Note on Tool Synergy:

Several strategies for regulating hyperfocus, time management, and sensory overload are outlined in detail in the ADHD and autism chapter and are equally applicable to AuDHD profiles. The following section expands on these with nuanced tools tailored to the interplay of both neurodivergent processing patterns.

6.3.1 Structure ↔ Novelty Tension

Spectrum Subtype: Paradox Navigator
Subtype Expression: Dual-Need Profile—structure-seeking and stimulus-driven

AuDHD individuals often experience a dynamic interplay between two core cognitive drivers: the autistic inclination toward predictability, coherence, and structured systems, and the ADHD-based demand for novelty, stimulation, and adaptive flexibility (Barkley, 2011; Ashinoff & Abu-Akel, 2021; Arnsten, 2009). This dual-need architecture does not indicate indecision or ambivalence—it reflects a paradox-integrating neurocognitive style that requires both order and stimulation for optimal regulation and engagement.

In workplace contexts, this profile frequently presents through oscillating work patterns: bursts of focused productivity when tasks are well-defined and meaningfully framed, followed by disengagement in environments that are either too rigid or lack stimulating variation. Observable behaviors may appear inconsistent or emotionally volatile, yet they often mirror competing internal needs for predictability and dynamic input.

In leadership roles, this cognitive configuration can support a rare adaptive capability: the capacity to stabilize systems while simultaneously disrupting stagnation. Leaders with this profile often bring strategic elasticity—able to uphold structure while redesigning it for responsiveness. This bidirectional fluency requires environments that do not penalize pacing shifts or interpret variability as instability.

Systemically, sustainable inclusion of this subtype relies on operational models that accommodate fluid engagement rhythms and dual-mode cognition. Modular workflows, periodic recalibration space, and strategic autonomy support consistent output without suppressing cognitive authenticity. Rather than viewing oscillation as a deviation, organizations can frame it as a performance rhythm aligned with complex processing demands.

While external environments shape performance, they are only half the equation. Equally critical is how internal processing interacts with how one is perceived. One of the most striking mismatches in AuDHD leadership is not spatial, but temporal: when verbal fluency masks delayed integration, and eloquence conceals exhaustion (Boucher, 2007).

6.3.2 *Verbal Fluency ↔ Processing Latency*

Spectrum Subtype: Eloquent Integrator
Subtype Expression: Outward fluency—inward delay

This AuDHD subtype combines verbal agility with delayed cognitive integration. Quick articulation, shaped by ADHD-associated spontaneity, often coexists with autistic-rooted depth processing that unfolds more gradually (Livingston & Happé, 2017). Fluency in expression can precede full conceptual or emotional clarity.

In collaborative settings, individuals with this profile often anchor group energy—facilitating dialogue, energizing ideation, or steering discussions. Their verbal presence signals confidence and cognitive momentum. However, when faced with ambiguity, interpersonal nuance, or layered decision-making, their processing rhythm may decelerate to accommodate complexity.

The discrepancy between expressive speed and integrative pacing can lead to interpretive gaps. Teams may assume readiness where synthesis is still unfolding, or overlook delayed insight that emerges post-interaction. This misalignment often results in feedback fatigue or overlooked contributions that crystallize after the formal moment has passed.

In leadership, this subtype often guides with linguistic precision and persuasive framing, yet requires recalibration time to consolidate input, emotional resonance, or long-range consequences. Verbal leadership is present, but it functions along a layered timeline—one that benefits from space, silence, and asynchronous reflection.

Sustainable integration of this profile relies on norms that distinguish expression from resolution. Cultural shifts—such as feedback deferral windows, silent work intervals, or post-meeting input channels—enable fuller contribution and reduce interpretive pressure.

Verbal fluency, in this context, is neither final nor exhaustive. It is one layer of cognitive presence—highly effective in motion, yet more powerful when paired with systems that respect integration time.

While verbal fluency may project cognitive ease, the underlying effort to regulate sensory input often remains hidden. This tension becomes even more pronounced in the next domain—where deep hyperfocus can coexist with heightened sensory vulnerability.

6.3.3 *Hyperfocus ↔ Sensory Overload*

Spectrum Subtype: Immersive Processor
Subtype Expression: Deep-focus capacity—sensory vulnerability

This AuDHD subtype combines intense cognitive immersion with pronounced sensory receptivity. Hyperfocus enables deep concentration, sustained momentum, and integrative clarity (Robertson & Baron-Cohen, 2017). Yet this same attentional intensity exists within a nervous system prone to sensory saturation, where environmental input—light, sound, texture, or interpersonal complexity—can quickly overwhelm (Porges, 2011).

The apparent contradiction reflects neurobiological design rather than inconsistency. Depth and sensitivity operate on shared circuitry. Without intentional calibration, immersive engagement risks tipping into overstimulation.

In team settings, this profile may appear highly productive and independent, often thriving in uninterrupted work phases. However, overstimulation—especially in open-plan offices, unpredictable routines, or extended social contact—can lead to abrupt disengagement, irritability, or shutdown. These shifts are rarely immediate; they build cumulatively and often go unnoticed until regulation capacity is exceeded.

Leaders with this profile may deliver strategic focus and visionary leadership, particularly when conditions support flow. Yet behind this clarity often lies a parallel strain: hidden exhaustion from sustained masking, sensory vigilance, and continuous adjustment to unspoken demands.

To support this subtype sustainably, organizations must prioritize environmental modulation. This includes sensory-responsive infrastructure (e.g., noise buffering, adjustable lighting), pacing autonomy, transition scaffolds, and predictable recovery windows. Equally important are social structures that allow for quiet integration post-interaction, asynchronous debriefs, and normalized periods of disengagement without reputational cost.

What appears as inconsistency or volatility is often the result of unmet regulatory needs. When supported, the Immersive Processor brings rare cognitive depth and emotional resonance—qualities that shape long-range vision, hold complexity, and offer grounded insight across dynamic leadership landscapes.

Even beyond sensory environments, AuDHD individuals face intense adaptive demands in social interactions—constantly decoding, mirroring, and adjusting behaviors to implicit norms. Many appear socially at ease, yet beneath this fluent exterior lies substantial hidden effort and resulting exhaustion.

6.3.4 Social Mirroring ↔ Social Fatigue

Spectrum Subtype: Adaptive Relator
Subtype Expression: Outward social ease—inward social depletion

AuDHD individuals frequently demonstrate a striking capacity for social adaptability—fluidly navigating interpersonal contexts through mirroring, intuitive attunement, and high verbal responsiveness. This externally fluent presentation, often reinforced by ADHD-linked sociability and spontaneity, can obscure a parallel autistic sensitivity to sensory environments and unspoken relational dynamics. While these individuals may appear confident and engaged in meetings, networking events, or emotionally complex interactions, the internal cost is often invisible: cumulative nervous system fatigue, relational disorientation, and eventual emotional depletion.

The paradox lies in the divergence between social performance and embodied experience. Fluency, while authentic, frequently depends on sustained cognitive and sensory labor—tracking tone, managing eye contact, decoding subtext, and modulating emotional expression under pressure. Because this effort is socially rewarded—interpreted as charisma, versatility, or leadership readiness—the underlying exhaustion is seldom recognized. Over time, this mismatch can lead to interpersonal burnout, blurred self-perception, and sudden withdrawal from relational or professional spaces (Hull et al., 2017; Milton, 2012).

Support requires reframing social output as a finite resource rather than a baseline expectation. Sustainable engagement depends on embedding relational recovery: sensory-neutral breaks, asynchronous response options, reduced-performance communication modes (e.g., written check-ins or low-verbal participation), and non-stigmatized opt-out mechanisms. Crucially, social agility must be understood as context-sensitive—a dynamic capacity, not a constant trait. Without recovery architecture, relational strength becomes a liability.

While each of the preceding profiles illustrates a distinct cognitive and relational dynamic within the AuDHD leadership spectrum, they share a common theme: performance depends not just on individual capacity, but on environmental alignment and structural reciprocity.

To translate these insights into practical strategy, the following section introduces a curated set of tools designed to stabilize energy, externalize executive function, and legitimize nonlinear engagement—across leadership and team roles alike.

6.4 Optional Tools to Try—Navigating Dual Wiring in Leadership

The co-occurrence of ADHD and autism creates paradoxical demands—simultaneous needs for structure and spontaneity, fluency and reflection, immersion and sensory withdrawal, social resonance and solitude (Table 6.2). These tools do not replace those found in the ADHD or autism chapters, but extend them to address specifically **co-activated tensions** that emerge in AuDHD leadership contexts.

6.4.1 AuDHD Paradoxes in Leadership: Precision Tools for Dual-Wired Performance

Lean interventions for common strain points across hybrid cognitive dynamics.

Table 6.2 Navigating AuDHD Leadership Paradoxes: Core Tensions and Precision Tools Targeted interventions for hybrid strain points in dual-wired leadership profiles This table outlines six recurring paradoxes in AuDHD leadership—each reflecting internal tensions that emerge from the co-expression of autistic and ADHD traits.

Paradox	*Leadership challenge*	*Targeted tool*
Structure ↔ Novelty	Needs both predictability and stimulation—routines can dull, chaos overwhelms	*Two-Track Taskboards*: Switch between structured and flexible task modes
Verbal Fluency ↔ Processing latency	Eloquent live, but slower to integrate—mistaken for instant readiness	*Dialogue-Lag Dashboard*: Schedule visible decompression slots post-interaction
Hyperfocus ↔ Sensory overload	Deep focus derailed by sensory input—performance depends on precision	*Focus Gate Protocol*: Use rituals to enter/exit deep work and manage re-entry
Social mirroring ↔ Social fatigue	Social ease masks depletion—risk of crash after high interaction	*Interaction Budgeting*: Cap and track weekly social load to preserve capacity
Cognitive mode fluctuation	Output varies with nervous system state—often misread as volatility	*Cognitive Mode Mapping*: Align task types to internal state windows
Recovery invisibility	High output hides the cost—no space for recalibration	*Recovery Anchors*: Ritualized breaks after cognitive or social sprints

1. Two-Track Taskboards

Design project workflows with both a structured and a flexible path—for example, predefined sequence vs. exploration-driven sprint. Leaders can toggle depending on internal state (e.g., seeking clarity vs. seeking stimulation).

→ Supports executive calibration and adaptive autonomy (Kerns et al., 2000; Barkley, 2011).

Application: Balances novelty-seeking (ADHD) and structure-craving (Autism, Dyspraxia) traits, enabling flexible access to task flow based on momentary cognitive state.

2. Dialogue-Lag Dashboards

Normalize integration time after high-verbal or fast-paced exchanges by embedding visible processing buffers in calendars. Signals pacing preferences to others without self-justification.

→ Grounded in asynchronous cognition and social tempo alignment (Crane et al., 2016; Austin & Pisano, 2017).

Application: Supports delayed processing in autism, HSPs, and APD profiles—reducing conversational exhaustion and improving input integration across tempo-diverse teams.

3. Interaction Budgeting

Track cumulative social load—calls, meetings, spontaneous chats—across the week. Set bandwidth caps (e.g., async-only communication after 3 PM or no calls on writing days) to prevent relational depletion.

→ Based on social masking and autistic burnout research (Milton, 2012; Raymaker et al., 2020).

Application: Reduces social overstimulation in autism, AuDHD, PTSD, and HSPs by providing clear boundaries for interactional energy management.

4. Cognitive Mode Mapping

Map fluctuations in cognitive access: Which days support analytical depth? Which support ideation, communication, or social presence? Use this data to cluster tasks or shift delivery expectations accordingly.

→ Informed by dynamic self-regulation and autonomy-motivation theory (Deci & Ryan, 2000).

Application: Optimizes cognitive rhythms in ADHD, bipolar, and gifted profiles—aligning task type with internal energy states to reduce friction and increase flow.

These tools provide a foundation, but their impact comes into focus when applied in real leadership contexts. The following case vignette illustrates how structural alignment enables sustainable performance and authentic presence.

6.5 Dual-Track Cognition, Purpose-Driven Innovation—AuDHD Leadership at the Intersection of Vision and Velocity

Systems thinking meets emotional insight.

Dr Temple Grandin, a professor of animal science and one of the most well-known individuals openly diagnosed with both autism and ADHD, exemplifies the AuDHD paradox: deep sensory-detail processing (autistic) paired with a relentless drive for creative problem-solving (ADHD). Her unique ability to think in visual sequences allowed her to pioneer humane livestock handling systems that blended innovation, ethics, and operational efficiency. While her sensory and social bandwidth was limited, she managed it through clear boundaries, structured routines, and a deep connection to purpose—a model of self-regulated, impact-driven leadership (Grandin, 2006).

AuDHD offers a bridge—a space where executive intensity meets social and sensory divergence. Yet, to fully appreciate the autistic dimensions within that overlap, we must step beyond duality.

While the interplay of ADHD and autistic traits creates complex leadership rhythms, autism alone presents a distinct cognitive architecture—marked by perceptual sensitivity, principled reasoning, and non-normative communication patterns. These traits are not simply one half of a hybrid profile. They form a leadership paradigm in their own right, often misinterpreted through neurotypical assumptions. We now shift from overlap to origin.

The following chapter approaches autism not as a fixed label, but as a distinct form of leadership intelligence—anchored in moral clarity, perceptual depth, and systemic precision. These capacities are often undervalued in conventional leadership cultures, yet essential for navigating complexity with integrity.

References

Antshel, K. M., Zhang-James, Y., Wagner, K. E., Ledesma, A., & Faraone, S. V. (2016). An update on the comorbidity of ADHD and ASD: A focus on clinical management. *Expert Review of Neurotherapeutics*, *16*(3), 279–293. https://doi.org/10.1586/14737175.2016.1146591

Arnsten, A. F. T. (2009). The emerging neurobiology of attention deficit hyperactivity disorder: The key role of the prefrontal association cortex. *The Journal of Pediatrics*, *154*(5), I–S43. https://doi.org/10.1016/j.jpeds.2009.01.018

Ashinoff, B. K., & Abu-Akel, A. (2021). Hyperfocus: The forgotten frontier of attention. *Psychological Research*, *85*, 1–12. https://doi.org/10.1007/s00426-019-01245-8

Austin, R. D., & Pisano, G. P. (2017). Neurodiversity as a competitive advantage. *Harvard Business Review*, *95*(3), 96–103.

Barkley, R. A. (2011). *Executive functions: What they are, how they work, and why they evolved*. Guilford Press.

Boucher, J. (2007). Memory and autism: A review and theoretical framework. *Journal of Child Psychology and Psychiatry*, *48*(1), 96–113. https://doi.org/10.1111/j.1469-7610.2006.01694.x

Crane, L., Goddard, L., & Pring, L. (2016). Autobiographical memory in adults with autism spectrum disorder: The role of depressed mood, rumination, working memory and theory of mind. *Autism*, *20*(2), 154–165. https://doi.org/10.1177/1362361311418690

Deci, E. L., & Ryan, R. M. (2000). The "what" and "why" of goal pursuits: Human needs and the self-determination of behavior. *Psychological Inquiry*, *11*(4), 227–268. https://doi.org/10.1207/S15327965PLI1104_01

Grandin, T. (2006). *Thinking in pictures: My life with autism*. Vintage Books.

Hull, L., Petrides, K. V., Allison, C., Smith, P., Baron-Cohen, S., Lai, M.-C., & Mandy, W. (2017). "Putting on my best normal": Social camouflaging in adults with autism spectrum conditions. *Journal of Autism and Developmental Disorders*, *47*, 2519–2534. https://doi.org/10.1007/s10803-017-3166-5

Kerns, K. A., McInerney, R. J., & Wilde, N. J. (2001). Time reproduction, working memory, and behavioral inhibition in children with ADHD. *Child Neuropsychology*, *7*(3), 162–171. https://doi.org/10.1076/chin.7.3.162.8744

Leitner, Y. (2014). The co-occurrence of autism and attention deficit hyperactivity disorder in children: What do we know? *Frontiers in Human Neuroscience*, *8*, 268. https://doi.org/10.3389/fnhum.2014.00268

Livingston, L. A., & Happé, F. (2017). Conceptualising compensation in neurodevelopmental disorders: Reflections from autism spectrum disorder. *Neuroscience & Biobehavioral Reviews*, *80*, 729–742. https://doi.org/10.1016/j.neubiorev.2017.06.005

Milton, D. E. M. (2012). On the ontological status of autism: The "double empathy problem". *Disability & Society*, *27*(6), 883–887. https://doi.org/10.1080/09687599.2012.710008

Porges, S. W. (2011). *The polyvagal theory: Neurophysiological foundations of emotions, attachment, communication, and self-regulation*. W. W. Norton & Company.

Raymaker, D. M., Teo, A. R., Steckler, N. A., Lentz, B., Scharer, M., Delos Santos, A., Arnold, S. R., & Nicolaidis, C. (2020). "Having all of your internal resources exhausted beyond measure and being left with no clean-up crew": Defining autistic burnout. *Autism in Adulthood*, *2*(2), 132–143. https://doi.org/10.1089/aut.2019.0079

Robertson, C. E., & Baron-Cohen, S. (2017). Sensory perception in autism. *Nature Reviews Neuroscience*, *18*(11), 671–684. https://doi.org/10.1038/nrn.2017.112

Chapter 7

Dyslexia

Visual Logic in a Verbal World

7.1 From Literacy Strain to Strategic Brilliance

Dyslexic cognition as a strategic asset.

This chapter analyzes the leadership potential and systemic challenges associated with dyslexia across five domains: big-picture systems thinking, visual-spatial reasoning, resilience and adaptive innovation, narrative and verbal strengths, and the friction patterns that emerge from systemic mismatch.

As Sir Richard Branson—himself dyslexic—has said: “Dyslexia should be seen as a sign of potential.” And indeed, dyslexic leaders frequently drive innovation not despite, but because of, their divergent processing style.

Dyslexia is a neurodevelopmental profile characterized by differences in phonological processing, working memory, and rapid automatized naming (RAN), which can affect reading fluency, spelling, and decoding of written language (Shaywitz, 2003). It is rooted in atypical patterns of brain activation in left-hemispheric language areas, often compensated by increased engagement in right-hemispheric regions responsible for visual-spatial reasoning and global pattern recognition.

According to the Yale Center for Dyslexia and Creativity, roughly 20% of the global population may be dyslexic (Shaywitz, 2020). Many remain undiagnosed, especially among adults in leadership roles who have developed compensatory strategies or masked their differences through overperformance.

Fully recognizing dyslexic talent means moving beyond deficit-based narratives and understanding dyslexia as a source of systemic advantage—particularly in complexity-rich, rapidly evolving environments. The following core traits illustrate how this cognitive profile translates into distinct leadership capacities and structural contributions (Table 7.1).

DOI: 10.4324/9781003681540-9

7.2 Dyslexia in Leadership: Patterns of Expression—Strength Zones and Strain Points

When linear paths misfit, dyslexic leaders reframe the map.

Table 7.1 Summarizes how core cognitive traits in dyslexic leaders translate into distinct strengths—and where systemic friction may arise when environments are not designed for nonlinear processing.

Cognitive modality	*Typical expression*	*Leadership strength*	*Systemic friction*
Visual-Spatial Thinking	Diagrams, whiteboards	Systems design, innovation	Slide decks, spreadsheets
Strategic Synthesis	Nonlinear pattern recognition	Big-picture vision, foresight	Rigid reporting formats
Verbal/Narrative Style	Oral storytelling	Alignment, motivation	Documentation, written updates
Adaptive Innovation	Workarounds, reframing	Process design, reinvention	Overcompensation, burnout risk

7.2.1 *Big-Picture Systems Thinking*

Spectrum Role: Strategic Synthesizer
Type: Strength—with processing mismatch

Dyslexic cognition is frequently characterized by holistic, associative, and systems-level thinking—prioritizing pattern recognition, conceptual integration, and nonlinear synthesis over sequential processing. This enables dyslexic leaders to detect trends, connect disparate information, and frame strategy in multidimensional ways, particularly in complex or ambiguous environments (Eide & Eide, 2011; von Karolyi et al., 2003).

These strengths may be obscured in work cultures that emphasize linear documentation, rapid written output, or strict adherence to stepwise logic. Dyslexic professionals often find traditional reporting tasks cognitively taxing because intuitive synthesis does not easily translate into standard formats—such as detailed reports or slide decks. Misalignments between big-picture cognition and detail-driven expectations can result in underestimation or self-censorship, particularly when intuitive leaps are misread as a lack of rigor.

Supporting this cognitive profile means building structures that legitimize strategic abstraction. Tools such as foresight mapping, analogy-based forecasting, and systems modeling can surface the unique visioning strengths of dyslexic thinkers. Without structural scaffolds that validate nonlinear processing, the result is frequently underrecognition of strategic value, despite consistently high-level systems thinking.

Once large-scale patterns are perceived and systemic coherence takes shape, dyslexic cognition often shifts further—from conceptual integration to spatial intuition, where relationships are not only understood but mentally visualized.

7.2.2 *Visual-Spatial Reasoning*

Spectrum Role: Conceptual Architect
Type: Strength—with operational mismatch

Dyslexic professionals frequently exhibit marked strengths in visual-spatial reasoning, enabling them to construct multidimensional mental models, synthesize abstract systems, and perceive relational patterns beyond linear sequences. This cognitive style supports high-level design thinking, process innovation, and strategic reframing—often grounded in intuitive coherence rather than stepwise articulation (Attree et al., 2009; Brunswick et al., 2010).

Visual insights may be misunderstood as imprecision when they resist immediate translation into conventional documentation formats. Strategic cognition in dyslexic minds tends to operate through pattern recognition, spatial scaffolding, and systemic logic—producing insights that are often more integrative than sequential. Yet when evaluative systems prioritize output form over conceptual substance, these strengths risk marginalization.

Systemically, inclusion demands structural calibration. Embedding visual modalities such as diagrams, mind maps, process schematics, or spatial modeling into standard workflows allows dyslexic professionals to lead and contribute in ways aligned with their cognitive architecture. For leaders, this might involve communicating strategy through conceptual blueprints rather than exhaustive text, or guiding teams using visual anchors that convey systems logic at a glance.

This spatial mode of reasoning not only supports how problems are perceived, but also how solutions are built—laying the foundation for adaptive strategies and resilient innovation, especially in environments where conventional paths falter.

7.2.3 *Resilience and Adaptive Innovation*

Spectrum Role: Adaptive Innovator
Type: Strength—with systemic friction

Persistent misalignment between cognitive style and systemic norms often cultivates design-based intelligence in dyslexic professionals. In environments that emphasize speed, linearity, and standardization, many develop friction-reducing strategies—modifying workflows, rethinking communication formats, and creating tools that enhance both individual performance and collective functionality (Nalavany et al., 2011).

These adjustments reflect applied systems thinking: insight grounded in the lived negotiation of structural constraints. Dyslexic leaders frequently act as embedded redesigners—shaping operational environments through necessity and, in doing so, building resilience into broader organizational processes.

Yet this adaptive labor too carries a cognitive cost. Without systemic recognition, chronic reconfiguration can result in overload, overfunctioning. Reflective design spaces, reverse mentoring, and the legitimization of informal insight loops help surface the strategic innovation embedded in dyslexic cognition (Alexander-Passe, 2008; Grant, 2010).

What begins as individual adaptation often evolves into organizational infrastructure. Dyslexic professionals, especially in team settings, frequently prototype visual aids and procedural anchors that improve pacing, clarity, and coherence at scale (McLoughlin et al., 2002). Recognizing these interventions not as workaround behavior but as expressions of operational intelligence enables organizations to retain and institutionalize their design value systemically.

7.2.3.1 *Dyslexic Leadership Strengths Grid*

What begins as compensation often becomes design intelligence.

While adaptive innovation reflects how dyslexic thinkers respond to complexity, it is often through language—especially storytelling, metaphor, and verbal framing—that these insights are made legible to others.

7.2.4 *Narrative and Verbal Strengths*

Spectrum Role: Story-Based Strategist
Type: Strength—with literacy mismatch

Dyslexic individuals often demonstrate pronounced strengths in storytelling, persuasive communication, and conceptual framing. These abilities are rooted in narrative cognition and episodic memory, enabling fluent synthesis of complex ideas, motivational clarity, and alignment of strategy with meaning and values (Tanner, 2009). Such strengths are particularly salient in leadership environments that rely on vision-building, relational resonance, and adaptive framing under uncertainty.

In leadership contexts, this misalignment can manifest in various ways—such as delayed documentation, reliance on verbal delegation, or a disproportionate investment of time and energy in producing written outputs that meet institutional standards. These adaptations may preserve performance appearance but obscure the underlying cost.

To mitigate this strain and enable access to full cognitive capacity, leadership systems may benefit from legitimizing alternative modalities of strategic communication. These can include recorded updates, voice notes, co-created written outputs, or facilitated synthesis through structured dialogue. Such practices not only reduce cognitive load but affirm verbal fluency as a legitimate and valuable leadership pathway.

And even when cognitive strengths are clearly articulated, systemic environments may remain misaligned—leading not to underperformance, but to chronic friction between individual processing styles and institutional expectations.

7.2.5 System Mismatch and Strain Patterns

Spectrum Role: Insightful Reframer
Type: Strain—with overlooked brilliance

Dyslexic professionals frequently demonstrate high-level insight, strategic reasoning, and systems thinking. However, these strengths often coexist with persistent strain in environments that equate competence with written precision, speed, and stylistic uniformity. The difficulty does not lie in intellectual capacity, but in the structural misalignment between dominant communication norms and neurocognitive processing profiles (Nalavany et al., 2011).

This mismatch can lead to cumulative fatigue, perfectionistic overcompensation, or avoidance in writing-intensive contexts—particularly where expectations for polished textual output are high and flexibility is limited. Over time, the cognitive load of sustaining written fluency under pressure may erode confidence and diminish visibility, especially when verbal strengths are overlooked or underutilized Leather et al., 2011).

Professionals may silently rely on scaffolding strategies—such as extensive editing, speech-to-text tools, or pre-scripted outlines—to meet expectations. When fluency becomes a proxy for credibility, core insights risk being delayed, diluted, or dismissed.

Sustainable leadership systems should move beyond ad hoc accommodation toward embedded inclusion—normalizing alternative modes of communication such as verbal debriefs, collaborative documentation processes, or visual frameworks. Such measures should not be viewed as remedial accommodations, but as intentional design interventions that broaden the conditions under which high-level cognitive contributions can emerge and be sustained(Gerber, 2012; Nalavany et al., 2011).

To translate these insights into practical alignment, the following tools offer structural support for dyslexic professionals in both leadership and team roles—reducing cognitive friction, legitimizing alternative processing styles, and enabling strategic contribution without exhaustion.

7.3 Optional Tools to Try—Dyslexia

These tools are designed to reduce reading-related strain, support cognitive flow, and allow dyslexic leaders to work in alignment with their natural strengths. They emphasize clarity over conformity—leveraging visual, auditory, and spatial processing to enable strategic contribution without overloading working memory or decoding systems.

1. Text-to-Speech Software

Tools like NaturalReader, Microsoft Immersive Reader, Speechify, or macOS VoiceOver enable auditory processing of dense text. Useful for reviewing reports, contracts, or emails without visual fatigue.

→ Supports comprehension and reduces cognitive overload (Doyle & Doyle, 2003).

Application: Ideal for dyslexia, ADHD, and APD profiles—where visual decoding or multimodal load creates friction; offloads textual strain and enables auditory strengths.

2. Visual Note-Taking and Mapping Apps

Use Miro, Notability, or analog mind maps to externalize information in visual-spatial formats. Enhances memory encoding and nonlinear processing.

→ Aligns with visual learning strengths often seen in dyslexia.

Application: Supports dyslexic, dyspraxic, and gifted profiles—particularly those who process best via patterning, abstraction, or spatial structuring.

3. Voice Memos and Audio Drafting

Record thoughts verbally before transcribing or refining. Particularly useful for ideation-heavy leadership roles where fluency of thought outpaces fluency of text.

→ Bridges expressive language and written communication (Snowling, 2000).

Application: Reduces expressive bottlenecks for ADHD, dyslexia, and AuDHD traits with high ideational flow but delayed linear writing capacity.

4. Font and Formatting Adjustments

Implement dyslexia-friendly fonts (e.g., OpenDyslexic, Lexend), larger spacing, and off-white backgrounds in your digital workspace. This reduces decoding strain and visual stress.

→ Increases reading efficiency and comfort (British Dyslexia Association, 2018).

Application: Especially helpful for dyslexia and visual processing strain; supports visual clarity for HSPs and those with post-traumatic visual sensitivity.

5. Collaborative Writing Platforms

Use real-time editors like Google Docs with comment threads and version history to reduce confusion, streamline collaboration, and avoid rework.

→ Prevents document overwhelm and supports clarity in co-creation.

Application: Aids ADHD and dyspraxic leaders who benefit from visible thinking, reduced revision chaos, and process transparency in text-based collaboration.

6. Meeting Replays or AI Summaries

Tools like Otter.ai, Fireflies, or Notion AI enable post-meeting review without relying solely on written minutes. Useful when simultaneous listening + note-taking is dysregulating.

→ Enhances retention and supports fair access to complex information.

Application: Supports APD, ADHD, and autistic profiles—especially where auditory processing lag, working memory strain, or contextual saturation reduces live comprehension.

While these tools offer concrete systems for dyslexic inclusion, their real impact becomes visible when translated into lived leadership practice. The following example illustrates how structural alignment can turn processing difference into strategic advantage.

7.3.1 Exploring How Dyslexic Modes of Visual Reasoning, Symbolic Synthesis, and Systemic Imagination Redefine Leadership and Creative Impact

Theoretical physicist, icon of innovative thought.

Though never formally diagnosed, Albert Einstein is frequently cited in neurodiversity discourse as an individual who may have exhibited traits consistent with dyslexia or related neurocognitive differences. He reportedly spoke late, struggled with rote memorization, and showed early difficulty with traditional schoolwork—particularly in language-dominant tasks.

Einstein often described his thinking as visual and spatial rather than verbal or sequential. He reported solving problems through mental imagery and kinesthetic intuition, rather than through verbal reasoning—a cognitive style common in many dyslexic individuals, who often excel in systems-level, integrative, and symbolic thinking.

Despite being misjudged by early educators, Einstein's work fundamentally transformed theoretical physics. His breakthrough contributions—including the theory of relativity—did not emerge from procedural mastery, but from deep imaginative insight, a hallmark of divergent cognition. His story underscores a recurring leadership truth: the inability to conform to a rigid system may, in fact, signal the capacity to change it.

> Imagination is more important than knowledge. For knowledge is limited… Imagination encircles the world.
>
> Albert Einstein

Einstein's legacy invites us to see dyslexia not as a deficit in literacy, but as a lens for visionary leadership.

While Einstein was never officially diagnosed, retrospective analyses suggest he may have experienced traits associated with dyslexia, ADHD, or autism spectrum conditions. See e.g., West, T. G. (1997). In the Mind's Eye: Creative Visual Thinkers, Gifted Dyslexics, and the Rise of Visual Technologies. Prometheus Books.

> Einstein once said that the words or the language, as they are written or spoken, do not seem to play any role in his mechanism of thought. Instead, he thought in visual and muscular images.
>
> (West, 1997, Kapitel 1)

Shaywitz, S. (2003). Overcoming Dyslexia: A New and Complete Science-Based Program for Reading Problems at Any Level. Alfred A. Knopf.

Einstein reportedly spoke late—around age three—and resisted traditional schooling, traits often discussed in the context of dyslexia's visual-spatial thinking.

While dyslexia often challenges our interaction with written language, dyscalculia disrupts something even more elemental: our internal sense of numbers, quantity, and spatial relationships. Where dyslexia affects how we decode text, dyscalculia influences how we comprehend magnitude, sequence, and the very structure of measurable information. It is not a lack of logic, but a divergence in how logic is processed—visually, symbolically, and emotionally. Before leaders can strategize or budget, delegate or forecast, they must first translate abstract quantity into cognitive clarity. Dyscalculia complicates that translation—not through lack of intelligence, but through a fundamentally different cognitive map.

References

Alexander-Passe, N. (2008). The sources and manifestations of stress amongst school-aged dyslexics, compared with sibling controls. *Dyslexia*, *14*(4), 291–313. https://doi.org/10.1002/dys.340

Attree, E. A., Turner, M. J., & Cowell, N. (2009). A virtual reality test identifies the visuospatial strengths of adolescents with dyslexia. *CyberPsychology & Behavior*, *12*(2), 163–168. https://doi.org/10.1089/cpb.2008.0199

British Dyslexia Association (BDA). (2018). *Dyslexia style guide 2018: Creating dyslexia friendly content.* https://accessiblewebsiteservices.com/dyslexia-style-guide-2018/

Brunswick, N., Martin, G. N., & Marzano, L. (2010). Visuospatial processing in adults and children with dyslexia: Evidence from eye movements during scene perception. *Journal of Research in Reading*, *33*(3), 247–263. https://doi.org/10.1111/j.1467-9817.2009.01414.x

Doyle, N., & Doyle, D. (2003). *Neurodiversity at work: A biopsychosocial model and the impact on working adults*. Dyslexia Foundation.

Eide, B. L., & Eide, F. F. (2011). *The dyslexic advantage: Unlocking the hidden potential of the dyslexic brain*. Hudson Street Press.

Gerber, P. J. (2012). The impact of learning disabilities on adulthood: A review of the evidenced-based literature for research and practice in adult education. *Journal of Learning Disabilities*, *45*(1), 31–46. https://doi.org/10.1177/0022219411426858

Grant, D. (2010). *That's the way I think: Dyslexia, dyspraxia, ADHD and dyscalculia explained*. Routledge.

Leather, C., Hogh, H., Seiss, E., & Everatt, J. (2011). Cognitive functioning and work success in adults with dyslexia. *Dyslexia*, *17*(4), 327–338. https://doi.org/10.1002/dys.435

McLoughlin, D., Leather, C., & Stringer, P. (2002). *The adult dyslexic: Interventions and outcomes*. Whurr Publishers.

Nalavany, B. A., Carawan, L. W., & Rennick, R. A. (2011). Psychosocial experiences associated with confirmed and self-identified dyslexia: A participant-driven concept map of adult perspectives. *Journal of Learning Disabilities*, *44*(1), 63–79. https://doi.org/10.1177/0022219410374237

Shaywitz, S. (2003). *Overcoming dyslexia: A new and complete science-based program for reading problems at any level*. Alfred A. Knopf.
Shaywitz, S. (2020). *The Yale center for dyslexia & creativity*. https://dyslexia.yale.edu
Snowling, M. J. (2000). *Dyslexia*. Blackwell Publishing.
Tanner, K. (2009). Adult dyslexia and the "conundrum of failure". *Disability & Society*, *24*(6), 785–797. https://doi.org/10.1080/09687590903160274
von Karolyi, C., Winner, E., Gray, W., & Sherman, G. F. (2003). Dyslexia linked to talent: Global visual-spatial ability. *Brain and Language*, *85*(3), 427–431. https://doi.org/10.1016/S0093-934X(03)00052-X
West, T. G. (1997). *In the mind's eye: Creative visual thinkers, gifted dyslexics, and the rise of visual technologies*. Prometheus Books.

Chapter 8

Dyscalculia

Quantity, Confidence, and the Leadership Cost of Number Strain

8.1 Dyscalculia in Leadership: When Numbers Obscure Insight

From quantitative friction to conceptual clarity.

This chapter examines how dyscalculia shapes leadership capacity and systemic friction across six intersecting domains: conceptual reasoning in place of numerical fluency, creative and nonlinear thinking, executive function challenges in time-based tasks, persistent compensation efforts, relational advocacy for diverse cognition, and symbolic-verbal patterning as a mode of strategic contribution.

Developmental dyscalculia is a specific learning difference characterized by persistent difficulties in processing numerical magnitude, performing arithmetic operations, and understanding mathematical relationships, despite adequate general intelligence, motivation, and educational exposure (Butterworth, 2005; Rubinsten & Henik, 2009). It is classified as a neurodevelopmental condition with a heterogeneous presentation, affecting an estimated 3–6% of the population (Shalev & Gross-Tsur, 2001). Often co-occurring with other neurodivergent profiles such as ADHD or dyslexia, dyscalculia remains significantly underdiagnosed and poorly understood in both educational and clinical domains.

Neuroscientific research has identified atypical functioning in the intraparietal sulcus (IPS)—a brain region implicated in basic numerical processing—as a core correlate of dyscalculia. Individuals with dyscalculia often show reduced activation or structural differences in the IPS during tasks involving magnitude comparison, number line estimation, or symbolic-to-quantity mapping (Butterworth & Laurillard, 2010; Kucian & von Aster, 2015). These neurofunctional differences may affect both non-symbolic numerosity (e.g., estimating which of two groups contains more objects) and symbolic number processing (e.g., associating "7" with its quantity),

DOI: 10.4324/9781003681540-10

leading to cumulative difficulty in arithmetic fluency, mental calculation, and numerical memory.

Cognitively, dyscalculia is not defined by the absence of reasoning ability, but by a disruption in how quantity-related information is encoded, retrieved, and manipulated. Many affected individuals struggle with procedural memory for numerical operations, spatial sequencing, and working memory under mathematical load. This can result in challenges with learning math facts, performing multi-step calculations, or interpreting visual-spatial representations such as graphs, timelines, or charts.

Importantly, dyscalculia is distinct from math anxiety, low motivation, or inadequate instruction. It persists across development and is often resistant to traditional pedagogical remediation unless supported by differentiated strategies that externalize, contextualize, or compensate for disrupted magnitude processing. Affective consequences—such as frustration, avoidance, or feelings of inadequacy—often emerge not from the condition itself, but from repeated experiences of failure in systems that implicitly assume numerical fluency.

In environments dominated by metrics and precision, dyscalculic individuals may struggle with execution fluency—yet bring uniquely valuable insight into what those numbers represent. The following patterns highlight how strategic leadership can arise from relational logic and meaning-first cognition in systems that privilege.

8.2 Dyscalculia in Leadership: Patterns of Expression—Strength Zones and Strain Points

Reframing numerical disfluency as a leadership asset in systems thinking, collaboration, and innovation.

8.2.1 Meaning over Metrics

Spectrum Role: Sense-Maker
Type: Strength—with number-based friction

Dyscalculia affects the ability to process numerical information fluently, yet many individuals with this profile exhibit pronounced strengths in contextual interpretation and meaning-making. Rather than focusing on numerical precision, they tend to extract significance from patterns, asking what quantitative data implies rather than what it explicitly states (Butterworth, 2019; Kaufmann et al., 2022). This mode of reasoning reflects a meaning-first orientation—linking data to purpose, ethics, and human impact.

In leadership contexts, such individuals often excel in identifying trends, reframing challenges, and aligning action with values. Their thinking supports ethical and narrative-based decision-making—particularly valuable in complex systems where numbers alone do not capture lived realities. However, in performance cultures that privilege fluency with budgets, dashboards, or KPIs, this contribution may remain underrecognized. Dyscalculic professionals may compensate by memorizing figures or rehearsing analytic scripts, masking their conceptual strengths under metric-oriented performance.

To support this leadership capacity, organizations can adopt hybrid evaluation frameworks that integrate qualitative indicators—such as stakeholder narratives, lived experience data, or impact stories—alongside quantitative outputs. This does not replace numerical analysis but expands its meaning context, allowing broader access to insight (Butterworth, 2005; Wilson et al., 2015).

If you work with someone showing this pattern, you might invite their input during the interpretation phase of data analysis—focusing not just on what the numbers are, but on what they mean. Consider framing analytics discussions through guiding questions such as: What does this trend suggest? What decisions does this inform?

When direct access to numerical precision is limited, dyscalculic thinkers often shift from calculation to connection—leveraging patterns, analogies, and relational logic to solve problems in ways that standard metrics might overlook.

8.2.2 Nonlinear Problem-Solving

Spectrum Role: Creative Synthesizer
Type: Strength—developed through adaptation

In the context of dyscalculia, problem-solving rarely follows conventional, stepwise models. When numerically driven pathways are inaccessible or inefficient, individuals frequently develop alternative strategies grounded in conceptual synthesis, pattern recognition, and analogical thinking (Price, 2020; Kaufmann, 2002). These adaptive mechanisms reflect a cognitive profile oriented toward lateral reasoning—connecting ideas through relationships rather than formulas, and drawing meaning from structure rather than calculation.

Such approaches often prove particularly effective in ambiguity-rich environments, where rigid procedures fall short and intuition, reframing, or systems thinking are required (Wilson et al., 2015; Rubinsten & Tannock, 2010). However, in settings that prioritize algorithmic precision or speed, these forms of insight may be overlooked or misjudged as imprecise—leading to missed opportunities for innovation and underrecognition of strategic capacity.

Organizations aiming to leverage this form of reasoning can create entry points for exploratory logic—through visual frameworks, speculative strategy sessions, or meaning-oriented design tools. These formats make space for ideation that is not prematurely constrained by linear metrics and allow for conceptual depth to emerge before formal modeling is imposed.

In a collaborative setting, it's important to integrate creative, narrative thinking early, especially in open-ended planning phases. Instead of immediately turning to predefined procedures, space should be created for metaphorical thinking, storytelling, or analogical mapping. These methods foster creativity and preserve the core concept before it becomes operational. In leadership, this approach externalizes problem-solving, easing the cognitive load of immediate formalization.

Nonetheless, even adaptive problem-solving carries unseen costs—particularly when the same cognitive architecture that supports lateral thinking struggles with sequencing, time estimation, or task pacing.

8.2.3 Temporal Friction and Sequencing Strain

Spectrum Role: Deep Diver
Type: Challenge—with hidden cognitive load

In individuals with dyscalculia, difficulties anticipating task duration, managing multi-step processes, or aligning timelines can result in persistent time blindness, even in the presence of high-level strategic thinking (Wilson et al., 2015). They may excel in vision and conceptual clarity, yet struggle with execution pacing—leading to deadline compression, inconsistent follow-through, or reliance on last-minute sprints.

In professional contexts, individuals may appear disorganized or delayed in follow-through, or struggle to operationalize timelines despite having strong conceptual clarity. If unacknowledged, this friction can lead to elevated stress, reduced confidence, and preventable breakdowns in team coordination. To reduce this load, organizations may benefit from implementing external temporal supports—such as shared task boards, visual sequencing tools, or retrospective time tracking focused on calibration rather than correction. Buffered transitions and flexible handovers can help distribute temporal responsibility across systems rather than individuals (Rubinsten & Tannock, 2010; Holmes et al., 2008).

If you lead with this pattern, it may be helpful to externalize sequencing priorities and delegate timeline ownership where appropriate. Focusing on interdependencies and structural pacing—rather than minute-by-minute tracking—can help sustain oversight without overwhelming executive bandwidth.

To manage these hidden frictions, many professionals adopt intensive compensatory strategies—often internalized over years of masking difficulty and striving to meet unspoken expectations of fluency.

8.2.4 Compensation and Overpreparation

Spectrum Role: Conscientious Overcomer
Type: Strain—with invisible labor

In numerically demanding professional environments, individuals with dyscalculia often develop extensive compensatory strategies to meet perceived expectations of fluency. Rather than disclosing processing difficulties, many invest substantial effort in overpreparation, memorization, and avoidance of high-risk tasks—patterns frequently rooted in early experiences of stigma, misrecognition, or performance anxiety (Price, 2007). These adaptations may sustain a surface of competence, but they impose a continuous cognitive and emotional burden, particularly in leadership roles where numerical ease is implicitly linked to strategic credibility.

This dynamic can contribute to chronic fatigue, reduced confidence in high-visibility roles, and an internalized sense of impostorism—especially in data-driven cultures. Yet beneath these compensatory patterns lies a distinct profile of conscientiousness, accountability, and interpersonal sensitivity, often shaped by a deep awareness of systemic exclusion.

To support sustainable leadership development, organizations may benefit from explicitly acknowledging cognitive variation in their definition of performance. Tools such as Strength-Based Role Mapping™ enable teams to align responsibilities with individual cognitive assets and energy rhythms—shifting the emphasis from silent overcompensation to transparent, needs-aware collaboration. When combined with collaborative workflows and permission-based communication models, this approach enables neurodivergent leaders to operate from areas of cognitive strength rather than under persistent adaptive pressure (Price & Ansari, 2013; Wilson et al., 2015).

But from this long arc of adaptation often emerges something deeper: a sharpened awareness of cognitive difference, and a commitment to shaping systems that no longer require such invisible labor.

8.2.5 *Relational Advocacy and Systemic Empathy*

Spectrum Role: Inclusive Strategist
Type: Strength—grounded in lived experience

Individuals with dyscalculia frequently develop a heightened sensitivity to cognitive difference, shaped by continuous engagement with systems misaligned to their processing style. This experience fosters not only personal resilience but also a deep capacity for interpersonal attunement and inclusive leadership orientation. Research suggests that challenges in numerical processing often co-occur with strengths in empathy, verbal reasoning, and perspective-taking—traits that support relational leadership and ethical stewardship (Butterworth, 2005; Homberg et al., 2016).

In professional settings, this pattern may express itself through a sustained commitment to psychological safety, inclusive communication practices, and structural fairness. Leaders with this profile often demonstrate strengths in mentoring, participatory decision-making, and systems reframing.

Their contributions frequently extend beyond task-level performance to the cultivation of trust, cohesion, and shared values within teams. This form of leadership is not only interpersonally effective but strategically valuable.

Organizations may benefit from explicitly positioning inclusion as an operational domain, supported by tools, structures, and shared accountability…embedding access, equity, and flexibility into workflows and participation models.

One expression of this commitment lies in communication itself—not through numbers, but through symbols, metaphors, and visual synthesis that render complexity not only accessible but meaningful.

While dyscalculic traits offer strategic insight, they often clash with systems built on numerical and procedural norms. The following tools support alignment by reducing executive friction—enabling contribution from strength without masking.

8.3 Optional Tools to Try—Dyscalculia

These tools are designed to reduce cognitive friction in number-heavy environments and support dyscalculic leaders in expressing their strengths through alternative formats of planning, reasoning, and communication. Rather than adapting to standard quantitative expectations, these strategies build on symbolic, sensory, and narrative capacities to enhance clarity, confidence, and leadership access.

1. Symbolic-Auditory Planning Tools

Use color-coded calendar blocks, narrative agendas, or audio reminders to translate abstract time or number-based expectations into sensory-accessible structures.

→ Improves working memory and temporal sequencing (Kaufmann & von Aster, 2012).

Application: Highly effective for dyscalculia, ADHD, and dyspraxia—where numeric abstraction is difficult but sensory or narrative anchors aid sequencing and time orientation.

2. Visual Framing for Metrics

Replace spreadsheets or raw data with dashboards, infographics, or conceptual mapping formats (e.g., KPI storyboards or journey metaphors).

→ Supports strategy input without numeracy overload (Butterworth et al., 2011).

Application: Ideal for dyscalculia, HSP, and gifted thinkers with high conceptual fluency but low metric resilience; reframes numbers into visual-conceptual systems.

3. Role-Based Math Delegation

Design leadership ecosystems where data translation is shared. Pair verbal-visual thinkers with numerate collaborators who can convert insight into metrics.

→ Preserves strategic authority while reducing cognitive strain (Geary, 2004).

Application: Supports dyscalculia and dyslexia in high-level roles; allows leaders to stay vision-centered while co-regulating numeric execution collaboratively.

4. Concept Anchoring Rituals

Use storytelling, analogies, or value-based reframing to "pin" numerical tasks into meaningful context—turning abstract tasks into purpose-driven action.

→ Enhances retention and engagement through semantic encoding (Ashcraft & Krause, 2007).

Application: Useful across dyscalculia, ADHD, and giftedness—particularly when executive function is enhanced through meaning rather than mechanics.

5. Sequencing Cue Cards

Support multi-step planning through laminated "flow cards" or digital prompt lists, which guide task order without numerical dependency.

→ Reduces anxiety and error rates during task transitions (Shalev et al., 2005).

Application: Supports dyspraxia, ADHD, and dyscalculia—especially where task breakdown and nonverbal sequencing increase autonomy and reduce overwhelm.

6. Emotional Regulation Pairing

Pair challenging tasks (e.g., budget planning) with grounding rituals such as co-working check-ins, compression tools, or movement breaks.

→ Prevents performance anxiety and supports nervous system regulation (Boetsch et al., 1996).

Application: Especially relevant for dyscalculia, HSP, and PTSD-linked profiles with numeracy anxiety or somatic stress linked to evaluative tasks.

7. Career Communication Toolkit

Develop bio or CV supplements that highlight conceptual contributions, relational leadership, and systems fluency—especially in numeracy-centric fields.

→ Reduces stereotype threat and reinforces narrative legitimacy (Fredrickson & Losada, 2005).

Application: Vital for dyscalculia, dyspraxia, and late-identified neurodivergent professionals whose value lies in system insight, not metric fluency.

While these tools provide structural alignment, real-world examples illustrate how dyscalculic individuals navigate and transform systems—not by conforming to numerical norms, but by reframing complexity through meaning, structure, and strategic clarity.

8.4 Systemic Trust over Numeric Precision: Larry Mullen Jr.'s Leadership through Collaboration and Rhythm

Leading without numbers.

U2's drummer, Larry Mullen Jr., revealed in December 2024 that he has dyscalculia, describing basic counting—like tracking musical bars—as feeling "like climbing Everest." Despite this, he's built one of the world's most enduring rock bands, navigating global tours, studio sessions, and complex performance schedules.

Rather than letting numeracy challenges hold him back, Mullen has demonstrated remarkable creative adaptability and systemic collaboration. He does not perform calculations intuitively but gains rhythm and structure through auditory anchors, memorized patterns, and collaborative support from his bandmates. His leadership shines not through number precision, but through live performance integrity, rhythmical trust, and team synchronization.

Today, he continues to create music and lead meaningful projects—such as composing for the documentary *Left Behind*, inspired by his own experiences and his son's dyslexia. His career exemplifies how dyscalculic leaders can shape culture, creativity, and coordination—without numerical instinct, yet entirely in sync with their environment.

While dyscalculia shapes how we conceptualize quantity, dyspraxia influences how we enact intention through movement, planning, and coordination. Executive functioning, spatial processing, and embodied action intersect here. We now transition from cognitive-symbolic navigation to the often invisible friction of motor planning and praxis in leadership roles.

References

Ashcraft, M. H., & Krause, J. A. (2007). Working memory, math performance, and math anxiety. *Psychonomic Bulletin & Review, 14*(2), 243–248. https://doi.org/10.3758/BF03194059

Boetsch, E. A., Green, P. A., Pennington, B. F., & Smith, S. D. (1996). A developmental behavior-genetic perspective on dyslexia: Evidence from the Colorado Reading Project. In C. Hulme & M. Snowling (Eds.), *Dyslexia: Biology, cognition and intervention* (pp. 3–24). Whurr.

Butterworth, B. (2005). Developmental dyscalculia. In J. I. D. Campbell (Ed.), *Handbook of mathematical cognition* (pp. 455–467). Psychology Press.

Butterworth, B. (2019). *Can fish count? What animals reveal about our uniquely mathematical minds*. Basic Books.

Butterworth, B., & Laurillard, D. (2010). Low numeracy and dyscalculia: Identification and intervention. *ZDM, 42*, 527–539. https://doi.org/10.1007/s11858-010-0267-4

Butterworth, B., Varma, S., & Laurillard, D. (2011). Dyscalculia: From brain to education. *Science, 332*(6033), 1049–1053. https://doi.org/10.1126/science.1201536

Cappelletti, M., Butterworth, B., & Kopelman, M. (2011). Spared numerical abilities in a case of semantic dementia. *Neuropsychologia, 49*(1), 207–218. https://doi.org/10.1016/j.neuropsychologia.2010.10.015

Fredrickson, B. L., & Losada, M. F. (2005). Positive affect and the complex dynamics of human flourishing. *American Psychologist, 60*(7), 678–686. https://doi.org/10.1037/0003-066X.60.7.678

Geary, D. C. (2004). Mathematics and learning disabilities. *Journal of Learning Disabilities, 37*(1), 4–15. https://doi.org/10.1177/00222194040370010201

Holmes, J., Adams, J. W., & Hamilton, C. J. (2008). The relationship between visuospatial sketchpad capacity and children's mathematical skills. *European Journal of Cognitive Psychology, 20*(2), 272–289. https://doi.org/10.1080/09541440701612702

Homberg, J. R., Karel, P., & Schmidt, M. (2016). *Cognitive and emotional processes in neurodevelopmental disorders*. Springer.

Kaufmann, L. (2002). More than mere problems with calculation: Developmental dyscalculia and numerical–arithmetic capabilities. *Journal of Learning Disabilities, 35*(4), 343–358. https://doi.org/10.1177/00222194020350040401

Kaufmann, L., & von Aster, M. (2012). The diagnosis and management of dyscalculia. *Deutsches Ärzteblatt International, 109*(45), 767–778. https://doi.org/10.3238/arztebl.2012.0767

Kaufmann, L., Vogel, S. E., Starke, M., Kremser, C., & Schocke, M. (2022). The role of the intraparietal sulcus in number processing: Evidence from fMRI-guided transcranial magnetic stimulation. *Cerebral Cortex, 32*(6), 1298–1310. https://doi.org/10.1093/cercor/bhab345

Kucian, K., & von Aster, M. (2015). Developmental dyscalculia. *European Journal of Pediatrics, 174*(1), 1–13. https://doi.org/10.1007/s00431-014-2455-7

Price, G. R. (2007). Dyscalculia: Characteristics, causes, and treatments. *Numeracy, 1*(1), Article 2. https://doi.org/10.5038/1936-4660.1.1.2

Price, G. R. (2020). Mathematical learning difficulties, dyslexia, and neuroscience: From basic research to educational practice. *Mind, Brain, and Education, 14*(1), 14–21. https://doi.org/10.1111/mbe.12217

Price, G. R., & Ansari, D. (2013). Dyscalculia: Characteristics, causes, and treatments. *Numeracy, 6*(1), Article 2. https://doi.org/10.5038/1936-4660.6.1.2

Rubinsten, O., & Henik, A. (2009). Developmental dyscalculia: Heterogeneity might not mean different mechanisms. Trends in Cognitive Sciences, 13(2), 92-99. https://doi.org/10.1016/j.tics.2008.11.002

Rubinsten, O., & Tannock, R. (2010). Mathematics anxiety in children with developmental dyscalculia. *Behavioral and Brain Functions, 6*(1), 46. https://doi.org/10.1186/1744-9081-6-46

Shalev, R. S., & Gross-Tsur, V. (2001). Developmental dyscalculia. *Pediatric Neurology, 24*(5), 337–342. https://doi.org/10.1016/S0887-8994(00)00258-7

Shalev, R. S., Manor, O., Kerem, B., Ayali, M., Badichi, N., Friedlander, Y., & Gross-Tsur, V. (2005). Developmental dyscalculia is a familial learning disability. *Journal of Learning Disabilities, 34*(1), 59–65. https://doi.org/10.1177/002221940103400107

Wilson, A. J., Revkin, S. K., Cohen, D., Cohen, L., & Dehaene, S. (2015). An open trial assessment of "The Number Race", an adaptive computer game for remediation of dyscalculia. *Behavioral and Brain Functions, 2*(1), 20. https://doi.org/10.1186/1744-9081-2-20

Chapter 9

Dyspraxia

Movement, Planning, and the Somatic Dimensions of Leadership

9.1 The Somatic Executive: Dyspraxia and the Architecture of Action

Embodied friction as a source of strategic redesign.

Dyspraxia's impact on leadership expression is examined through five interrelated areas: movement and planning difficulties, invisible motor load, processing latency in time-bound tasks, resilient problem-solving strategies, and the interpersonal toll of navigating embodied difference within normative professional settings.

Dyspraxia—also known as Developmental Coordination Disorder (DCD)—is often misunderstood as mere clumsiness. In reality, it's a complex neurodevelopmental profile affecting motor coordination, spatial awareness, planning, sequencing, and sometimes speech and working memory. It's not a reflection of low intelligence or lack of effort. It reflects a brain that organizes movement and action differently.

In professional environments, dyspraxia can manifest in subtle ways: difficulty with fine or gross motor tasks, challenges with time perception or spatial planning, or an unspoken exhaustion from translating thoughts into physical action. These friction points are often invisible—and often misread. Adults with dyspraxia are frequently mislabeled as disorganized or inefficient, when in fact they're relying on compensatory strategies that demand significant cognitive energy.

Yet alongside these challenges often exist powerful strengths: creative problem-solving, deep empathy, and a remarkable capacity for persistence. Many individuals with dyspraxia develop strong adaptive intelligence—not because things came easily, but because they rarely did. Their insight often comes from navigating complexity, not bypassing it.

Despite affecting an estimated 5–6% of children (APA, 2013; Lingam et al., 2009), dyspraxia remains underrecognized in adult life—particularly in professional settings. Like many forms of neurodivergence, it is

DOI: 10.4324/9781003681540-11

frequently masked through compensatory behaviors such as overpreparation, perfectionism, or heightened relational effort. While often concealed from view, its effects can significantly influence well-being, task execution, and long-term performance.

To understand dyspraxia in professional contexts is to expand what counts as competence: to make space not only for different ways of thinking, but for different ways of doing. It requires attentiveness to the cognitive labor behind outward fluency, and an appreciation for process as well as output. Not all brilliance is fluid; not all coordination is physical.

Yet it is precisely this friction—between intention and execution, sequencing and response—that fosters adaptive strategies marked by foresight, persistence, and creative restructuring. The following patterns explore how dyspraxic individuals navigate high-coordination environments, and how leadership can emerge through the reordering of process under pressure.

9.2 Dyspraxia in Leadership: Patterns of Expression—Strength Zones and Strain Points

When sequencing meets systems insight: Navigating leadership through embodied adaptation.

9.2.1 Movement, Sequencing, and Motor Planning

Spectrum Role: Process-Oriented Integrator
Type: Strength—with coordination friction

Dyspraxia affects the integration of motor planning, spatial sequencing, and action coordination across both physical and cognitive domains. These disruptions stem from atypical development in neural circuits involved in procedural learning, visuomotor control, and executive sequencing (Kirby et al., 2008; Blank et al., 2019). As a result, individuals often encounter cumulative friction when executing multi-step tasks, adapting to dynamic conditions, or translating internal intention into timely action.

In leadership contexts, these coordination demands may surface as delayed verbal articulation, reduced spontaneity in unstructured group interactions, or friction in tasks requiring simultaneous cognitive and motor output—such as live facilitation, real-time diagramming, or high-speed decision-making. While often misread as hesitation or disengagement, such patterns reflect the elevated translation and planning load associated with dyspraxic neurocognition.

When environments support anticipatory processing—through advance preparation, external planning aids, or modular workflows—dyspraxic professionals frequently demonstrate pronounced strengths in systems thinking, procedural clarity, and strategic problem-solving.

Organizationally, providing visual planning scaffolds, enabling structured transitions, and legitimizing paced decision frameworks helps reduce avoidable friction and foster cognitive sustainability (Zwicker et al., 2012; Blank et al., 2019).

Yet even beyond visible coordination tasks, dyspraxic professionals often contend with a subtler challenge: the hidden motor demands embedded in everyday work practices.

9.2.2 *Motor Execution as Cognitive Labor*

Spectrum Role: Kinetic Strategist
Type: Challenge—with invisible labor

Dyspraxia increases the cognitive effort required for routine professional tasks involving physical coordination—such as handwriting, equipment handling, or gestural interaction (Kirby et al., 2008). These demands often remain invisible, yet they place a significant load on executive resources and can influence role preferences, participation style, and confidence—especially in environments that favor spontaneity or physical agility.

In team contexts, this pattern may show up as hesitation in high-speed collaboration, difficulty with interactive tools, or a preference for asynchronous or conceptual contributions. Individuals may thrive in domains like systems thinking, pattern recognition, or long-form analysis—especially when timelines are predictable and physical demands are minimized.

To manage strain, many rely on mental modeling, preparation, and strategic avoidance of high-effort settings. Reduced physical engagement may be misinterpreted as passivity, even when cognitive contribution remains high.

Organizations can reduce this friction by offering flexible input formats, ergonomic design, and predictable workflows. It may be normalized to embed alternative contribution methods—such as voice input, visual synthesis, or delegated physical tasks. In that case, participation would not be tied to physical immediacy (Tal-Saban et al., 2014).

This ongoing kinetic effort doesn't exist in isolation—it often overlaps with slowed cognitive sequencing, creating time strain in environments that privilege speed over integration.

9.2.3 Processing Lag and Time Strain

Spectrum Role: Sequential Strategist
Type: Challenge—with adaptive depth

Dyspraxic professionals often require extended time to sequence thoughts, organize responses, and verbalize ideas. This cognitive pacing reflects not a deficit in comprehension, but a different mode of executive orchestration—one that favors deliberate processing over rapid iteration (Blank et al., 2019). When temporal space is respected, these individuals often produce highly structured, integrative contributions that strengthen long-range logic and conceptual coherence.

In high-speed environments, however, this pacing mismatch can create friction. Delayed responses are frequently misread as disengagement, indecision, or insufficient expertise—especially in meetings that privilege verbal immediacy and spontaneous exchange. The pressure to keep up may lead to premature conclusions, surface-level input, or withdrawal from group discourse.

Importantly, processing lag is not the same as avoidance. It often indicates a higher-order synthesis process that is still unfolding. The value lies not in the speed of delivery, but in the precision and system coherence of the eventual insight.

To access the full strengths of sequential thinkers, organizations can implement reflective workflows—such as asynchronous input rounds, written debriefs, or post-meeting voice memos—as legitimate formats for strategic contribution (Lingam et al., 2009; Pfeiffer et al., 2018). These alternatives do not hinder efficiency; they reframe participation from immediate presence to sustained clarity.

In leadership contexts, this sequential mode often enables high-fidelity sensemaking, procedural foresight, and scenario planning. Dyspraxic leaders may not dominate the room in rapid debate, but they frequently surface the insights that bring coherence after complexity.

Over time, however, the mental and emotional labor involved in continually adapting to mismatched systems can accumulate—often leading to masking behaviors and hidden depletion beneath outward performance.

9.2.4 Emotional Labor and Masking

Spectrum Role: Quiet Overcomer
Type: Strain—with invisible depletion

For many dyspraxic professionals, the energy required to meet normative expectations—whether in coordination, pacing, or outward polish—carries a cumulative cost. Shaped by prior misrecognition, this often results in masking behaviors, hyper-preparation, or perfectionistic overcompensation. While these efforts may preserve external functionality, they frequently lead to hidden depletion and diminished leadership sustainability—especially in cultures that conflate competence with uninterrupted visibility or seamless execution (APA, 2013; Pfeiffer et al., 2015) (Figure 9.1).

To address this, organizations can adopt energy-conscious leadership frameworks that legitimize nonperformative contribution styles and asynchronous workflows. Recognizing masking as labor, rather than avoidance, reframes the conversation around authenticity and regulation. Support structures should shift focus from output frequency to energy-attuned consistency.

This is less a matter of time management than of energy alignment—ensuring that cognitive, motor, and emotional demands match individual processing rhythms and recovery cycles.

A practical approach is the Energy-Focus Method™: a rhythm-based mapping practice that tracks individual peaks in clarity, availability, and coordination. By aligning high-effort tasks with these windows—and buffering motor-intensive demands—leaders can optimize performance without overextension. Designed for both personal use and team alignment, the method reframes leadership as calibrated contribution, grounded in strategic presence rather than continuous polish.

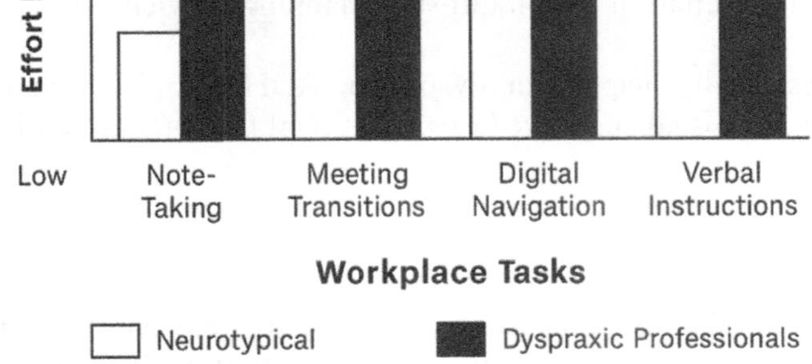

Figure 9.1 The invisible effort spectrum: Dyspraxia and workplace performance.

This figure illustrates the often-unseen cognitive and motor demands associated with dyspraxia by contrasting typical workplace tasks with the internal effort required to perform them. Research indicates that individuals with dyspraxia expend significantly more executive and physical energy to complete everyday professional activities—such as handwriting, spatial navigation, or time-sensitive coordination—despite outwardly similar performance (Kirby et al., 2011; Missiuna et al., 2008). These discrepancies, while rarely visible to colleagues, represent a measurable increase in cognitive load and highlight the need for systems that recognize performance sustainability—not just outcome parity.

To translate these traits into sustainable practice, the following tools support dyspraxic professionals in aligning effort with impact—reducing hidden labor while enabling structured contribution.

9.3 Optional Tools to Try—Dyspraxia

9.3.1 Neurodivergent Leadership Profile: The Sequential Strategist

These tools aim to reduce friction in planning, sequencing, and executive flow—externalizing complexity instead of forcing internal compensation. They support consistency through structure, not rigidity, and honor the cognitive depth behind seemingly small tasks. Designed for leaders who think in systems but struggle with stepwise execution, these strategies make invisible effort visible—and manageable.

1. Sequencing Scaffolds

Use visual workflow aids such as step-based checklists, kanban boards, or mind maps. These provide structure for transitions, reduce cognitive load, and support clear action sequencing.

→ Enhances task initiation and multi-step planning (Zwicker et al., 2012).

Application: Especially helpful for dyspraxia, ADHD, and dyslexia, where step clarity and visual cueing reduce executional friction and working memory load.

2. Motor Planning Buffers

Build extra time into schedules for tasks requiring spatial navigation, fast adaptation, or fine motor control (e.g., live presentations, travel setups).

→ Reduces time-based anxiety and prevents cascading dysregulation.

Application: Crucial for dyspraxic profiles and autistic leaders with sensory-motor friction—prevents panic under time pressure and supports smoother role performance.

3. Digital Workspace Anchors

Standardize platforms with automation features—calendar templates, recurring reminders, smart folders, and document history. These reduce executive overload from constant mental tracking.

→ Supports environmental predictability (Kirby et al., 2011).

Application: Beneficial for dyspraxia, ADHD, and working memory variability—offloads sequencing and supports continuity in high-interruption settings.

4. Voice Notes and Verbal Processing Aids

Use tools like speech-to-text dictation or private audio journaling to process and record ideas fluidly, especially when handwriting or typing is a bottleneck.

→ Bridges ideation and expression without penalizing motor strain.

Application: Supports dyspraxia, dysgraphia, and ADHD—ensures fluency of thought isn't blocked by physical execution constraints.

5. Post-Task Decompression Routines

After complex tasks or socially dense interactions, use short physical resets (stretching, slow walks, pressure stimulation) to discharge sensory-motor tension.

→ Supports nervous system recalibration (Pfeiffer et al., 2015).

Application: Highly relevant for dyspraxic and HSP profiles—minimizes somatic overload and restores motor-emotional regulation.

6. Co-Pilot Delegation Strategy

Identify a trusted colleague or assistant for high-friction executional tasks (e.g., note-taking, formatting, logistics) without sacrificing decision-making authority.

→ Honors autonomy while reducing burnout (Kirby & Sugden, 2007).

Application: Enables dyspraxic and dyslexic leaders to focus on high-value conceptual work while minimizing performance drag in friction-heavy zones.

7. Pacing Protocols

Use energy mapping or weekly rhythm check-ins to distribute demanding tasks evenly. Avoid overloading "good days" that lead to rebound fatigue.

→ Promotes sustainable productivity patterns in fluctuating energy cycles.

Application: Supports dyspraxia, ADHD, and chronic pain-adjacent profiles where energy dips are nonlinear and task timing requires anticipatory strategy.

While the strategies above offer practical scaffolding, real-world examples illustrate how dyspraxic leaders translate these supports into adaptive strength—navigating complexity not through polish, but through process clarity, resilience, and quiet redesign.

9.4 Leading with Precision beyond Coordination: The Dyspraxic Advantage in Complex Systems

Beyond motion lies imagination—leading through visual logic and resilient design.

Diagnosed with dyspraxia, Dr Maggie Aderin-Pocock has built a distinguished career in science and technology, serving as a systems engineer on major aerospace projects including the James Webb Space Telescope. As a technical leader, she has managed complex teams and cross-disciplinary innovations while navigating the motor coordination and sequencing challenges typical of dyspraxia.

Rather than being deterred by her coordination difficulties, she has credited her dyspraxia with enhancing her ability to think visually and unconventionally—especially in complex problem-solving and systems integration. Beyond technical leadership, she has also become one of the UK's most prominent science communicators, hosting BBC programs and promoting inclusivity in STEM. Her trajectory demonstrates how dyspraxic thinkers, when supported, can lead through imagination, persistence, and systems fluency (Aderin-Pocock, 2010; National Autistic Society, 2016).

Both dyspraxia and high sensitivity engage the nervous system—though in different languages. Where dyspraxia speaks through motor complexity and fatigue, HSP traits express through heightened emotional and sensory responsivity. In leadership, both profiles may struggle with overstimulation, yet bring profound attunement to detail, ethics, and relational dynamics. We now explore this sensitivity not as fragility, but as depth of perception.

References

Aderin-Pocock, M. (2010). *It's not rocket science: Discover the science in everyday life*. BBC Books.

American Psychiatric Association. (2013). *Diagnostic and statistical manual of mental disorders* (5th ed.). https://doi.org/10.1176/appi.books.9780890425596

Blank, R., Smits-Engelsman, B., Polatajko, H., & Wilson, P. (2019). European Academy for Childhood Disability (EACD) recommendations on the definition, diagnosis and intervention of developmental coordination disorder (long version). *Developmental Medicine & Child Neurology, 61*(3), 242–285. https://doi.org/10.1111/dmcn.14132

Kirby, A., & Sugden, D. (2007). Children with developmental coordination disorder. *Journal of the Royal Society of Medicine, 100*(4), 182–186. https://doi.org/10.1177/014107680710011414

Kirby, A., Edwards, L., & Sugden, D. (2011). Emerging adulthood and developmental co-ordination disorder. *Journal of Adult Development, 18*(3), 107–113. https://doi.org/10.1007/s10804-011-9123-1

Kirby, A., Edwards, L., & Sugden, D. (2011). Emerging adulthood in developmental coordination disorder: Parent and young adult perspectives. *Research in Developmental Disabilities, 32*(4), 1351–1360. https://doi.org/10.1016/j.ridd.2011.01.003

Kirby, A., Williams, N., Thomas, M., & Hill, E. L. (2008). Self-reported mood, general health, wellbeing and employment status in adults with suspected DCD. *Research in Developmental Disabilities, 29*(4), 314–332. https://doi.org/10.1016/j.ridd.2007.05.001

Lingam, R., Hunt, L., Golding, J., Jongmans, M. J., & Emond, A. (2009). Prevalence of developmental coordination disorder using the DSM-IV at 7 years of age: A UK population-based study. *Pediatrics, 123*(4), e693–e700. https://doi.org/10.1542/peds.2008-1770

Missiuna, C., Moll, S., King, S., Stewart, D., & Macdonald, K. (2008). Life experiences of young adults who have coordination difficulties. *Canadian Journal of Occupational Therapy, 75*(3), 157–166. https://doi.org/10.1177/000841740807500307

National Autistic Society. (2016). *Inspirational women: Maggie Aderin-Pocock*. https://www.autism.org.uk/advice-and-guidance/stories/maggie-aderin-pocock

Pfeiffer, B., Clark, G. F., & Arbesman, M. (2015). Effectiveness of cognitive and occupation-based interventions for children with challenges in sensory processing and integration: A systematic review. *American Journal of Occupational Therapy, 72*(1), 7201190040p1–7201190040p9. https://doi.org/10.5014/ajot.2018.028233

Tal-Saban, M., Ornoy, A., & Parush, S. (2014). Young adults with developmental coordination disorder: A longitudinal study. *American Journal of Occupational Therapy, 68*(3), 307–316. https://doi.org/10.5014/ajot.2014.009563

Zwicker, J. G., Harris, S. R., & Klassen, A. F. (2012). Quality of life domains affected in children with developmental coordination disorder: A systematic review. *Child: Care, Health and Development, 39*(4), 562–580. https://doi.org/10.1111/j.1365-2214.2012.01379.x

Chapter 10

Highly Sensitive Persons

Depth Processing, Emotional Precision, and Sensory Boundaries

10.1 Quiet Power, Loud Systems: High Sensitivity in Fast-Moving Work Cultures

Reframing sensory sensitivity as strategic insight in high-demand environments.

This chapter investigates the leadership dynamics of high sensitivity across five dimensions: depth-oriented insight and pattern recognition, sensory saturation and overstimulation, relational intelligence and emotional absorption and burnout risk, and the ethical strain that arises in decision-intensive environments.

High Sensitivity—also known as Sensory Processing Sensitivity (SPS)—is a neurobiological trait marked by heightened depth in cognitive and emotional processing (Aron & Aron, 1997). Affecting roughly 15–20% of the population (Greven et al., 2019), it involves increased responsiveness to subtle stimuli and greater vulnerability to overstimulation—not due to fragility, but to the intensity of simultaneous input.

Neuroscientific research shows that Highly Sensitive Persons (HSPs) display greater activation in brain regions associated with empathy, awareness, and reflective decision-making—such as the insula, precuneus, and anterior cingulate cortex (Acevedo et al., 2014). Their perceptual systems are finely tuned, often leading to enriched inner experiences, but also a need for thoughtful pacing and recovery. When misunderstood or unsupported, this depth-oriented processing can result in sensory overload or emotional exhaustion—particularly in high-stimulus, fast-response environments.

While HSP is not classified as a clinical neurodivergence, it is widely recognized within the broader neurodiversity spectrum as a neurologically distinct processing style—with meaningful implications for how individuals navigate work, leadership, and social environments.

To better understand how high sensitivity shapes leadership, the following expressions trace distinct yet interconnected patterns—ranging from

DOI: 10.4324/9781003681540-12

sensory processing and relational attunement to ethical discernment and emotional load. Each highlights a unique strength–strain dynamic, alongside implications for sustainable leadership practice.

10.2 HSP in Leadership: Patterns of Expression—Strength Zones and Strain Points

Leveraging high sensitivity for relational, ethical, and systemic leadership.

10.2.1 Depth-Oriented Insight and Pattern Recognition

Spectrum Role: Nuance-Focused Strategist
Type: Advanced Strength—Commonly Overlooked

As outlined above, heightened sensory and emotional attunement in highly sensitive individuals enables depth-integrated processing and early recognition of subtle systemic shifts (Acevedo et al., 2014). This perceptual orientation supports nuanced pattern detection, contextual awareness, and meaning-making—especially in emotionally complex or ambiguous environments. Sensitivity in this sense is not limited to interpersonal affect, but extends to the ability to perceive emerging dynamics across social, emotional, and sensory domains.

In professional settings, this often translates into anticipatory insight. HSP individuals may intuit relational undercurrents, identify tensions before they escalate, or sense when alignment is drifting—all before these signals become overt. Their contributions can strengthen group cohesion, ethical grounding, and long-range perspective.

At the same time, fast-paced or overstimulating environments may challenge this processing depth. Delayed responses, hesitation under pressure, or the need for retreat can be misread as indecision or disengagement when they are, in fact signs of cognitive saturation. Structures that legitimize reflective processing—such as quiet work zones, visual synthesis formats, or pacing accommodations—can reduce overload and help translate insight into action (Aron & Aron, 1997; Homberg et al., 2016). When adequately supported, HSP cognition becomes a systemic asset: attuned, integrative, and responsive to complexity.

Yet the same depth that enables nuanced foresight and meaning-making can also leave highly sensitive leaders vulnerable to saturation—particularly when perceptual input accumulates faster than it can be integrated.

10.2.2 Sensory Saturation

Spectrum Role: Environmental Integrator
Type: Challenge—with perceptual depth

Highly sensitive individuals exhibit amplified responsiveness to sensory and emotional input, underpinned by increased neural activity in regions linked to awareness, empathy, and sensory integration (Aron & Aron, 1997; Acevedo et al., 2014). This heightened attunement supports subtle situational tracking—enabling early recognition of emotional undercurrents, ethical friction, or environmental dissonance that may go unnoticed by others.

However, this perceptual openness can become overwhelming in high-stimulus or fast-paced environments. Sensory input, social complexity, or emotional intensity may exceed processing capacity, leading to cognitive saturation or temporary withdrawal. What may appear as indecision or low resilience often reflects a responsive system actively managing input load.

In team and organizational settings, sustained performance depends on recognizing sensory regulation as a structural need and not a personal preference. Measures such as reducing ambient noise, legitimizing sensory tools (e.g., headphones, tinted lighting), and avoiding back-to-back emotionally charged meetings can support nervous system stability. Recovery time after high-input tasks and asynchronous contribution options also help preserve clarity and participation over time.

For individuals with HSP traits, aligning task rhythms with sensory thresholds can increase sustainability. This may involve front-loading demanding tasks into quieter periods, inserting transitional buffers between emotionally dense and strategic work, or integrating calming rituals—such as silent breaks, movement, or visual thinking—into daily routines. When honored systemically, this sensitivity becomes a strategic resource for attuned, values-driven contribution.

Still, when environmental demands are attuned to their processing rhythm, HSP leaders frequently shift from sensory overload to relational depth—transforming heightened perception into emotional attunement and trust cultivation.

10.2.3 Emotional Absorption and Relational Burnout

Spectrum Role: Empathic Anchor
Type: Strength–Strain Duality

Highly sensitive individuals often bring a relational depth marked by emotional resonance, careful listening, and intuitive awareness of unspoken dynamics. Their presence can foster psychological safety, strengthen interpersonal trust, and support cohesion—particularly in emotionally complex or mission-driven environments (Aron et al., 2012; Pluess, 2015).

Emotional input is frequently experienced not as distant observation but as direct transmission—others' stress or urgency is often felt as one's own. This heightened responsiveness, underpinned by intensified mirror neuron activity and deep emotional integration (Acevedo et al., 2014), can be a powerful connector. At the same time, it increases susceptibility to overload, especially when emotional boundaries remain implicit or support structures are lacking.

Over time, this relational labor can become invisible—expressed through constant availability, conflict buffering, or the quiet absorption of group tension. What may appear outwardly as steadiness or warmth may internally reflect cognitive strain or empathic saturation. Misreadings are common: emotional depth may be mistaken for indecision, relational sensitivity for mood fluctuation.

To support sustainability, it is essential to recognize emotional presence as effortful, not infinite. Team and organizational systems can respond by acknowledging relational labor explicitly—through reflective rituals, shared debriefs, or distributed emotional support roles. Emotional supervision and structural containment (e.g., protected downtime, relational boundaries, role clarity) enable long-term coherence.

For individuals with HSP traits, relational discernment may be just as vital as empathic openness. Sustained contribution depends on practices that restore internal boundaries—whether through journaling, peer processing, or deliberate disengagement. When relational intelligence is embedded into collective rhythm rather than carried silently, sensitivity becomes a strategic asset—not a hidden liability.

However, a deep connection carries its own complexity. Without clear emotional boundaries, the same empathic resonance that sustains trust can gradually erode internal clarity through unconscious absorption. As moral attunement deepens, many HSP leaders encounter a second form of load: ethical strain and decisional fatigue.

10.2.4 Ethical Strain and Decision Fatigue

Spectrum Role: Integrity Compass
Type: Hidden Stressor

Highly sensitive individuals, moral reasoning is often rooted in deep internal alignment—guided by values such as systemic coherence, human dignity, and long-range responsibility (Aron et al., 2012). This principled orientation enhances trust and ethical clarity, especially in emotionally complex or ambiguous contexts. However, when personal ethics conflict

Misinterpretation	Reality (HSP Trait)
"Too sensitive"	Deep perceptual processing
"Takes things personally"	Strong ethical/ empathic attunement
"Slow to decide"	Integrative decision-making
"Avoids feedback"	Overprocessing + emotional load

Figure 10.1 Illustrates common misinterpretations of HSP traits in professional settings and reframes them through a neurobiologically accurate and strength-based lens. This comparison aims to dismantle stereotypes and validate the leadership capacities of Highly Sensitive Persons.

with organizational expectations, implicit pressures, or strategic compromises, internal dissonance can arise. What may appear externally as hesitation often reflects a deeper alignment check—not indecision, but conscientious pause.

Systemic relief comes from distributing ethical reflection across the organization. Transparent escalation paths, value-based review processes, and shared accountability structures help reduce the pressure to privately resolve moral ambiguity (Lionetti et al., 2018). When ethical signals are treated as indicators of system tension rather than personal blocks, integrity becomes a collective capacity.

To support this, organizations can normalize practices that externalize ethical reasoning—such as clarifying decision principles upfront, surfacing non-negotiables, or embedding reflective dialogue into high-stakes planning. These approaches reduce rumination and strengthen cohesion by transforming ethical sensitivity from silent burden into visible strategic depth.

To translate these insights into sustainable practice, leaders can draw on targeted tools that support emotional clarity, boundary regulation, and value-centered decision-making. The following strategies are designed to improve recovery, distribute relational labor, and transform perceptual sensitivity into stable leadership presence—without eroding integrity or well-being.

10.3 Optional Tools to Try—Highly Sensitive Persons

These tools are designed to protect cognitive clarity and emotional bandwidth in overstimulating environments. They support intentional pacing, sensory regulation, and values-centered alignment—so that sensitivity becomes a leadership asset, not a liability. Instead of dampening intensity, these strategies create containers where depth, intuition, and resonance can thrive without depletion.

1. Emotional Bandwidth Tracker

Conduct daily or weekly self-checks to map emotional input/output. Track patterns of overstimulation, emotional resonance, or energy drain.

→ Supports anticipatory planning and adaptive load balancing.

Application: Ideal for HSP and emotionally attuned leaders who experience relational intensity, empathic absorption, or post-interaction fatigue. Helps identify invisible energy drains and recalibrate boundaries.

2. Sensory Regulation Kit

Assemble personalized regulation tools such as noise-dampening earbuds, soft clothing textures, or dimmable lighting. These reduce environmental input during high-sensitivity moments.

→ Increases cognitive resilience during overload (Aron, 2004).

Application: Vital for HSP and autism-adjacent sensory profiles where tactile, auditory, or visual input rapidly exceeds thresholds—supports grounded functioning in overstimulating work settings.

3. Buffer Zone Planning

Use calendar blocks to schedule decompression time before or after emotionally intense or high-stimulus activities (e.g., feedback sessions, large meetings, travel).

→ Protects nervous system recovery and decision-making clarity.

Application: Supports all leaders whose nervous systems require transitional buffering; especially effective for leadership roles with frequent high-stakes engagement.

4. Values Alignment Journal

Use structured journaling prompts to reflect on alignment between personal values and current professional choices—especially useful when emotional overwhelm blurs direction.

→ Anchors internal clarity amid relational or sensory turbulence.

Application: Anchors ethical clarity for HSP, autistic, or gifted leaders with strong integrity drives; prevents moral fatigue in high-ambiguity systems.

5. Low-Stimulus Productivity Mapping

Identify windows of peak focus and environments that match sensory readiness (e.g., early mornings, nature-facing desks). Align deep work with calm zones.

→ Optimizes output without triggering overstimulation.

Application: Effective for HSP and sensory-divergent professionals who perform best in controlled, low-distraction contexts; boosts sustainable deep work.

6. Empathic Detachment Cues

Develop internal scripts or somatic cues (e.g., "This isn't mine to hold," or hand-to-heart grounding) to avoid emotional enmeshment.

→ Preserves presence without burnout (Aron & Aron, 1997).

Application: Especially helpful for HSP leaders in relationally intensive roles (coaching, mediation, team care); protects against empathic depletion while maintaining compassionate leadership.

7. Team Sensitivity Brief

Offer a short, optional summary or team dialogue that introduces HSP traits, work preferences, and communication boundaries. Focuses on strength-framing, not pathology.

→ Enhances team trust and prevents misinterpretation.

Application: Normalizes sensory-emotional boundaries especially for HSP, ADHD, autism, or AuDHD profiles in leadership, enabling relational safety and collective clarity without disclosure pressure.

Abstract tools become transformative when grounded in lived experience. The following example highlights how one HSP leader operationalized emotional boundaries and value-centered clarity under pressure.

10.3.1 When Compassion Leads: Regulated Presence in Times of Crisis

In crisis, compassion becomes command presence.

As Prime Minister of New Zealand (2017–2023), Jacinda Ardern led with a leadership style often described as compassionate, emotionally attuned, and relationally grounded—hallmarks of high sensitivity. Her response to the Christchurch mosque shootings, which emphasized empathy, swift protective action, and cultural respect, illustrated a deep capacity to absorb emotional nuance without bypassing action. Ardern also spoke candidly about the emotional weight of leadership, setting a precedent for transparency and regulation in high-responsibility roles. Rather than shielding from intensity, she consistently channeled it into presence and purpose—demonstrating how sensitivity, when supported, becomes a strategic strength rather than a liability.

Heightened sensitivity can manifest inwardly—as empathy, sensory receptivity, and emotional depth—but in the case of tic disorders, it may also surface through involuntary expression. Tics, both motor and vocal, challenge the norm of smooth, polished communication. As we transition, we ask: What does it mean to lead when your nervous system speaks out loud?

References

Acevedo, B. P., Aron, E. N., Aron, A., Sangster, M. D., Collins, N., & Brown, L. L. (2014). The highly sensitive brain: An fMRI study of sensory processing sensitivity and response to others' emotions. *Brain and Behavior, 4*(4), 580–594. https://doi.org/10.1002/brb3.242

Aron, E. N. (2004). *The highly sensitive person: How to thrive when the world overwhelms you*. Broadway Books.

Aron, E. N., & Aron, A. (1997). Sensory-processing sensitivity and its relation to introversion and emotionality. *Journal of Personality and Social Psychology, 73*(2), 345–368. https://doi.org/10.1037/0022-3514.73.2.345

Aron, E. N., Aron, A., & Jagiellowicz, J. (2012). Sensory processing sensitivity: A review in the light of the evolution of biological responsivity. *Personality and Social Psychology Review, 16*(3), 262–282. https://doi.org/10.1177/1088868311434213

Greven, C. U., Lionetti, F., Booth, C., Aron, E., Fox, E., Schendan, H. E., Pluess, M., Bruining, H., Acevedo, B., Bijttebier, P., & Homberg, J. (2019). Sensory Processing Sensitivity in the context of Environmental Sensitivity: A critical review and development of research agenda. *Neuroscience & Biobehavioral Reviews*, 98, 287–305. https://doi.org/10.1016/j.neubiorev.2019.01.009

Homberg, J. R., Schubert, D., & Gaspar, P. (2016). New perspectives on the neurobiology of sensitivity. *Trends in Neurosciences, 39*(11), 712–723. https://doi.org/10.1016/j.tins.2016.09.001

Lionetti, F., Aron, A., Aron, E. N., Burns, G. L., Jagiellowicz, J., & Pluess, M. (2018). Dandelions, tulips and orchids: Evidence for the existence of low-sensitive, medium-sensitive and high-sensitive individuals. *Translational Psychiatry, 8*(1), 24. https://doi.org/10.1038/s41398-017-0090-6

Pluess, M. (2015). Individual differences in environmental sensitivity. *Child Development Perspectives, 9*(3), 138–143. https://doi.org/10.1111/cdep.12120

Chapter 11

Tics and Tourette Syndrome

Expression, Control, and Visibility under Pressure

11.1 Involuntary Expression and the Social Gaze

How visibility, perception, and suppression shape the lived experience of Tourette Syndrome in professional settings.

This chapter explores the leadership dynamics associated with Tourette-related neurodivergence across five dimensions: sensorimotor overflow and task interruption, pattern disruption and systems-level innovation, cognitive co-occurrence and executive load, real-time adaptability under pressure, and the social interpretation of tics in visibility-sensitive environments.

Tics are sudden, repetitive, and non-rhythmic motor or vocal expressions that are experienced as involuntary. When both types persist for more than a year, a diagnosis of Tourette Syndrome (TS) may be made—typically during childhood (Robertson, 2000). Public understanding of TS is still shaped by media caricatures that overemphasize rare symptoms and underrepresent the daily complexity of living with tics. Particularly in leadership contexts, the experience demands a more nuanced and respectful discourse.

Tourette Syndrome is neurologically based, not behaviorally chosen. Yet in professional environments, visible tics are frequently subject to misinterpretation, requiring those affected to navigate constant vigilance: when to disclose, how to manage others' reactions, and whether to suppress. This invisible labor carries a neurophysiological cost. Suppressing tics—even temporarily—draws on working memory, increases stress levels, and can lead to rebound effects or emotional fatigue, especially under conditions of scrutiny or sensory overload (Cohen et al., 2013; Cavanna et al., 2012).

Tics often fluctuate in intensity depending on stress, fatigue, or environmental stimuli. Their visibility exposes leaders to persistent

DOI: 10.4324/9781003681540-13

micro-misreadings—such as interpreting a facial tic as sarcasm or a vocal tic as interruption—which can accumulate over time and shape perceptions of professionalism. This is compounded by frequent co-occurrence with ADHD, OCD, anxiety, or autism traits, creating what might be described as executive complexity: a layered cognitive profile requiring ongoing internal negotiation (Freeman et al., 2000; Hirschtritt et al., 2015).

Yet these demands often give rise to distinctive leadership strengths—shaped not in spite of difference, but through it.

11.2 The Cognitive Cost beneath the Surface of Tourette Syndrome

Beneath each tic lies a discipline few ever see.

The leadership experience of Tourette Syndrome extends beyond visible tics to the hidden cognitive costs they generate. Suppression, self-monitoring, and social calibration consume executive resources, shaping performance and sustainability in ways often overlooked. Recognizing these invisible demands provides essential context for understanding expression, perception, and adaptive capacity in professional settings (Table 11.1).

The expressions below outline key leadership patterns associated with Tourette-related traits. Together, they illustrate how sensorimotor unpredictability, cognitive layering, and social scrutiny shape both the challenges and the adaptive capacities of individuals with tics.

Table 11.1 Visualizes the contrast between outward expressions of tics in leadership (left column) and the hidden regulatory effort required to manage them (right column). It highlights how visible behaviors often misrepresent the significant cognitive and emotional labor involved.

Visible expression	*Invisible effort*
Repetitive facial or motor tics	Suppression effort; working memory strain
Vocal sounds or interruptions	Emotional self-monitoring; fear of social misinterpretation
"Nervous" body language	Anticipatory stress; energy spent masking
Pauses or disrupted flow	Internal regulation; recovery from executive overload
Unexpected reactions or gestures	Co-occurring processing (e.g., OCD, ADHD, sensory input)
Avoidance of group visibility	Risk calculation; self-protection from misunderstanding

11.3 Tics and Tourette Syndrome in Leadership: Patterns of Expression—Strength Zones and Strain Points

Rethinking Disruption, Presence, and Performance through a Neurodynamic Lens.

11.3.1 Sensorimotor Overflow and Task Interruption

Spectrum Role: Kinetic Interrupter
Type: Challenge—with sporadic visibility

Tourette Syndrome (TS) involves involuntary sensorimotor expressions—tics—that can interrupt ongoing tasks, alter perceived presence, and affect how leadership behaviors are interpreted. These neurological expressions vary in frequency and intensity, often intensifying under stress, fatigue, or sensory overload (Robertson, 2000; Cavanna & Termine, 2012). While they are not under voluntary control, the effort to navigate professional expectations amid unpredictable physical impulses draws heavily on cognitive and emotional resources.

Externally, visible tics are often misread. Behaviors rooted in neurology may be mistaken for distraction, agitation, or disinterest, creating relational friction and undermining trust in ways that have little to do with actual competence. Internally, the need to manage these responses alongside task demands can fragment attention and elevate the baseline effort required to maintain presence and continuity.

In leadership and team roles, these dynamics introduce a unique form of complexity: performance quality may remain high, but its rhythm and presentation diverge from normative expectations. The impact is often disproportionate to visibility—occasional interruptions or fluctuations may carry outsized interpretive weight, especially in environments that prioritize composure and consistency.

Organizational cultures that default to surface-read assessments may overlook the depth of adaptation and resilience TS requires. Misattributions—such as associating interruption with instability or emotional volatility—can distort perceptions of capacity and overlook the systemic load of navigating expression within unaccommodating environments.

When structural awareness is present, kinetic variation becomes less disruptive and more intelligible. Leadership with TS often brings sharpened attunement to social nuance, resilience in high-pressure contexts, and a grounded understanding of how bodily expression intersects with performance culture. These insights are not secondary—they arise directly from embodied negotiation with complexity.

Yet navigating constant interruption can also sharpen a different capacity: the ability to question assumptions and disrupt default patterns from within.

11.3.2 Pattern Disruption and Innovation

Spectrum Role: Norm Challenger
Type: Strength—with unconventional insight

Tourette-related cognition is often marked by a heightened sensitivity to implicit norms, behavioral expectations, and structural rigidity. This orientation can foster a first-principles approach—questioning unexamined assumptions, reframing challenges, and identifying systemic blind spots (Robertson, 2000). Rather than accepting established pathways, individuals with TS frequently navigate through divergent reasoning, pattern disassembly, and conceptual redirection.

Such cognitive tendencies are particularly valuable in contexts requiring innovation, strategic reset, or resistance to groupthink. Where others follow precedent, norm challengers often detect friction points and propose alternative models—offering early signals of dysfunction or stagnation that may otherwise remain unexamined.

However, these strengths may be misread within environments that favor polish, linearity, and consensus. Unconventional input can be dismissed as tangential or disruptive, especially when it challenges comfortable assumptions. The result is often a disconnect between insight and uptake—not due to lack of relevance, but because communicative form diverges from institutional expectations.

To benefit from this form of systemic intelligence, organizations must decouple value from delivery style. Disruption should be interpreted not as defiance, but as diagnostic acuity—a means of exposing tensions and surfacing alternatives. Formal structures that accommodate divergence—such as foresight functions, challenge-based strategy formats, or neurodivergent-led audits—can help translate pattern disruption into collective gain.

When integrated rather than resisted, this form of insight contributes not just to creativity, but to resilience. In times of complexity or constraint, the ability to reconfigure assumptions becomes a leadership asset—one rooted in cognitive variability rather than behavioral conformity.

While disruptive insight is a strength, it often coexists with layered executive demands—especially when Tourette traits intersect with ADHD, OCD, or sensory sensitivities.

11.3.3 Cognitive Co-Occurrence and Executive Load

Spectrum Role: Layered Processor
Type: Strain—with dual-tasking cost

Tourette Syndrome (TS) frequently coexists with other neurocognitive profiles such as ADHD, OCD, and anxiety-related traits. These overlapping dimensions contribute to layered executive functioning—where impulsivity, perfectionism, hyperfocus, and emotional reactivity intersect in complex ways (Freeman et al., 2000; Hirschtritt et al., 2015). This convergence often supports high-level insight, rapid pattern recognition, and innovative thinking—but it also amplifies cognitive load, especially under time pressure or high-context demands.

The challenge lies less in capacity than in coordination. Competing internal demands—such as attentional redirection, emotional filtering, and memory management—can interfere with task transitions, temporal sequencing, and administrative follow-through. In professional contexts, these dynamics may present as variability in rhythm, delayed responses, or fluctuating clarity—despite consistent underlying competence.

Because these regulatory demands are largely invisible, misinterpretation is common. In systems that reward speed, polish, or unbroken presence, divergence from linear pacing may be seen as disorganization or lack of reliability. Yet such assumptions obscure the ongoing internal effort required to maintain function across multiple cognitive channels.

Structural clarity supports performance more effectively than compensatory effort. Clear segmentation of tasks, multimodal communication pathways, and pacing that allows for cognitive recalibration reduce the mismatch between internal processing and external expectation. When variability is normalized as part of cognitive diversity—not treated as a disruption—sustainability becomes more feasible.

Recognition of cognitive co-occurrence shifts the evaluative lens. Rather than viewing fluctuations as deficits, they can be understood as manifestations of parallel processing demands—calling for rhythm-aware design and thoughtful role alignment. In team environments, this enables contributions to be assessed not by surface steadiness, but by the depth and integrity of what is delivered over time.

Still, under these layered pressures, many leaders develop a surprising strength: real-time adaptability forged through the necessity of continuous internal recalibration.

11.3.4 Real-Time Adaptability and Presence under Pressure

Spectrum Role: Reflexive Improviser
Type: Strength—forged through unpredictability

Marked by rapid shifts in attention, heightened contextual awareness, and improvisational responsiveness, many individuals with Tourette Syndrome (TS) bring a unique capacity for real-time adaptation—particularly in dynamic or high-pressure situations. This flexibility, as outlined before, is often shaped by overlapping cognitive profiles such as ADHD, OCD, or anxiety-spectrum traits, which introduce layered processing demands and amplify both reactivity and regulation.

Rather than following linear or uniform cognitive patterns, these individuals navigate complex internal landscapes—constantly recalibrating between competing stimuli, impulses, and situational cues. This makes them especially adept at responding to sudden shifts, anticipating emerging needs, and steering group attention in the moment.

Yet these strengths come with a cost: the same reflexive capacity that supports live problem-solving can hinder sustained focus, task sequencing, or administrative follow-through. Output rhythms may appear irregular—not due to lack of competence, but because cognitive load is being managed across multiple simultaneous channels. In standardized work cultures, such fluctuation is easily misread as inconsistency or underperformance.

Creating space for this kind of adaptive cognition requires structural responsiveness. Systems that allow for temporal variability, modular input, and strategic pacing can absorb fluctuations without compromising collective output. By designing for real-time strength rather than penalizing asynchronous rhythm, organizations gain access to a form of leadership intelligence forged through continuous internal negotiation with unpredictability.

Yet this capacity to stay present under pressure is often complicated by how visible traits—like tics—are socially read, misinterpreted, or stigmatized in professional settings.

11.3.5 Social Interpretation and Visibility Anxiety

Spectrum Role: Misread Communicator
Type: Strain—with relational complexity

Tics—whether motor or vocal—can introduce expressive ambiguity in professional environments. As involuntary yet visible behaviors, they are often misread: motor tics may be mistaken for anxiety or disrespect, vocal tics for sarcasm or interruption. This misinterpretation intensifies in digital settings, where screen fragmentation and reduced nonverbal cues diminish contextual clarity (Cavanna et al., 2012).

To reduce the risk of being misread, individuals with Tourette Syndrome (TS) may adjust participation—limiting verbal input, avoiding video calls, or preferring asynchronous formats. While these adaptations support self-regulation, they are often misinterpreted as disengagement, lack of initiative, or low leadership potential. The cumulative effort to manage others' perceptions can lead to emotional fatigue, hypervigilance, or withdrawal from visibility-heavy roles.

These patterns do not stem from communicative deficit but from a mismatch between normative expectations and neurophysiological expression. As Cavanna and Rickards (2013) note, communicative divergence in TS represents an alternative mode of presence—often marked by clarity, reflexive responsiveness, and high social awareness.

Systemic inclusion requires structural clarity. Norms should accommodate varied expression styles through pre-meeting framing, silent input options, and flexible participation formats. Decoupling verbal fluency from perceived competence and legitimizing diverse pacing and delivery strengthens team trust and reduces relational strain.

When expression is interpreted through a neurological rather than normative lens, visibility becomes less about conformity and more about contribution.

Addressing visibility anxiety and cognitive strain requires more than awareness—it requires tools that reshape participation, communication, and pacing at the system level. The following strategies offer entry points for embedding Tourette-informed inclusion into leadership practice and team design.

11.4 Optional Tools to Try—Tics and Tourette Syndrome

Leadership with tics often involves managing visibility, timing, and energy under social scrutiny. These tools aim to reduce anticipatory stress, support nervous system balance, and create spaciousness around self-expression. The goal is not suppression, but sovereignty—enabling focus, presence, and authenticity without unnecessary vigilance.

1. Visibility Choice Board

Create a matrix for visibility-related choices—e.g., live vs. asynchronous formats, prep windows, or off-camera presence.

→ Enhances agency and reduces anticipatory overload in exposure-heavy situations (Robertson, 2000).

Application: Supports leaders with Tourette, social anxiety, or HSP traits; reduces masking pressure by legitimizing format variation.

2. Structured Transition Scripts

Develop verbal reset cues (e.g., "Let me regroup," "Give me a second to reset") for regaining flow after tic activity.

→ Maintains communication continuity; normalizes real-time adaptation (Cavanna & Rickards, 2013).

Application: Helpful for people with TS, dysfluency, AuDHD, or dyspraxia—supports graceful re-entry during interaction lag.

3. Cognitive Load Tracker

Log daily mental bandwidth, tic intensity, and co-occurring trait impact (e.g., ADHD-driven impulsivity or OCD-related mental loops).

→ Externalizes internal fluctuations and enables pacing calibration.

Application: Useful for people with Tourette and overlapping profiles (e.g., ADHD, OCD); supports self-awareness, team alignment, and access planning.

4. Asynchronous Leadership Tools

Use recorded briefings, collaborative docs, or dashboard updates instead of real-time speech-heavy formats.

→ Protects nervous system regulation and output coherence (Conelea & Woods, 2008).

Application: Valuable for TS, autistic, or dyslexic professionals with expressive pacing variation or verbal fatigue.

5. Environmental Modulation Plan

Identify sensory triggers (e.g., flickering lights, sharp noises) and make subtle environmental adaptations—seat choice, meeting length, etc.

→ Lowers tic activation threshold through contextual alignment.

Application: Applies to TS, HSP, AuDHD, and epilepsy-adjacent cognitive variation—reduces stress-induced neuro-motor escalation.

6. Ally Briefing Templates

Equip close collaborators with a brief, respectful overview of tics, nervous system needs, and communication preferences.

→ Promotes team fluency and preempts stigma without oversharing.

Application: For TS and other visible/invisible neurodivergent expressions (e.g., stimming, verbal dysregulation); helps shift team culture through proactive normalization.

7. Restorative Regulation Menu

Create a menu of sensory reset options (e.g., texture tools, breathwork, proprioceptive input) to use between meetings or after intense control effort.

→ Mitigates rebound tics and nervous system strain from extended regulation.

Application: Especially effective for professionals with tic-related suppression, executive fatigue, or emotional overcontainment (TS, AuDHD, trauma-informed profiles).

These tools support everyday regulation and autonomy. The following real-life example shows how one public figure integrates them into daily life.

11.4.1 *From Tic to Trust: Public Vulnerability as Relational Authority*

Leading with vulnerability and visibility.

During his 2023 Glastonbury performance, singer-songwriter Lewis Capaldi—who lives with Tourette Syndrome—experienced an intense tic episode that made it difficult to finish his set. Instead of masking or exiting the stage, he stayed present, visibly vulnerable. The crowd stepped in, singing his lyrics back to him in a powerful act of shared dignity.

While not a traditional workplace setting, this moment exemplified emotionally intelligent leadership: modeling transparency, trust, and collective resilience. Capaldi's openness about his condition has also helped destigmatize Tourette Syndrome in the public eye—turning personal struggle into cultural advocacy.

At first glance, giftedness may seem disconnected from motor expression or sensory overload—but many gifted individuals experience co-occurring tics, compulsions, or regulation struggles. The shared thread is intensity: of thought, emotion, or neurobiological activity. As we enter the realm of giftedness, we leave behind the expectation of linearity—and begin exploring the cognitive multiverse through a strength-first lens.

References

Cavanna, A. E., & Rickards, H. (2013). The psychopathological spectrum of Gilles de la Tourette syndrome. *Neuroscience & Biobehavioral Reviews, 37*(6), 1008–1015. https://doi.org/10.1016/j.neubiorev.2012.11.017

Cavanna, A. E., & Termine, C. (2012). Tourette syndrome. In M. J. Aminoff, F. Boller, & D. F. Swaab (Eds.), *Handbook of clinical neurology* (Vol. 106, pp. 583–590). Elsevier. https://link.springer.com/chapter/10.1007/978-1-4614-0653-2_28

Cavanna, A. E., David, K., Bandera, V., Termine, C., Balottin, U., Schrag, A., & Selai, C. (2012). Health-related quality of life in Gilles de la Tourette syndrome: A decade of research. *Behavioural Neurology, 25*, Article 120296. https://doi.org/10.3233/BEN-120296

Cohen, S. C., Leckman, J. F., & Bloch, M. H. (2013). Clinical assessment of Tourette syndrome and tic disorders. *Neuroscience & Biobehavioral Reviews, 37*(6), 997–1007. https://doi.org/10.1016/j.neubiorev.2012.11.013

Conelea, C. A., & Woods, D. W. (2008). The influence of contextual factors on tic expression in Tourette's syndrome: A review. *Journal of Psychosomatic Research, 65*(5), 487–496. https://doi.org/10.1016/j.jpsychores.2008.03.005

Freeman, R. D., Fast, D. K., Burd, L., Kerbeshian, J., Robertson, M. M., & Sandor, P. (2000). An international perspective on Tourette syndrome: Selected findings from 3,500 individuals in 22 countries. *Developmental Medicine & Child Neurology, 42*(7), 436–447. https://pubmed.ncbi.nlm.nih.gov/10972415/

Hirschtritt, M. E., Lee, P. C., Pauls, D. L., Dion, Y., Grados, M. A., Illmann, C., ... & Mathews, C. A. (2015). Lifetime prevalence, age of risk, and genetic relationships of comorbid psychiatric disorders in Tourette syndrome. *JAMA Psychiatry, 72*(4), 325–333. https://doi.org/10.1001/jamapsychiatry.2014.2650

Robertson, M. M. (2000). Tourette syndrome, associated conditions and the complexities of treatment. *Brain, 123*(3), 425–462. https://doi.org/10.1093/brain/123.3.425

Chapter 12

Giftedness

Cognitive Intensity, Asynchrony, and the Challenge of Containment

12.1 Cognitive Intensity, Emotional Asynchrony, and the Challenge of Containment

Giftedness in leadership is a distinct cognitive architecture, not a surplus of skill.

This chapter explores giftedness in leadership across four interrelated dimensions: asynchronous development and accelerated cognition, perfectionism linked to risk sensitivity, emotional intensity shaped by existential purpose, and multipotentiality as a challenge to linear career norms. Together, these patterns illustrate how high intellectual capacity can enhance strategic vision and innovation—while also generating unique forms of strain when internal rhythms diverge from organizational expectations.

Giftedness is often misunderstood as a straightforward cognitive advantage—an abstract "high IQ" that implies ease, success, or genius in a narrow domain. In practice, it reflects a qualitatively distinct neurocognitive orientation shaped by heightened intensity, developmental asynchrony, and a strong drive for meaning, justice, or systemic coherence (Piechowski, 1999; Webb et al., 2016). It often involves a depth of perception that is as disorienting as it is generative (Silverman, 2013; Neihart et al., 2016). Gifted individuals may exhibit exceptional cognitive speed or insight in one area while simultaneously navigating challenges such as dyscalculia, sensory sensitivity, or emotional hyperreactivity—making popular depictions of giftedness both reductive and misleading.

Traditionally defined by an IQ two standard deviations above the mean (≥130), giftedness tends to manifest across multiple domains—cognitive, emotional, creative, and sensorimotor. Yet this expression is rarely linear or evenly distributed. A gifted leader might synthesize systems-level insights with extraordinary speed, yet struggle to tolerate inefficiency, adapt to emotionally incongruent settings, or sustain patience with bureaucratic structures (Peters, 2020). Their thinking may be abstract, nonlinear, and

DOI: 10.4324/9781003681540-14

anticipatory—while their emotional pacing or social regulation may lag behind. This internal dissonance, often referred to as asynchronous development, is one of the most defining—and most misunderstood—features of gifted profiles.

12.2 Prevalence of Giftedness

The estimated prevalence of giftedness depends on how it is defined:

Prevalence estimates for giftedness vary depending on the thresholds and criteria applied, ranging from narrow IQ-based definitions to broader multidimensional approaches (Table 12.1). Population-level figures provide only a baseline, as actual representation in professional and leadership contexts is likely higher.

Emotionally, many gifted adults experience what Dabrowski termed *overexcitabilities*—heightened responsiveness in intellectual, emotional, imaginational, psychomotor, and sensory domains (Piechowski, 1999). These sensitivities often fuel innovation, moral clarity, and deep engagement—but can also lead to overload, internal conflict, and difficulty disengaging from unresolved ethical tension.

To understand what this means in concrete leadership practice, the following expressions examine four key dynamics through which giftedness manifests—each with its own interplay of cognitive strength, systemic friction, and adaptive strategy.

12.3 Giftedness in Leadership: Patterns of Expression—Strength Zones and Strain Points

Exploring the dual edge of intellectual acceleration in organizational contexts.

Table 12.1 While these estimates apply to the general population, the actual proportion in academic and professional leadership contexts—such as technology, science, strategy, or the arts—is likely significantly higher. Still, giftedness is rarely acknowledged openly in these settings. Many gifted adults do not self-identify with the label, or actively avoid it for social or professional reasons (Probst & Kämpfe, 2019).

Definition	*Estimated prevalence*	*Notes*
IQ ≥ 130	~2–3% of the population	Classic psychometric threshold (2 SD above the mean)
IQ ≥ 145	~0.1–0.2%	Often referred to as "exceptionally gifted"
Broader definitions	Up to 5–10%	Includes creative, emotional, sensory, or social dimensions

12.3.1 *Asynchronous Development and Intellectual Overclocking*

Spectrum Role: Accelerated Integrator
Type: Strength–Strain Duality

Giftedness often involves asynchronous development: advanced cognitive capabilities coexist with uneven progress in emotional regulation, social pacing, or executive functioning (Silverman, 2013; Peterson, 2009). This internal divergence can lead to friction—especially in systems that expect synchronized development across domains.

Such individuals may demonstrate rapid synthesis, strategic foresight, and deep conceptual alignment. Yet the same profiles may encounter strain when navigating ambiguity, pacing collaborative processes, or translating abstract insight into stepwise delivery. Intensity—especially when rooted in ethical clarity or systems-level insight—can be misunderstood as impatience, aloofness, or resistance to feedback.

In team contexts, this pattern may appear as uneven contribution rhythms: bursts of high-impact input followed by silence, or deep analysis that feels disconnected from procedural steps. Emotional and cognitive bandwidth are often tightly linked—when internal coherence is disrupted, outward engagement may decline. These rhythms are frequently misread, leading to isolation or misattribution of intent.

Supportive environments acknowledge this duality and offer structures that integrate cognitive velocity with shared operational clarity. This might include planning formats that allow for conceptual input at early stages, collaborative scaffolds that align visionary thinking with tactical pacing, and reflective practices that bridge high abstraction with relational transparency.

Rather than diluting complexity, such approaches translate it—making depth legible without forcing flattening. When teams interpret intensity as a signal of alignment-seeking rather than critique, and when systems are designed to hold cognitive variability without penalizing it, gifted profiles can thrive not in spite of their asynchronous architecture, but through it.

However, the pace and intensity of intellectual acceleration frequently incur a hidden cost: an elevated internalized pressure to control outcomes, whereby elevated cognitive standards evolve into perfectionistic tendencies and a persistent fear of inadequacy.

12.3.2 *Perfectionism and Risk Aversion*

Spectrum Role: Precision Driver
Type: Strain—masked as reliability

Perfectionism in gifted individuals often arises from an internally anchored need for precision, coherence, and integrity—driven less by external reward than by complex, self-generated standards (Greenspon, 2000). This orientation can yield exceptional outcomes, but also inhibit flexibility in ambiguous or iterative settings. The pursuit of internal alignment may take precedence over timeliness, exploration, or collaborative trial phases—slowing processes even in otherwise high-performing environments.

This pattern may manifest as overpreparation, delayed output, or hesitation to share unpolished ideas. While such individuals are frequently described as diligent or dependable, the underlying experience may involve cognitive overload, decision fatigue, or anxiety linked to reputational risk. In group dynamics, these tendencies can unintentionally constrain momentum—especially when speed, iteration, or emergent insight is valued.

The external expression of perfectionism often includes highly controlled delivery, cautious participation in undefined tasks, or selective silence when standards cannot be met. These behaviors may preserve credibility, but at the cost of creative friction, relational ease, or adaptive flow.

Organizationally, perfectionism benefits from system-level shifts rather than individual correction. Mechanisms such as written ideation scaffolds, opt-in iteration rounds, or reflective buffer zones help retain conceptual depth without reinforcing overextension. These approaches normalize emergent contribution and reduce the pressure to perform polish before clarity.

At the developmental level, cultivating discernment between precision and perfection can foster healthier decision thresholds. The ability to define contextual sufficiency, tolerate ambiguity, and externalize partial thinking strengthens long-range impact without exhausting internal alignment mechanisms.

Beneath this pursuit of precision lies something deeper still—a profound emotional and ethical investment that drives not only what gifted individuals do, but why they lead in the first place.

12.3.3 Emotional Intensity and Existential Drive

Spectrum Role: Depth-Seeker
Type: Strength—with emotional bandwidth cost

Gifted individuals often operate from a pronounced existential orientation—marked by a search for coherence, contribution, and moral significance across domains of life (Piechowski, 1997; Neihart, 2006). This inner drive is frequently accompanied by emotional intensity and ethical sensitivity, shaping how decisions are made, relationships are formed, and meaning is assigned to professional activity.

In team settings, this can surface as passionate involvement, discomfort with superficiality, and a strong response to value incongruence. While this depth often enriches collaboration and strategic clarity, it can also generate emotional strain—especially when organizational realities diverge from internally held standards. Misalignment between purpose and practice is not merely frustrating; it can feel existentially disorienting.

The same intensity that fosters long-range vision and principled action may create difficulty in boundary setting, emotional detachment, or navigating compromise. Internalizing systemic shortcomings as personal moral failure is common—and may lead to overidentification with mission, withdrawal, or rigidity when ethical coherence feels threatened.

In systems that rely on emotional neutrality or detachment as markers of professionalism, this intensity is easily misread as volatility or overinvestment. Yet what appears affectively disproportionate may in fact reflect refined ethical perception and deep systemic awareness.

Supportive environments acknowledge this orientation as a form of cognitive-emotional integration rather than pathology. Structures that foster philosophical alignment—such as value-integrated planning, dialogic decision processes, and space for principled dissent—allow existential depth to function as a stabilizing system force rather than a personal liability.

Sustainability for individuals with this profile rests less on emotion management than on meaning regulation: ensuring that what is invested emotionally corresponds to what is returned structurally. When depth is met with resonance, the result is often not burnout, but durable commitment.

And while depth anchors meaning, it often coexists with breadth. Many gifted leaders don't follow linear paths—they navigate across disciplines, fueled by curiosity rather than convention.

12.3.4 Multipotentiality and Career Nonlinearity

Spectrum Role: Polymath Navigator
Type: Strength—with structural friction

Multipotentiality—defined by the capacity to excel across diverse domains—represents a hallmark of many gifted profiles (Freeman, 2010; Kerr & Sodano, 2003). Rather than advancing along a singular disciplinary track, multipotential individuals often pursue nonlinear trajectories shaped by pattern recognition, interdisciplinary synthesis, and strategic agility. This breadth is not a deviation from depth, but a different cognitive architecture—optimized for complexity, cross-sectoral navigation, and integrative insight.

Within organizational structures that reward vertical progression, deep specialization, or clearly delineated roles, these profiles frequently encounter friction. Nonlinear contributions—such as bridging silos, reframing entrenched problems, or connecting weak signals across systems—may remain underrecognized when they fall outside standard evaluation metrics or title-based hierarchies.

In team contexts, multipotential individuals often operate as translational anchors—linking abstract strategy with operational realities, and identifying cross-functional leverage points before they surface formally. Their impact often lies in second-order insight: recognizing ripple effects, ecosystem dependencies, and reframing opportunities that others overlook.

Structural misalignment emerges when institutional frameworks equate reliability with role continuity, or depth with disciplinary isolation. When range is interpreted as lack of direction, and adaptability as wavering, the result is often reduced visibility or diminished strategic influence—despite high systems value.

Sustainable engagement for multipotential profiles benefits from models that legitimize lateral thinking and layered contribution. Role architectures that accommodate portfolio work, rotational design, or functionally fluid mandates can reduce cognitive dissonance and organizational underutilization. Capability mapping that reflects synthesis, translation, and anticipatory foresight—rather than singular expertise—allows polymathic thinkers to operate from coherence rather than fragmentation (Kerr & McKay, 2013; Frederiksen, 2020).

For polymathic leaders, the task is not to defend variation, but to articulate throughlines—constructing narratives that reveal coherence across diverse experiences. For those evaluating or collaborating with them, the challenge is to look past chronology and domain loyalty, and toward design-level thinking. What appears nonlinear is often deliberate, strategic development: a model of systems leadership shaped by breadth, agility, and complex pattern recognition.

12.4 Optional Tools to Try—Giftedness in Leadership

Gifted leaders often navigate rapid cognition, layered insight, and intensity mismatches with their environment. These tools help channel complexity into focused contribution, support collaboration across pacing gaps, and maintain inner coherence without dulling depth. The aim: contain brilliance without constraining it.

1. Thought Tree Mapping

Use branching diagrams, visual ideation apps (e.g., Miro, Milanote), or analog sketching to map layered ideas.

→ Aids in translating abstract or nonlinear cognition into shareable models (cf. Silverman, 2013).

Application: Helpful for gifted, AuDHD, and dyslexic thinkers who synthesize across domains. Supports clarity in systems thinking and strategic leadership.

2. Nonlinear Career Narrative Templates

Reframe resumes, bios, or intros around strengths clusters and impact themes rather than chronology.

→ Shifts narrative from "fragmented" to intentionally polymathic (Kerr & Sodano, 2003).

Application: Ideal for gifted, multipotential, or dyslexic professionals with nonlinear trajectories; reduces self-censorship and misrecognition.

3. Perfectionism Reframe Sheet

Map internal standards and assess where they stem from fear vs. values. Translate into "healthy precision zones."

→ Helps decouple inner worth from flawless performance (Greenspon, 2000).

Application: Supports gifted, OCD-adjacent, or dyspraxic professionals with high internal pressure. Encourages compassionate rigor over burnout loops.

4. Ethical Tension Tracker

Keep a log of situations that triggered ethical dissonance. Note root causes and boundary violations.

→ Makes invisible moral strain visible; supports coherence (Piechowski, 1997).

Application: Useful for gifted, HSP, autistic, or trauma-impacted professionals; protects against integrity erosion in high-stakes settings.

5. "Slow Thinking" Time Blocks

Schedule non-output time for systems visioning, strategic reframing, or values synthesis.

→ Anchors philosophical integration and reduces urgency bias (Kahneman, 2011; Silverman, 2013).

Application: Critical for gifted, ADHD, and autistic thinkers operating in pattern mode; prevents cognitive overspeeding.

6. Peer Calibration Sessions

Engage 1–2 trusted peers to test assumptions, reality-check insights, and reduce abstraction fatigue.

→ Fosters resonance and metacognitive feedback in high-altitude thinking.

Application: Especially helpful for gifted, twice-exceptional, or socially misread leaders; strengthens psychological safety and cognitive grounding.

7. Multipotentiality Focus Wheel

Draw a radial diagram: center = current focus; surrounding = adjacent skills, latent interests, long-term aims.

→ Contains cognitive sprawl; supports strategic self-alignment.

Application: Designed for gifted and AuDHD polymaths; helps reconcile range with role clarity.

The effectiveness of these tools becomes visible in practice. The examples below highlight how gifted individuals convert cognitive breadth and emotional depth into strategic contribution—when supported by the right conditions.

12.4.1 *Visionary Integration: How Gifted Cognition Shapes Ethically Aligned, Systemic Leadership*

When intellect meets integrity, systems transform.

Dr Fei-Fei Li, co-director of the Stanford Human-Centered AI Institute and a pioneer in computer vision, exemplifies gifted leadership through her rapid cognitive synthesis, deep ethical orientation, and cross-disciplinary fluency. A child prodigy who emigrated from China at age 16, she earned her PhD in electrical engineering from Caltech and went on to lead AI efforts at Google Cloud. Her leadership is marked by the ability to connect high-level technical innovation with humanistic purpose—demonstrating classic traits of multipotentiality, intellectual depth, and values-driven intensity. She has also spoken publicly about the need for emotional intelligence and inclusivity in the future of tech, underlining how gifted leaders can integrate cognitive and relational intelligence to shape transformative systems.

While the preceding chapters have explored core neurodivergent constellations in depth—each with distinct patterns of cognitive strength, regulation, and systemic friction—other profiles also shape leadership in meaningful ways. The following section briefly acknowledges additional expressions of neurodivergence that hold growing relevance for inclusive leadership design and neurodiversity-informed practice.

12.5 Supplementary Profiles of Neurodivergent Leadership

Where cognitive friction reveals overlooked forms of divergence.

While this volume explores nine core neurodivergent profiles in dedicated chapters, several additional configurations—often underrepresented or diagnostically ambiguous—merit brief acknowledgment due to their relevance in leadership contexts. These profiles are not elaborated in full, but frequently intersect with themes of executive function, relational processing, or regulatory strain addressed throughout the book.

12.5.1 Neurocognitive Profiles

12.5.1.1 Nonverbal Learning Disorder

Nonverbal Learning Disorder (NVLD) is characterized by challenges in visual-spatial reasoning, abstract integration, and nonverbal communication, often paired with strong verbal abilities and articulate expression. In leadership, this profile may manifest as difficulty navigating visual data, reading unspoken group dynamics, or synthesizing loosely structured inputs. Professionals with NVLD may bring high linguistic clarity, yet require explicit scaffolding in ambiguous or nonverbal contexts. Conversely, some may be misread as literal, disengaged, or "missing the big picture," when in fact the issue lies in spatial or inferential load rather than intent or effort.

Strengths. Individuals with NVLD often excel in verbal analysis, analytical precision, and structured problem-solving. Their linguistic clarity and capacity to articulate complex ideas can strengthen communication, documentation, and knowledge transfer within leadership and team contexts.

Leadership Application. Provide explicit scaffolding for visual, spatial, or nonverbal tasks. Use structured formats and verbal explanations to reduce ambiguity and enable strengths in linguistic and analytical reasoning.

This profile shows how uneven cognitive strengths can create both clarity and friction in leadership contexts, a pattern that also appears in auditory processing, though with a different form of divergence.

12.5.1.2 Auditory Processing Disorder

Auditory Processing Disorder (APD) involves impaired neurological decoding of auditory information despite normal peripheral hearing. This can create significant friction in real-time dialogue, fast-paced meetings, or multi-voice conversations—especially when verbal overload coincides with decision-making pressure. In leadership, APD may be masked through compensation strategies such as anticipatory scripting or overpreparation, but the underlying auditory strain can still lead to fatigue, delayed responses, or miscommunication. In team contexts, APD may surface as apparent distractibility or detachment, underscoring the need for multimodal communication norms and pacing flexibility.

Strengths. Leaders and team members with APD frequently develop advanced visual learning, pattern recognition, and written communication skills. Their reliance on alternative processing pathways can foster careful preparation, attentiveness to detail, and creative integration of non-auditory information, all of which enhance leadership resilience in complex environments.

Leadership Application. Adopt multimodal communication practices—pairing verbal with visual or written formats—and allow processing time in meetings to minimize fatigue and reduce misinterpretation.

As with APD, where alternative processing channels can strengthen leadership capacities, the discussion of Intellectual Disability highlights how different modalities of understanding and participation expand the scope of inclusive leadership.

12.5.1.3 Intellectual Disability

Traditionally excluded from executive discourse, Intellectual Disability (ID) is increasingly relevant in reimagined models of peer-based and supported leadership. Defined by limitations in cognitive functioning and adaptive behavior, ID does not preclude meaningful contribution or relational leadership—particularly in systems designed around collaboration, lived experience, and task-specific intelligence.

Strengths. Individuals with ID often bring authenticity, consistency, and a relational presence that strengthens team cohesion. Their contributions frequently emphasize lived experience, practical wisdom, and loyalty, creating steady anchors in collaborative settings. In well-designed environments, these strengths can translate into trustworthy peer leadership, resilience in routine processes, and unique insights into inclusion practices.

Leadership Application. Ensure clarity in roles and expectations, respect autonomy, and maintain process transparency. Emphasize collaborative structures that honor practical contributions, strengthen mutual trust and team coherence.

Just as ID foregrounds the importance of clarity, autonomy, and relational trust in inclusive leadership, the upcoming episodic and trauma-linked profiles shift the focus toward rhythm and fluctuation—highlighting how leadership must adapt when cognition and regulation unfold in cycles rather than in static patterns.

12.5.2 *Episodic and Trauma-Linked Profiles in Leadership*

When leadership moves in cycles, systems must learn to flex with them.

While Section 12.5.1 outlined underrecognized neurocognitive patterns marked by continuous cognitive processing differences—this section turns to a distinct group of profiles characterized by episodic, state-dependent, or trauma-mediated fluctuation. These include Bipolar Disorder, Obsessive-Compulsive Disorder (OCD), epilepsy-related cognitive variation, and Post-Traumatic Stress Disorder (PTSD).

12.5.2.1 *Bipolar Disorder*

Bipolar Disorder is a mood-based neurodivergence marked by cyclical shifts in cognition, energy, and affect—ranging from high-activation phases (hypomania or mania) to periods of reduced drive and processing capacity (Goodwin & Jamison, 2007). These fluctuations affect executive function, goal orientation, and interpersonal engagement—not as instability, but as rhythm-based variation.

In leadership contexts, individuals may exhibit exceptional bursts of insight, strategic vision, and emotional commitment during activated phases. These may be followed by the need for withdrawal, recalibration, or decreased output—patterns often misunderstood as inconsistency. Yet when structurally supported, this rhythmic intensity can fuel innovation, systemic thinking, and deep relational work.

Challenges arise when organizational systems expect sustained, uniform performance. Without flexible pacing models, task redistribution protocols, or psychological safety for fluctuation, bipolar leaders may overextend, mask, or face legitimacy strain. Equally, teams may struggle to interpret nonlinear engagement without clear language for rhythm-based productivity.

Strengths. Leaders with bipolar profiles often bring visionary capacity, creative intensity, and an ability to mobilize deep emotional commitment. Their capacity for expansive thinking during activated phases can drive innovation and systemic foresight, while reflective periods often foster strategic depth and empathic leadership.

Leadership Application. Build flexible pacing models that honor cycles of high activation and recovery. Use workload modulation and clear boundaries around rest to sustain performance without overextension.

Understanding leadership as cyclical prepares the ground for epilepsy-related divergence, in which periods of fatigue or reduced responsiveness alternate with clarity and foresight.

12.5.2.2 *Epilepsy-Related Cognitive Variation*

Epilepsy-related neurovariation often extends beyond seizure events, encompassing episodic shifts in cognitive clarity, sensory processing, and executive functioning (Hermann et al., 2008; Kwan et al., 2011). These fluctuations—marked by mental fatigue, slowed processing, or verbal unavailability—disrupt expectations of consistent pacing and real-time responsiveness.

In leadership, such rhythms may result in temporary dips in presence or processing bandwidth. Without anticipatory structures, individuals may overcompensate, mask cognitive strain, or experience misrecognition. Teams may, in turn, misinterpret variability as disengagement or unreliability, especially in high-tempo environments.

Such patterns call for frameworks that transform episodic variability into structured opportunities for foresight, preparation, and adaptive clarity, ensuring that temporary fluctuations do not diminish long-term contribution.

Strengths. Individuals with epilepsy-related cognitive variation frequently cultivate foresight, disciplined preparation, and resilience through navigating unpredictability. Their lived experience can translate into heightened situational awareness, adaptive clarity under shifting conditions, and commitment to sustainable team pacing.

Leadership Application. Build flexible pacing models that honor cycles of high activation and recovery. Use workload modulation and clear boundaries around rest to sustain performance without overextension.

As the next section will show, PTSD-informed leadership brings similar lessons—though its rhythms are shaped less by neurology than by lived trauma, regulatory vigilance, and relational safety.

12.5.2.3 *Post-Traumatic Stress Disorder*

Post-Traumatic Stress Disorder (PTSD) alters how the nervous system processes threat, safety, and relational cues. Beyond clinical symptoms, its impact on leadership is often shaped by hypervigilance, emotional sensitivity, and a heightened need for predictability and psychological control (Yehuda & LeDoux, 2007; Bremner, 2006).

In workplace setting, individuals with PTSD may exhibit strong ethical discernment, situational awareness, and relational commitment, alongside heightened reactivity under ambiguity, difficulty with rapid pivots, or withdrawal in overstimulating environments.

Such individuals may be perceived as deeply principled, meticulous, or emotionally tuned-in—yet also as occasionally rigid, risk-averse, or prone to interpersonal shutdown. When misread, this dynamic can erode trust on both sides.

Strengths. Professionals with PTSD-informed profiles often demonstrate strong ethical grounding, acute situational vigilance, and principled decision-making. Their heightened sensitivity to trust, fairness, and relational dynamics can foster cultures of safety, accountability, and moral clarity within organizations.

Leadership Application. Prioritize predictability, relational safety, and clear communication rhythms. Embed trust-building practices and structured feedback loops to reduce ambiguity and support sustainable presence.

PTSD-informed leadership reminds us that regulation is relational and contextual. Inclusion here is not just a matter of access, but of co-regulation, transparency, and protected space for adaptive strategies to be enacted without stigma.

While PTSD centers on threat sensitivity and trauma regulation, the next profile—Obsessive-Compulsive Dynamics—raises a different leadership question: what happens when precision, control, and cognitive recursion become central organizing principles? OCD-informed leadership reflects regulation patterns shaped by compulsion, certainty-seeking, and executive load, rather than vigilance rooted in trauma.

12.5.2.4 Obsessive-Compulsive Disorder

Obsessive-Compulsive Disorder (OCD) is marked by recurrent intrusive thoughts (obsessions) and repetitive behaviors or mental rituals (compulsions) aimed at reducing anxiety or restoring a sense of control. Though often mischaracterized in popular discourse as a personality quirk, OCD reflects a neurocognitive regulation pattern centered on uncertainty, perfection, and internal conflict (Abramowitz & Jacoby, 2015).

Strengths. Individuals with OCD-informed traits may demonstrate exceptional strengths in detail sensitivity, procedural integrity, and systems thinking—often going beyond surface-level solutions to anticipate downstream effects and ethical blind spots. Their commitment to thoroughness and accountability strengthens quality assurance, compliance, and ethical oversight, offering organizations a safeguard against error and short-termism.

However, this strength can carry hidden costs. Under pressure, cognitive load may rise sharply due to mental looping, checking behaviors, or decision paralysis. Leaders may find it difficult to delegate, release incomplete work, or tolerate ambiguity—resulting in overextension, strained timelines, or relational rigidity. Such patterns are often perceived as diligence combined with distance, perfectionism, or limited adaptability.

Leadership Application. Define explicit scope boundaries and introduce closure rituals to prevent cognitive looping. Support delegation with transparent protocols that protect precision while preserving bandwidth, and structured feedback loops that interrupt recursive thinking without judgment.

OCD-informed leadership highlights how precision, certainty-seeking, and recursive processing intersect with broader neurodivergent patterns. These traits rarely exist in isolation; in combination with other profiles, they create layered forms of both friction and strength that require systemic, mixed-profile approaches.

12.5.2.5 Cross-Profile Resonance

These profiles share key dynamics with core neurodivergent expressions explored throughout this book—such as the invisible labor of regulation (cf. dyspraxia), emotional load under misalignment (cf. giftedness, HSP), and nonlinear engagement patterns (cf. ADHD, AuDHD). Accordingly, many of the tools, role structures, and co-regulation strategies presented across earlier chapters are relevant here as well.

Leadership thrives on the variability of experience and depends on systems that respect and accommodate it. These profiles illustrate that neurodivergence is defined less by diagnostic categories than by the ways in which a mind interacts with its environment and the degree to which surrounding structures provide support.

12.6 From Profile to Practice

When difference enters the room, design decides what happens next.

The preceding chapters have illuminated the intrapersonal dimensions of neurodivergence—mapping distinct cognitive profiles and their leadership implications across a range of domains. Yet neurodivergence does not manifest in isolation; it emerges and gains relevance within social systems, particularly in team-based environments where collaboration, communication, and role clarity are continuously negotiated.

As we transition from individual expression to collective dynamics, the analytical focus necessarily expands: from traits and tendencies to the structural and relational conditions that enable or constrain neurodivergent contribution. Leadership, in this context, is not merely about recognition—it becomes an active process of system design.

As Edmondson (1999) notes, "teaming is inherently interpersonal," requiring psychological safety, mutual respect, and openness to learning from difference. This is particularly true when cognitive differences intersect with communication norms and power hierarchies.

Recent research by Pelicano and den Houtling (2022) further underscores that meaningful neurodivergent inclusion depends less on individual adaptation and more on collective willingness to redesign norms, environments, and expectations in ways that reflect pluralistic forms of cognition.

The following chapter examines neurodiversity not as a demographic feature to be managed, but as a foundational dimension of team ecology—one that demands adaptive frameworks, attuned communication, and a rethinking of productivity, participation, and psychological safety.

> *Neurodiversity is not a dis*ability rights *issue. It's a human rights issue. It's a social justice issue. It's about shifting our entire cultural understanding of what it means to be a person.*
>
> Walker, *Neuroqueer Heresies*, 2021

References

Abramowitz, J. S., & Jacoby, R. J. (2015). Obsessive-compulsive disorder in adults. In R. L. Leahy, S. L. Hofmann, & E. A. Bailey (Eds.), *Treatment plans and interventions for depression and anxiety disorders* (2nd ed., pp. 113–160). Guilford Press.

Bremner, J. D. (2006). Traumatic stress: Effects on the brain. *Dialogues in Clinical Neuroscience*, *8*(4), 445–461.

Edmondson, A. C. (1999). Psychological safety and learning behavior in work teams. *Administrative Science Quarterly*, *44*(2), 350–383. https://doi.org/10.2307/2666999

Frederiksen, D. N. (2020). Leading like a polymath: Integrating multipotentiality in leadership. *Journal of Leadership Studies, 14*(2), 27–32. https://doi.org/10.1002/jls.21775

Freeman, J. (2010). *Gifted lives: What happens when gifted children grow up*. Routledge.

Goodwin, F. K., & Jamison, K. R. (2007). *Manic-depressive illness: Bipolar disorders and recurrent depression*. Oxford University Press.

Greenspon, T. S. (2000). "Healthy perfectionism" is an oxymoron! Reflections on the psychology of perfectionism and the sociology of science. *The Journal of Secondary Gifted Education*, *11*(4), 197–208. https://doi.org/10.4219/jsge-2000-629

Hermann, B., Seidenberg, M., & Bell, B. (2008). The neurodevelopmental impact of childhood-onset epilepsy on brain and cognitive functioning. *Epilepsia*, *49*(5), 697–707.

Kahneman, D. (2011). *Thinking, fast and slow*. Farrar, Straus and Giroux.

Kerr, B. A., & McKay, R. (2013). Searching for multipotentiality: Challenges and solutions. *Journal of Counseling Psychology*, *60*(4), 549–559. https://doi.org/10.1037/a0033991

Kerr, B. A., & Sodano, S. M. (2003). Career assessment with intellectually gifted students. *Journal of Career Assessment*, *11*(2), 168–186. https://doi.org/10.1177/1069072702250310

Kwan, P., Arzimanoglou, A., Berg, A. T., Brodie, M. J., Allen Hauser, W., Mathern, G., ... & French, J. (2011). Definition of drug resistant epilepsy: Consensus proposal by the ad hoc Task Force of the ILAE Commission on Therapeutic Strategies. *Epilepsia*, *51*(6), 1069–1077. https://doi.org/10.1111/j.1528-1167.2009.02397.x

Neihart, M. (2006). Dimensions of emotional intelligence and giftedness. In T. Cross & P. Olszewski-Kubilius (Eds.), *Social and emotional development of gifted children: What do we know?* (pp. 103–112). Prufrock Press.

Neihart, M., Reis, S. M., Robinson, N. M., & Moon, S. M. (2016). *The social and emotional development of gifted children: What do we know?* (2nd ed.). Prufrock Press.

Pellicano, E., & den Houting, J. (2022). Annual research review: Shifting from 'normal science' to neurodiversity in autism science. *Journal of Child Psychology and Psychiatry*, *63*(4), 381–396. https://doi.org/10.1111/jcpp.13534

Peterson, J. S. (2009). Myth 17: Gifted and talented individuals do not have unique social and emotional needs. *Gifted Child Quarterly*, *53*(4), 280–282. https://doi.org/10.1177/0016986209346946

Piechowski, M. M. (1997). Emotional giftedness: The measure of intrapersonal intelligence. In N. Colangelo & G. A. Davis (Eds.), *Handbook of gifted education* (2nd ed., pp. 366–381). Allyn & Bacon.

Probst, J., & Kämpfe, M. (2019). *Hochbegabte Erwachsene im Berufsleben: Herausforderungen und Chancen*. Beltz.

Peters, S. J. (2020). From test scores to talent development: Building a new paradigm for gifted education. *Gifted Child Today*, *43*(3), 144–152. https://www.jstor.org/stable/26977208

Silverman, L. K. (2013). *Giftedness 101*. Springer Publishing Company.

Tracy, J. L., & Robins, R. W. (2004). Show your pride: Evidence for a discrete emotion expression. *Psychological Science*, *15*(3), 194–197. https://doi.org/10.1111/j.0956-7976.2004.01503008.x

Walker, N. (2021). *Neuroqueer heresies: Notes on the neurodiversity paradigm, autistic empowerment, and postnormal possibilities*. Autonomous Press.

Webb, J. T., Amend, E. R., Webb, N. E., Goerss, J., Beljan, P., & Olenchak, F. R. (2016). *Misdiagnosis and dual diagnoses of gifted children and adults: ADHD, bipolar, OCD, Asperger's, depression, and other disorders* (2nd ed.). Great Potential Press.

Yehuda, R., & LeDoux, J. (2007). Response variation following trauma: A translational neuroscience approach to understanding PTSD. *Neuron*, *56*(1), 19–32.

Part III

Systemic Integration

Leading Neurodiverse Teams and Self

Chapter 13

Neurodiversity in Teams

Integrating Difference without Friction

13.1 From Accommodation to Integration

Reframing neurodiversity as a core dimension of leadership strategy.

Having established the systemic relevance of neurodivergent inclusion in organizational leadership (CIPD, 2022; Austin & Pisano, 2017), it becomes necessary to examine how such commitments can be translated into design practices that are structurally embedded—transforming intention into lasting organizational infrastructure. Effective leadership in cognitively diverse teams cannot be reduced to standardized toolkits. Individuals contribute distinct constellations of cognitive traits, environmental influences, and lived experience—often exhibiting greater variation within neurodivergent populations than between divergent and neurotypical groups (Armstrong, 2010; Singer, 1999).

At the same time, it is important to acknowledge that not all workplaces are structurally positioned to implement adaptive strategies in full or at once. In high-stakes environments such as emergency response units or tightly regulated manufacturing settings, flexibility may be constrained by operational demands. A surgeon cannot pause mid-procedure to align with a preferred cognitive rhythm—yet support in preparation and recovery remains essential. Such measures often depend on individuals feeling safe enough to articulate their needs in the first place.

Nonetheless, simply fostering awareness of cognitive variation—and making space for its consideration in decision-making—holds significant value. Each step toward greater inclusion, no matter how small, is a step in the right direction.

This chapter offers a synthesis of evidence-informed strategies that serve as entry points for designing environments conducive to sustained engagement and inclusive participation. Rather than prescribing fixed solutions, it provides adaptable approaches to help make that inclusion a lived, structural reality.

DOI: 10.4324/9781003681540-16

13.2 Strategic Foundations for Neuroinclusive Leadership

From theory to practice: designing for the lived, structural reality of neurodivergence.

While there is no universal manual for inclusive leadership across all contexts, the following clusters offer a flexible repertoire of principles that support cognitive diversity in organizational practice. Rather than serving as prescriptive checklists, they function as adaptive design heuristics—meant to be iteratively engaged, contextually refined, and aligned with the lived realities of diverse teams.

Grounded in neuroscience, organizational theory, and inclusion research, these strategies aim to redefine leadership as structurally inclusive, cognitively plural, and adaptively intelligent. Rooted in neuroinclusive design, their benefits extend to all team members across all neurotypes (Edmondson, 1999; Deloitte, 2022).

The strategies are organized into four interrelated clusters, each addressing a distinct layer of inclusive transformation:

- **Awareness**: Cultivates perceptual clarity and epistemic humility regarding cognitive difference. This includes identifying bias, interrogating defaults, and embedding neurodivergence into leadership discourse as a legitimate domain of variation.
- **Adaptation**: Focuses on responsive practices that reduce friction and foster participation—without requiring disclosure. Adaptive strategies acknowledge sensory, pacing, and regulatory needs as integral to equity.
- **Integration**: Embeds neuroinclusion into the fabric of team design, leadership behavior, and operational logic. Integration shifts inclusion from reactive accommodation to proactive systems alignment.
- **Infrastructure**: Establishes lasting structures that sustain neuroinclusion over time and reduce dependency on individual advocacy.

Together, these clusters articulate a multidimensional framework for systemic inclusion—advancing beyond discursive commitments to diversity and into the operational core of leadership praxis (Figure 13.1).

13.2.1 Section I: Awareness

1. Interrupting Bias and Micro-Exclusion in Organizational Practice
2. Embedding Neuroinclusion in Leadership Development and Organizational Literacy
3. Reframing Universality: Neurodiversity Across Cultures and Systems
4. Neurodivergent Leadership: Visibility, Legitimacy, and the Weight of Representation

Figure 13.1 Illustrates the evolution from awareness to infrastructure in neuroinclusive leadership. Rather than treating inclusion as an add-on, the arc visualizes how cognitive diversity becomes a design principle embedded in leadership practice, organizational systems, and team architecture.

> We don't see things as they are; we see them as we are.
>
> Anaïs Nin

Awareness begins with perception. The assumptions we carry—about competence, clarity, and contribution—shape what we notice, how we evaluate, and whom we include. In cognitively diverse environments, leadership may cultivate not only technical knowledge, but also epistemic humility: a willingness to question whose ways of thinking are recognized, and whose are rendered invisible.

These strategies foster foundational understanding and perceptual clarity around neurodiversity, implicit bias, and the conditions under which inclusion becomes structurally possible. They form the cognitive infrastructure upon which all other inclusive practice is built.

1. Interrupting Bias and Micro-Exclusion in Organizational Practice

Rethinking competence: beyond fluency and performance style.

Despite growing awareness, systemic bias against neurodivergent professionals remains prevalent—particularly in how competence, leadership potential, and promotability are assessed. Evaluation mechanisms often favor neurotypical proxies while undervaluing other forms of cognition like pattern recognition, reflective insight, or conceptual synthesis (Bottema-Beutel et al., 2021). These biases are seldom explicit; they persist through informal norms—who appears confident, who speaks without hesitation, who conforms to dominant interaction styles.

Such tacit preferences are reinforced not only through formal evaluations but also through everyday interactions. Neurodivergent professionals frequently report being interrupted mid-thought, misread as aloof or abrasive, or receiving feedback focused more on tone than substance (Kattari et al., 2020). These moments, while subtle in isolation, accumulate into a form of social exclusion that erodes psychological safety, reinforces masking, and diminishes confidence in one's professional legitimacy.

Challenging these dynamics requires a dual recalibration: of systems and of norms. Organizations should revise performance frameworks to reflect cognitive plurality, separating effectiveness from stylistic conformity and embedding fairness indicators into decision-making. At the same time, teams may normalize inclusive interaction habits—such as reflective pauses, multimodal input formats, and routine checks for underrepresented voices. As Sue et al. (2007) note, microaggressions are "brief and commonplace… slights and insults" that signal exclusion. Their opposite—micro-inclusions—should be equally deliberate.

Bias is not only embedded in policies—it lives in tone, timing, and tacit assumptions. Designing for neuroinclusion means rethinking how excellence is defined, how contribution is noticed, and whose presence is expected to fit without friction.

2. Embedding Neuroinclusion in Leadership Development and Organizational Literacy

Teaching what we can no longer assume: Neuroinclusion as a core leadership skill.

Leadership development and learning systems rarely treat it as a strategic competency. Most programs focus on broad DEI principles, yet overlook the specific dynamics of cognitive variation that shape team interaction and leadership efficacy (Austin & Pisano, 2017; CIPD, 2022).

To shift from symbolic inclusion to operational fluency, neuroinclusion must be embedded across leadership curricula, evaluation frameworks, and onboarding practices. This includes training in psychological safety, strength-based delegation, and bias-aware feedback. Tools such as the SBI-Care™ model expand traditional feedback by combining Situation, Behavior, and Impact with four additional steps—Clarify expectations, Align on solutions, Reframe the learning, and Empower the next step—to foster bias-aware, constructive, and growth-oriented dialogue. By anchoring observations in context and affirming relational intent, SBI-Care reduces attribution error and fosters psychological safety (Figure 13.2).

The SBI-CARE™ Framework: How Each Step Reduces Bias and Increases Psychological Safety

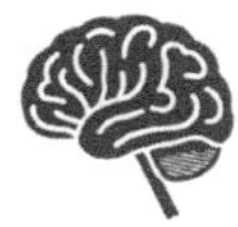

Step	Purpose	Bias Awareness Mechanism	Example	Evidence / Source
S - Situation	Establish time, place, and context.	Grounds feedback in time/context to avoid overgeneralization and reduce recall bias.	"In yesterday's client call when we reviewed the Q3 dashboard..."	Situation-specific framing reduces misattribution (Heider, 1958).
B - Behavior	Describe observed actions without judgment.	Focuses on actions, not traits—crucial for decoding neurodivergent expression without stereotype filters.	"You paused for about 20 seconds before answering the metrics question."	Objective observation reduces interpretation bias (Stone & Heen, 2014).
I - Impact	Explain the effect the behavior had.	Names outcomes without implying intent—opens space for shared interpretation.	"That pause created some uncertainty for the client about whether the data was ready."	Feedback anchored in impact increases perceived fairness (Kluger & DeNisi, 1996).
C - Clarify Expectations	Re-establish shared norms and goals.	Makes implicit norms explicit—reduces neurotypical default bias.	"In this meetings, quick responses are often read as confidence—even when content is less solid."	Makes implicit norms visible and negotiable (Dweck, 2006; Edmondson, 1999).
A - Align on Solutions	Co-develop actionable steps.	Encourages joint problem-solving—avoids top-down correction.	"Would it help to note upfront that you process more carefully and will respond in 10 seconds?"	Collaborative repair fosters mutual trust (Carnegie Mellon, 2020).
R - Reframe the Learning	Highlight what can be learned, not just what went wrong.	Shifts focus from error to insight—disrupts deficit narratives.	"This is a great insight into how diverse pacing can shape client expectations —we can design around it."	Growth framing increases resilience (Dweck & Leggett, 1988).
E - Empower the Next Step	End with agency and forward movement.	Restores agency—prevents learned helplessness and role freeze.	"Let's test one strategy in the next call—you choose what fits best and we'll debrief after."	Autonomy in feedback improves uptake (Deci & Ryan, 1985).

Highlights how each component of the SBI-CARE™ framework disrupts common bias patterns in feedback interactions—particularly where neurodivergent expression risks misinterpretation. The table links each step to its specific bias-reduction function, supporting more equitable and psychologically safe leadership communicatio

Figure 13.2 Bias-Awareness Functions of the SBI-CARE™ Feedback Framework. Outlines how each feedback step addresses common bias patterns—particularly in neurodivergent leadership contexts—by clarifying context, reducing attribution error, and reinforcing psychological safety.

Key performance indicators (KPIs) should likewise be revised to reflect adaptability, inclusion, and relational integrity—not just efficiency or visibility—as core leadership metrics.

More than a matter of knowledge, this shift represents an epistemic transformation. Leaders may learn to recognize how their assumptions about competence, clarity, or professionalism are shaped by neurotypical defaults. Integrating lived-experience voices, multimodal learning formats, and behaviorally grounded training helps make invisible norms visible—and actionable.

As outlined in earlier SAP's Autism at Work initiative illustrates what such integration can look like in practice: onboarding protocols were adapted for sensory and communication preferences, leadership training included neurodiversity content, and neurodivergent professionals were placed in core roles. The result: increased innovation, process gains, and stronger collaboration across neurotypes. The next strategy addresses how neurodivergence intersects with culture, identity, and power—and why universal models of inclusion often fail to capture what lived difference really means.

3. Reframing Universality: Neurodiversity across Cultures and Systems

Inclusion without borders: Decentering norms to recenter equity.

Contemporary neuroinclusion discourse remains heavily shaped by Western, industrialized, and often white-majority paradigms—privileging norms such as linear time orientation, verbal assertiveness, and individual autonomy (Hofstede, 2001; Gannon et al., 2021). These frameworks, while foundational, risk universalizing cognitive expectations and marginalizing divergent cultural expressions of neurodivergence.

Local constructs of professionalism, feedback, and sociality deeply influence how neurodivergent traits—such as sensory sensitivity, processing time, or affective expression—are interpreted and judged. For instance, indirectness may be normative in some Global South contexts, reframing what in Western settings might be pathologized as "masking" or "social withdrawal."

Intersectionality further deepens the complexity of neurodivergent experience. Professionals who are simultaneously navigating racialization, gender marginalization, or systemic exclusion encounter compounded barriers to diagnosis, legitimacy, and inclusion in leadership contexts (Botha, Hanlon, & Williams, 2021). As Gannon (2020) notes, "intersectionality is not additive—it is architectural": it configures the very frameworks through which neurodivergence becomes intelligible, acknowledged, or erased.

In this context, organizational narratives—conveyed through policies, symbolic language, and case visibility—serve as cultural blueprints. To be truly inclusive, such narratives must resist tokenization, embrace plural epistemologies of competence, and recognize neurodivergence not as an exception to be managed, but as a legitimate mode of insight and participation.

4. Neurodivergent Leadership: Visibility, Legitimacy, and the Weight of Representation

Beyond symbolism: Making neurodivergent leadership structurally viable.

When neurodivergent professionals hold formal authority, inclusion shifts from abstract commitment to the concrete negotiation of legitimacy and structural alignment. Yet visibility without systemic reinforcement risks reducing leadership presence to symbolic representation. Those who choose to disclose often carry a dual burden: meeting role expectations while informally embodying institutional progress (Clouder et al., 2020; Botha, 2021).

Without clear policy safeguards, adaptive leadership frameworks, or sponsorship mechanisms, this symbolic load can generate precarity rather than protection. Many face a persistent "legitimacy gap"—a disconnect between how leadership is performed and how it is normatively recognized, often privileging fluency, affective conformity, and neurotypical presence (Eagly & Chin, 2010). The result is a demand for continuous self-regulation and relational translation—forms of cognitive labor rarely acknowledged in conventional performance metrics.

To address this, structural neuroinclusion may go beyond representation. Sustainable leadership equity requires embedded peer networks, revised evaluation standards, and board-level sponsorship. Importantly, disclosure must always remain voluntary, limited to trusted contexts—such as a direct line manager—and never treated as a prerequisite for access or adaptation.

When neurodivergent leadership is positioned as systemically valid rather than exceptional, it expands who leads and also redefines how leadership is enacted, resourced, and understood.

13.2.2 Section II: Adaptation

5. Psychological Safety as a Structural Prerequisite
6. Designing for Enablement: Sensory Alignment and Autonomy
7. Enabling Task Mastery Through Tools, Technology, and Temporal Flexibility
8. Cultivating Growth Through Iterative Learning Structures

It is not the strongest of the species that survives, nor the most intelligent, but the one most responsive to change.

Leon C. Megginson

Adaptive leadership responds to cognitive diversity by adjusting context, rather than demanding conformity. The following strategies promote flexibility in interaction, workflow, and expectation—making space for neurodivergent strengths without requiring self-disclosure or exception status.

5. Psychological Safety as a Structural Prerequisite

From Sentiment to Structure: Building Psychological Safety into Leadership Architecture

Psychological safety is widely recognized as a cornerstone of effective teamwork, yet in neuroinclusive leadership, it requires translation into concrete structures. Beyond fostering openness, it must be operationalized through routines, environments, and accountability systems that make trust durable and visible (Table 13.1).

6. Designing for Enablement: Sensory Alignment and Autonomy

Moving from environment as background to environment as enabler.

Cognitive performance is directly influenced by environmental conditions. Sensory factors such as lighting, acoustics, spatial design, and digital density shape focus, regulation, and interaction—particularly for neurodivergent individuals (Robertson & Ne'eman, 2008). Inclusive features like quiet zones, dimmable lighting, noise-reduction tools, and low-stimulus interfaces enhance cognitive clarity and reduce overload across diverse teams.

In addition, as discussed earlier, inclusive environments extend beyond sensory calibration. They also provide structural autonomy in pacing, communication, and workflow design. Empirical research highlights that flexible conditions—where individuals co-shape their working rhythms—enhance performance, mitigate burnout, and support creative output, particularly in cognitively diverse teams (Austin & Pisano, 2017; EY, 2020).

To operationalize this, adaptive options should be embedded into team norms—such as focus time agreements, asynchronous collaboration, and flexible deadlines—without requiring disclosure. These practices normalize self-regulation and reduce the pressure to mask. Likewise, clarity in instructions, timelines, and expectations minimizes interpretive friction and promotes inclusion through design rather than exception.

Inclusive design, therefore, is not limited to sensory responsiveness; it is defined by its capacity to enable autonomy, communicative reliability, and sustainable cognitive engagement.

7. Enabling Task Mastery through Tools, Technology, and Temporal Flexibility

Normalizing tools as core infrastructure, not compensatory add-ons.

Assistive technologies function as performance enhancers across neurotypes (Al-Azawei et al., 2017; Burgstahler, 2015). These tools reduce unnecessary mental load and support sustained focus, adaptability, and precision in complex environments.

This being said, the mere availability of support does not guarantee its use; without structural normalization, uptake remains low—often due to stigma, prior exclusion, or concerns about perceived competence.

13.2.3 Augmented Clarity: Tech-Enabled Support for Neurodivergent Thinking

An overview of technological scaffolds that enhance perceived competence and enable cognitive diversity in practice.

Technology becomes inclusive when it shifts from compensatory aid to a systemic scaffold. In leadership contexts, tech-enabled clarity is less about fixing deficits than about expanding the range of how cognition can operate effectively (Burgstahler, 2015). Table 13.2 illustrates how targeted tools align with distinct neurodivergent profiles, transforming hidden friction into visible capacity and embedding diversity into daily workflow.

To operationalize inclusion, organizations should incorporate assistive technologies into standard onboarding—complete with guided exploration, opt-in customization, and visual setup aids. When framed as tools for optimizing workflow rather than as special accommodations, such infrastructure supports all employees managing complexity.

8. Cultivating Growth through Iterative Learning Structures

Protecting the Right to Learn by Design, Not Exception.

Mistake intolerance remains a pervasive barrier to innovation—particularly in cognitively diverse teams, where historical experiences of

Table 13.1 Outlines key dimensions of psychological safety as operationalized within neuroinclusive leadership. By linking systemic functions with neurodivergent relevance, the table highlights how inclusive environments are not defined by intent alone, but by the structural integration of regulation, responsiveness, and cognitive equity.

Leadership focus	*Systemic function*	*ND-specific benefit*
Feedback culture	Enables open, non-punitive communication	Reduces masking and supports clarity
Regulation practices	Integrates pacing and co-regulation into routine	Prevents overload and supports rhythm
Normalized adjustments	Frames accommodations as standard practice	Lowers disclosure pressure and stigma
Temporal flexibility	Allows dynamic scheduling and recovery points	Aligns with variable energy and focus patterns
Reflective supervision	Creates structured processing and recalibration	Supports sustainable decision-making
Responsive environments	Adapts space, noise, and workflow conditions	Enhances presence and reduces sensory strain

Table 13.2 Illustrative tools categorized by core support functions across neurodivergent profiles. Designed to inform inclusive leadership and team design.

Neurodivergent profile	*Support focus*	*Tool types/categories*
Dyslexia	Reading, writing, idea structuring	Text-to-speech, speech-to-text, mind mapping, dyslexia-friendly fonts
ADHD	Focus, task management, distraction control	Project boards, Pomodoro timers, distraction blockers, voice note apps
Autism (ASD)	Sensory regulation, asynchronous communication	Noise reduction, visual schedules, async messaging, environmental aids
Dyscalculia	Numerical comprehension, planning	Step-by-step calculators, visual data tools, budget planners
Dyspraxia	Task sequencing, motor coordination	Routine planners, calendar visualizers, ergonomic tools, speech input
Tourette Syndrome	Stress regulation, motor relief	Hands-free input, mindfulness aids, physical accommodations
HSPs	Emotional regulation, sensory filtering	Background noise apps, mood tracking, lighting adjusters, async platforms
Giftedness	Complexity management, intellectual stimulation	Concept mapping, nonlinear planning tools, high-input learning platforms

overcorrection or misattribution often produce risk aversion (Russell et al., 2019). Yet complex problem-solving and strategic reframing—hallmarks of neurodivergent contribution—require space for trial, error, and refinement.

Reframing failure as an acronym—**First Attempt in Learning (FAIL)**—can serve as a powerful cultural reframe. When leadership treats iteration as a normative process rather than as an indicator of deficit, it enables risk-tolerant environments where divergent strategies are explored, not prematurely corrected.

To systematize this mindset, organizations should implement debrief structures that decouple learning from personal judgment, prioritize experimentation over polish, and actively model reflective inquiry. Learning cultures are not built through rhetoric, but through repeatable rituals that normalize uncertainty and protect adaptive pacing.

Inclusive feedback should differentiate not only *how* input is delivered—timing, tone, and modality—but also *what* is being evaluated. Co-created review formats, opt-in reflection sessions, and depersonalized feedback loops enable sustained development without triggering defense or shame responses, particularly in neurodivergent professionals.

13.2.4 Section III: Integration

9. Reconceptualizing Productivity through Cognitive Equity
10. Operationalizing Neuroinclusion through Role and Team Design
11. From Accommodation to Architecture: Systemic Design for Neurodivergent Teams

Culture does not change because we desire to change it. Culture changes when the organization is transformed; the culture reflects the realities of people working together every day.

Frances Hesselbein

Integration means translating awareness into sustained action. By embedding neuroinclusive logic into operational design, these strategies ensure that leadership, team dynamics, and evaluative mechanisms reflect inclusion as enacted practice rather than aspirational intent.

9. Reconceptualizing Productivity through Cognitive Equity

When inclusion measures what matters: reframing productivity through equity-aligned metrics.

Traditional productivity norms—such as constant availability or visible activity—often misrepresent the working patterns of neurodivergent professionals, whose contributions may emerge through nonlinear pacing, episodic hyperfocus, or deep-focus intervals.

Productivity models that prioritize output quality and strategic autonomy over stylistic conformity are associated with stronger innovation, performance, and retention (Deloitte, 2022; CIPD, 2020). In contrast, rigid systems tend to equate presence with value and fluency with competence, marginalizing less conventional forms of excellence.

Leaders can address this by embedding cognitive equity into team design: normalize asynchronous rhythms, co-create outcome-based deliverables, and reduce structural friction. Practical steps include protected focus time, streamlined meeting culture, and flexible deadlines aligned with cognitive pacing.

10. Operationalizing Neuroinclusion through Role and Team Design

Strategic energy regulation: Enabling sustainable high performance.

When roles and environments align with diverse patterns, neurodivergent professionals contribute distinct strengths in innovation, systems thinking, and adaptive strategy. Inclusive organizations move beyond rigid job profiles by implementing dynamic role architectures that activate strengths such as hyperfocus, nonlinear reasoning, or conceptual synthesis.

To institutionalize this, strength-based tools—such as energy mapping, collaborative workstyle inventories, and adaptive role matrices—should be embedded into core HR practices. One such approach, the Energy-Focus Method™, offers a strategic self-regulation framework that helps leaders align cognitive intensity with task relevance and pacing. By mapping energy availability and prioritizing tasks based on focus quality—rather than elapsed time—this model supports sustainable performance, particularly for neurodivergent professionals navigating oscillations between hyperfocus and executive fatigue. Together, these tools mark a shift from traditional performance management to strengths orchestration, reducing friction and enhancing cognitive alignment across teams.

At the team level, cognitive complementarity becomes a guiding principle: ideators work alongside implementers, synthesists with operational anchors, asynchronous thinkers with live facilitators. Such configurations enhance coordination and innovation, particularly when supported by shared pacing norms, transparent communication, and distributed ownership (Stenning & Rosqvist, 2021).

When flexibility, clarity, and neurocognitive fit are embedded into the operating model, difference functions as a strategic resource. To sustain this at scale, organizations must shift from reactive accommodations toward proactive architecture, embedding equity as foundational design logic.

11. From Accommodation to Architecture: Systemic Design for Neurodivergent Teams

When inclusion evolves from case-by-case adjustments to embedded design logic.

Accommodation models frame neurodivergence as deviation—addressed through individualized requests and negotiated exceptions. This reinforces disclosure pressure and sustains marginality. An architectural approach, by contrast, treats cognitive diversity as a baseline condition. Equity is not added on; it is engineered into workflows, evaluation criteria, and leadership systems (Shore et al., 2011).

Systemic neuroinclusive architecture operates across three dimensions:

Structural—role expectations, progression pathways, and evaluation systems are designed with variability assumed. **Relational**—co-regulation, inclusive communication rhythms, and repair practices are institutionalized as leadership norms. **Environmental**—sensory conditions, digital density, and temporal pacing are calibrated to enable regulation and presence.

This shift redefines inclusion as an infrastructural guarantee. By embedding divergence into the organizational blueprint, leaders mobilize difference as a source of resilience and innovation. *Yet architecture alone is not sufficient; it must be reinforced through lived infrastructure. Section 13.2.6 examines the peer structures, evaluative metrics, and optional strategies that ensure neuroinclusive leadership is continuously sustained in practice.*

13.2.5 Section IV: Infrastructure

12. Embedding Peer Infrastructure and Leadership Pathways
13. Metrics for Neuroinclusive Evaluation
14. Overview for optional strategies

You do not rise to the level of your goals. You fall to the level of your systems.

James Clear

Infrastructure strategies embed neuroinclusion into the organizational architecture—beyond personal intention or individual accommodations. They formalize support, build systemic resilience, and ensure that inclusive practices persist, even when individual leaders or champions change.

12. Embedding Peer Infrastructure and Leadership Pathways

Inclusion becomes sustainable when peer support is structured, not spontaneous.

Navigating implicit norms, high-context communication, and unwritten behavioral expectations can impose significant cognitive load on neurodivergent professionals—especially in leadership trajectories. Yet inclusion cannot rely on informal generosity or individual resilience. It requires systemic scaffolding that supports both everyday functioning and long-term advancement.

Peer-based infrastructure—such as strength buddies, onboarding partners, or norm translators—makes the invisible navigable. When formalized and supported through basic neuroinclusion training, these roles surface hidden rules, calibrate interpersonal rhythms, and reduce the pressure to self-disclose. Rather than ad hoc support, they become embedded mechanisms that strengthen team coherence and accelerate contribution across neurotypes.

At the same time, equitable career development must be designed—not assumed. Neurodivergent professionals remain underrepresented in leadership not due to talent scarcity, but due to design gaps in development systems. Inclusive organizations embed neurodiversity considerations across the talent lifecycle—from recruitment and onboarding to advancement and succession—treating cognitive difference not as a barrier, but as a strategic asset.

By aligning peer infrastructure with recalibrated career pathways, organizations transform episodic accommodation into enduring inclusion architecture—ensuring that neurodivergent potential is not only welcomed, but fully realized.

13. Metrics for Neuroinclusive Evaluation

What gets measured tends to shape what is ultimately valued.

Neuroinclusive infrastructure becomes actionable when abstract principles are translated into visible structures. Table 13.3 illustrates how these elements can be operationalized across leadership design, ensuring that systemic commitment is paired with practical anchors.

14. Overview: From Intention to Embedded Practice

Summarizing key infrastructure strategies for neuroinclusive leadership.

To embed sustainable neuroinclusion, organizations must go beyond individual accommodations and design systems that structurally enable cognitive diversity. The following overview consolidates the strategic categories introduced throughout this chapter—each representing a critical layer of neuroinclusive infrastructure:

- **Interaction Infrastructure** ensures accessible, multimodal communication.
- **Relational Infrastructure** formalizes peer scaffolding and norm navigation.
- **Regulation Infrastructure** supports self-management of energy and attention.
- **Structural Flexibility** aligns roles and tasks with cognitive strengths.
- **Psychological Infrastructure** embeds safety protocols and reflexive space.

Table 13.3 This table summarizes key metrics that shift inclusion from symbolic representation to measurable impact, embedding cognitive equity into performance and cultural evaluation frameworks.

Metric	*Brief description*	*Evaluative purpose*
Lived experience feedback	Systematic integration of neurodivergent perspectives into evaluation cycles.	Aligns organizational learning with real-world needs and insights.
Equity-informed KPIs	Indicators for rhythm alignment, inclusion literacy, and masking reduction.	Measures cognitive fit and inclusive efficacy beyond output metrics.
Participatory review formats	Co-definition of evaluation criteria by neurodivergent team members.	Enhances transparency, legitimacy, and stakeholder relevance.
Indirect inclusion markers	Indicators such as autonomy, modality choice, and feedback responsiveness.	Captures psychological safety and systemic coherence.

- **Data Infrastructure** tracks inclusion metrics, masking load, and rhythm fit.
- **Structural Commitment** codifies neuroinclusive values in governance and policy.
- **Operational Support** provides standardized tools, templates, and processes.
- **Digital Infrastructure** adapts collaboration platforms to diverse work styles.

Together, these infrastructures form a systemic backbone—reducing reliance on disclosure, mitigating ambiguity, and enabling neurodivergence as an embedded asset rather than an exception. These dimensions are consolidated (see Table 13.4), which organizes the strategies by functional domain and demonstrates how infrastructure translates principles into practice.

Table 13.4 This table outlines core strategies for building neuroinclusive infrastructure. Each strategy is categorized by its functional domain—ranging from communication and regulation to governance and digital systems—and supports sustainable inclusion through structural design.

Strategy	*Description*
Cognitive communication design	Standardized, multimodal communication (e.g., visual task boards, written recaps, structured check-ins) to reduce semantic ambiguity.
Peer-based scaffolding	Formalized partnerships (e.g., onboarding allies, "strength buddies") that clarify implicit norms and support cognitive diversity.
Strength-aligned role design	Use of tools such as energy maps, workstyle profiles, and dynamic role matrices to align responsibilities with cognitive strengths.
Embedded safety protocols	Structural safeguards like reflection spaces, pacing agreements, and supervisory check-ins to sustain psychological safety.
Neurodiversity dashboards	Anonymous monitoring systems tracking inclusion KPIs, communication pacing, and masking-related load.
Governance anchors	Formal integration of neuroinclusive principles into ethics codes, leadership frameworks, and policy agreements.
Regenerative leave policies	Rhythmic recovery formats (e.g., interval breaks, ND-sensitive sabbaticals) supporting nervous system resilience.
Neuroinclusion toolkits	Standardized team resources (e.g., onboarding scripts, sensory maps, check-in templates) for inclusive daily practices.
ND-centered platform design	Collaboration and HR platforms designed with focus filters, paced notifications, and nonverbal engagement signals.

13.3 From Supporting Neurodivergent Teams to Leading While Neurodivergent

While this chapter has explored how inclusive systems can support neurodivergent team members, one critical configuration remains: when the leader themselves is neurodivergent. In such instances, inclusion transcends managerial design—it becomes a lived, embodied negotiation of legitimacy, regulation, and structural expectation.

The next chapter examines this convergence: where neurodivergence is central to how leadership is experienced, enacted, and redefined.

References

Al-Azawei, A., Serenelli, F., & Lundqvist, K. (2017). The effect of Universal Design for Learning (UDL) application on e-learning acceptance: A structural equation model. *International Review of Research in Open and Distributed Learning, 18*(6), 54–87. https://doi.org/10.19173/irrodl.v18i6.2880

Armstrong, T. (2010). *The power of neurodiversity: Unleashing the advantages of your differently wired brain*. Da Capo Press.

Austin, R. D., & Pisano, G. P. (2017). Neurodiversity as a competitive advantage. *Harvard Business Review, 95*(3), 96–103.

Bottema-Beutel, K., Kapp, S. K., Lester, J. N., Sasson, N. J., & Hand, B. N. (2021). Avoiding ableist language: Suggestions for autism researchers. *Autism in Adulthood, 3*(1), 18–29. https://doi.org/10.1089/aut.2020.0014

Botha, M. (2021). Academic, activist, or advocate? Angry, entangled, and emerging: A critical reflection on autism knowledge production. *Autism, 25*(3), 621–625. https://doi.org/10.3389/fpsyg.2021.727542

Botha, M., Hanlon, J., & Williams, G. L. (2021). Does language matter? Identity-first versus person-first language use in autism research: A response to Vivanti. *Journal of Autism and Developmental Disorders, 51*(12), 4461–4464. https://doi.org/10.1007/s10803-020-04858-w

Burgstahler, S. (2015). *Universal design in higher education: From principles to practice* (2nd ed.). Harvard Education Press.

CIPD. (2022). *Neurodiversity at work: Guide for HR professionals*. Chartered Institute of Personnel and Development. https://www.cipd.org/uk/knowledge/bitesize-research/neurodiverse-workforces/

Clouder, L., Karakus, M., Cinotti, A., Ferreyra, M. V., Fierros, A. G., & Rojo, P. (2020). Neurodiversity in higher education: A narrative synthesis. *Higher Education, 80*, 757–778. https://doi.org/10.1007/s10734-020-00513-6

Deloitte. (2022). *Neurodiversity in the workplace*. Deloitte Insights. https://www.deloitte.com/us/en/insights/topics/talent/neurodiversity-in-the-workplace.html

Eagly, A. H., & Chin, J. L. (2010). Diversity and leadership in a changing world. *American Psychologist, 65*(3), 216–224. https://doi.org/10.1037/a0018957

Edmondson, A. (1999). Psychological safety and learning behavior in work teams. *Administrative Science Quarterly, 44*(2), 350–383. https://doi.org/10.2307/2666999

EY. (2020). *Neurodiversity in the workplace: Creating an environment for success*. Ernst & Young Global.

Gannon, S. (2020). Intersectionality and the matrix of domination. In N. Rodríguez & D. Morrison (Eds.), *Handbook of critical race theory in education* (2nd ed., pp. 123–135). Routledge.

Gannon, S., Hall, W., & Cross, C. (2021). Decolonizing neurodiversity: Toward an anti-racist model of difference. *Journal of Disability Studies in Education, 1*(1), 45–67. https://doi.org/10.1163/25888803-bja10001

Hofstede, G. (2001). *Culture's consequences: Comparing values, behaviors, institutions and organizations across nations* (2nd ed.). SAGE Publications.

Kattari, S. K., Lavery, A., & Hasche, L. (2020). Differences in experiences of microaggressions between autistic and non-autistic people. *Autism in Adulthood, 2*(2), 152–161.

Robertson, S. M., & Ne'eman, A. (2008). Autistic acceptance, the college campus, and technology: Growth of neurodiversity in society and academia. *Disability Studies Quarterly, 28*(4). https://doi.org/10.18061/dsq.v28i4.146

Russell, G., Steer, C., & Golding, J. (2019). Social and demographic factors associated with diagnosis of autistic spectrum disorders: An analysis of data from the Avon Longitudinal Study of Parents and Children (ALSPAC). *European Child & Adolescent Psychiatry, 28*, 993–1003.

Shore, L. M., Randel, A. E., Chung, B. G., Dean, M. A., Ehrhart, K. H., & Singh, G. (2011). Inclusion and diversity in work groups: A review and model for future research. Journal of Management, 37(4), 1262–1289. https://doi.org/10.1177/0149206310385943

Singer, J. (1999). Why can't you be normal for once in your life? From a "problem with no name" to the emergence of a new category of difference. In M. Corker & S. French (Eds.), *Disability discourse* (pp. 59–67). Open University Press.

Stenning, A., & Rosqvist, H. B. (2021). Neurodiversity studies: Mapping out possibilities for research and practice. *Disability & Society, 36*(9), 1532–1537. https://doi.org/10.1080/09687599.2021.1919503

Sue, D. W., Capodilupo, C. M., Torino, G. C., Bucceri, J. M., Holder, A. M. B., Nadal, K. L., & Esquilin, M. (2007). Racial microaggressions in everyday life: Implications for clinical practice. *American Psychologist, 62*(4), 271–286. https://doi.org/10.1037/0003-066X.62.4.271

Chapter 14

Leading While Neurodivergent

Navigating Leadership from the Inside Out—Clarity, Capacity, and Cognitive Fit

14.1 Against the Grain

When leadership diverges: Legitimacy, structure, and cognitive difference.

This chapter explores the lived realities of neurodivergent leaders through seven thematic lenses—ranging from regulatory strain and structural bias to visibility and credibility gaps. It examines the paradox of role modeling under pressure, the cost of translating divergent cognition into socially legible leadership, and the toll of masking within normative systems.

Eagly and Chin's (2010) concept of the "legitimacy gap" captures this dynamic: leaders who diverge from dominant behavioral expectations face heightened scrutiny and must often overperform to be perceived as credible.

Leadership norms are never context-neutral (Hofstede, 2001; Meyer, 2014). The manifestation—and marginalization—of neurodivergent leadership is deeply shaped by organizational culture and sectoral architecture. A neurodivergent executive in a flat, innovation-driven tech start-up may navigate bias differently than a public-sector leader embedded in hierarchical bureaucracies. Norms around pace, authority expression, and communication vary widely across industries, leadership cultures, and regional expectations. These contextual dynamics modulate both the visibility of divergence and the strategies leaders deploy to sustain legitimacy.

Crucially, effective leadership in neurodivergent contexts begins with differentiated self-awareness. Leaders benefit from understanding how their cognitive style interacts with stress, and how patterned responses under pressure may compromise clarity, relational safety, or sustainability. These patterns reflect individual modes of nervous system dysregulation.

Whether through structured tools like the Stress Signature Spectrum™ or other reflective practices, leaders can learn to identify their dominant stress tendencies, such as overfunctioning (e.g., micromanaging, urgency-driven control), withdrawal (e.g., emotional shutdown, disengagement), or

DOI: 10.4324/9781003681540-17

reactivity (e.g., irritability, impulsivity). Recognizing these early markers enables proactive regulation before escalation occurs.

More than a self-management tool, this awareness fosters relational attunement: leaders who track their own stress responses are better equipped to notice dysregulation in others, model recovery, and embed pacing culture as a collective norm.

While disclosure of neurodivergent identity can foster understanding, such sharing must always remain voluntary. Respecting individual preferences—whether a leader chooses to self-identify or whether a team member wishes to keep their divergence confidential—is foundational to psychological safety. However, when thoughtfully navigated, open dialogue around needs, boundaries, and stress patterns can reduce misinterpretation and enhance collective resilience.

14.2 Dual Burden Leadership: Navigating the Paradox of Regulation and Role Modeling

When leading requires both holding the room and holding yourself together.

Neurodivergent leaders often navigate a dual workload—shouldering the visible responsibility of guiding others while simultaneously managing the invisible labor of continuous self-regulation. This is not merely a matter of multitasking; it constitutes a structural paradox that demands *metacognitive leadership*: the capacity to lead while constantly monitoring how one's own cognition is perceived, adjusted, or constrained. As Wood, Petriglieri, and Petriglieri (2012) note, minoritized leaders frequently operate within "identity workspaces," where authority is continually negotiated through translation, self-surveillance, and emotional buffering.

This paradox becomes especially acute under pressure. Leaders with sensory processing differences may endure overstimulating environments to avoid drawing attention to their needs—often at the cost of dissociative fatigue or diminished presence. Autistic executives may script informal interactions to maintain communicative fluency, while leaders with ADHD may engage in exhaustive preparation to compensate for working memory fluctuations—only to have their nonlinear expression misread as disorganization.

When neurodivergent leaders manage neurodivergent teams, interpersonal complexity intensifies. While shared lived experience can foster mutual understanding, it does not neutralize divergent cognitive rhythms or regulatory profiles. A leader operating in a state of hyperfocus may inadvertently flood a sensory-sensitive team member with unfiltered ideation, while an autistic leader who privileges asynchronous processing may encounter friction when attempting to co-regulate with an ADHD colleague who relies on rapid, verbally mediated exchange.

14.3 The Cost of Translation

When communication is measured by performance, not clarity, neurodivergent individuals pay the toll.

For neurodivergent leaders, the challenge is rarely what to say—but how it is heard. Communication is not neutral. It is filtered through expectations around pace, fluency, tone, timing, and emotional resonance. In leadership contexts, these norms quietly become gatekeepers of perceived competence.

Verbal fluency is often equated with credibility. Pauses, indirect phrasing, or delayed response times may be misread as disengagement or indecision. Leaders who communicate through monotone delivery, reduced eye contact, or nonlinear sequencing often find themselves explaining the mode before the message.

This burden increases in high-velocity organizational environments where speed is conflated with decisiveness. In executive settings that prioritize rapid, real-time decision-making, leaders who rely on reflective or asynchronous processing styles are often misperceived as unprepared or indecisive—despite demonstrating greater analytical depth and strategic acuity when afforded temporal flexibility.

Emotional expression carries its own asymmetries. A flat affect may be read as apathy. Expressiveness may be labeled "too much." Such judgments, shaped by neurotypical norms, often manifest indirectly—through feedback mechanisms that privilege fluency over depth (Bottema-Beutel et al., 2021).

The result is a quiet tax on clarity: a constant effort to meet unspoken communication norms that may bear little relationship to leadership impact. These tensions, along with strategies for more inclusive communication, are summarized in practical guidance for leadership contexts (Figure 14.1).

> *The most valuable insights may come from those least fluent in dominant communication codes—unless we decenter fluency as a metric, we risk filtering out wisdom for polish.*
>
> (paraphrased from Bottema-Beutel et al., 2021)

Leadership in Action: Inclusive Communication Design

- Structure turn-taking and post-meeting buffers to ease performance pressure.
- Use asynchronous channels to separate value from fluency.
- Clarify communication norms to protect diverse expression styles.
- Provide pre-briefing tools for high-stakes interactions.

Figure 14.1 Practical strategies for neuroinclusive communication. This figure outlines leadership actions that decouple communication performance from credibility and support cognitively diverse contribution formats.

14.4 Self-Regulation in Power Dynamics

Authority requires clarity—but for neurodivergent leaders, clarity begins with internal coherence.

Leadership entails continuous exposure—to decision-making pressure, scrutiny, and relational demands. For neurodivergent leaders, this exposure extends beyond the psychological to the neurobiological: navigating authority while simultaneously regulating sensory input, executive load, and emotional arousal demands sustained internal calibration—typically unseen, and rarely systemically supported.

Stress hits differently in neurodivergent profiles. Heightened cortisol reactivity, rejection sensitivity, and co-occurring anxiety can amplify routine demands into cascading overload (Dinkler et al., 2022). Decision fatigue emerges more rapidly; self-doubt intensifies; cognitive presence degrades—particularly when regulation needs remain unrecognized or unsupported.

Consider the AuDHD leader who absorbs sensory overload during a town hall, modulates emotional undercurrents in a team conflict, and delivers high-stakes fiscal strategy in an executive meeting—all before lunch. This sequence demands continuous executive override, activating cumulative stress pathways that tax both cognitive clarity and physiological resilience.

This is where leadership tools—such as recognizing your stress persona and understanding its effects—become critical. Strategies like the Pre-Vent™ Protocols, a proactive regulation framework that helps leaders stabilize before high-stakes interactions, offer practical scaffolding for maintaining clarity and safeguarding relational trust.

Yet the deeper paradox remains: Who regulates the regulator? Neurodivergent leaders are often expected to be emotional anchors without reciprocal scaffolding. This imbalance is unsustainable—and antithetical to psychologically safe leadership cultures. These dynamics, along with actionable strategies for resilience-oriented regulation, are outlined in Figure 14.2.

> *Leadership presence is often mistaken for composure—but for neurodivergent leaders, it is built through layered self-regulation—not inherited ease.*
>
> (inspired by Wood & Petriglieri, 2012; Evers et al., 2020)

14.5 Adaptive Strategy Design

Effective neurodivergent leadership doesn't replicate norms—it rewrites systems for sustainability.

Conventional leadership norms often conflict with the cognitive realities of neurodivergent leaders. Sustainable leadership emerges through honest self-mapping and structural alignment with one's neurological profile.

This means naming both energetic constraints and strategic strengths. A visionary with ADHD may excel in ideation but struggle with stepwise follow-through. An autistic leader might bring systems fluency and pattern clarity, yet find rapid pivots or ambiguous tasks destabilizing. Leadership here is about strategic alignment, rather than overcompensation.

Cognitive complementarity represents a strategic design principle in neurodivergent leadership: pairing distinct cognitive strengths to create interdependent scaffolding within teams. Delegation, in this context, functions as an intentional act of architectural alignment. Leadership thus becomes a matter of structural intelligence, not performative conformity.

Frameworks like the Energy-Focus Method™ and Strength-Based Role Mapping™ support this shift by centering energy as a primary metric of

Leadership in Action: Regulating for Resilience

- Embed regulation rituals into daily leadership practice.
- Identify stress patterns early using tailored diagnostics.
- Anticipate triggers with proactive regulation strategies.
- Establish reciprocal support through peer mentorship.
- Normalize rest as a condition for sustained clarity.

Figure 14.2 Core strategies for enhancing self-regulation in leadership contexts to maintain cognitive clarity and decision-making capacity under pressure.

performance, rather than time or visibility. The Energy-Focus Method™ helps leaders identify cognitive peak zones and align them with high-impact tasks, while Strength-Based Role Mapping facilitates relational architectures that distribute both load and innovation according to individual capacity—mapped across cognitive strengths, learned skills, energy rhythms, and relational working styles.

As Botha et al. (2023) emphasize, sustainability is the real predictor of thriving in leadership. These principles are further synthesized into actionable strategies (Figure 14.3).

14.6 Managing Bias from the Top

Neurodivergent leaders may navigate not only bias but the expectation to transcend it flawlessly.

Leadership, contrary to assumption, does not immunize against structural doubt. In fact, it often renders leaders more visible, more scrutinized, and more isolated. Formal authority rarely shields against informal bias; instead, divergence from normative leadership prototypes—whether cognitive, communicative, or emotional—invites interpretive distortion and

Leadership in Action:
Designing from Cognitive Profile

- Map cognitive and energetic patterns to guide focus and regulation.
- Align tasks with strengths; delegate for processing complementarity.
- Redesign decision rhythms to match executive functioning.
- Communicate leadership cadence to foster clarity and cohesion.
- Build support structures that balance load and amplify innovation.

Figure 14.3 Strategic actions for aligning leadership practice with individual cognitive and energetic profiles to enhance sustainability, clarity, and system coherence.

heightened skepticism.

This dynamic is especially pronounced for those who become "the first," "the only," or "the representative" of neurodivergence in a leadership role. In such cases, individual presence becomes entangled with collective symbolism. Decisions, expressions, and emotional responses are no longer judged on their own terms—they are read as referenda on neurodivergence itself. Leaders are asked to perform competence and embody hope, resilience, and transformation on behalf of others. This representational pressure often unfolds without structural reinforcement—creating a gap between symbolic expectation and systemic support.

The performance of authenticity becomes conditional. Organizations may celebrate difference rhetorically, while expecting it to remain legible, inspiring, and non-disruptive. Leaders should frequently calibrate disclosure, curating identity in ways that are coherent, palatable, and strategically intelligible.

Managing bias from a leadership position requires more than personal resilience—it demands strategic fluency. First, leaders may develop a language of self-advocacy that affirms both their authority and their neurodivergence—without apology or dilution. Second, narrative authorship becomes critical: defining visibility not as vulnerability but as design, where personal identity serves clarity and cultural transformation without becoming a consumable performance. Third, institutional leverage must be used to reshape assumptions—through policy, modeling, and the redefinition of what leadership looks like.

As Wood, Petriglieri, and Petriglieri (2012) remind us, authentic leadership cannot be sustained by courage alone; it must be scaffolded by systems that legitimize divergence—not as a deviation from the norm, but as a new paradigm of value. These dynamics are distilled into practical strategies that address bias, positioning, and systemic legitimacy (Figure 14.4).

14.7 Building Restorative Rhythms

Sustainable leadership requires nervous system stewardship, rather than heroic endurance.

Neurodivergent leadership often demands deeper regulation, instead of greater output. The ongoing effort to translate, adapt, and self-monitor within systems built around neurotypical norms takes a cumulative toll.

Leadership in Action:
Legitimacy Without Performance

- Prepare bias-aware responses that affirm identity without overexplaining.
- Set internal limits before systems set external expectations.
- Anchor credibility in clarity, not overcompensation.
- Transform role expectations by modeling divergent legitimacy
- Build peer constellations that reinforce presence

Figure 14.4 Strategies for confronting bias while leading neurodivergently—highlighting self-positioning, peer scaffolding, and the systemic dynamics of legitimacy and misrecognition.

Without intentional rhythm design, leaders risk cycles of overfunctioning, adrenal fatigue, and misaligned decision-making.

These dynamics call for structured approaches to recovery. The 4R Rest™ Framework identifies four key domains of sustainable regulation: Rest (physiological decompression), Rhythm (alignment with cognitive pacing), Relevance (task-attunement and priority reset), and Realignment (strategic recalibration of focus and boundaries). Together, they provide a scaffolding for restorative interruption—helping leaders preserve clarity and adaptive functioning under prolonged internal strain.

Restorative leadership begins by redefining pace as strategic alignment. Leadership cadence should reflect internal energy rhythms rather than external hustle expectations.

Yet boundaries alone are insufficient. Many neurodivergent leaders—particularly those socialized into hypercompetence—struggle to rest without guilt. Saying no without retreating, and pausing without needing to justify, must be relearned.

Nonetheless, lived credibility holds transformative potential. Leaders who integrate—rather than suppress—their neurodivergent identity not only safeguard their internal rhythm—they model a reframed, sustainable paradigm of leadership. One grounded in presence, relational clarity, and cognitive integrity. It is precisely this paradigm that Gentle Leading™ seeks to operationalize. These principles are translated into recovery- and regulation-focused practices that embed sustainability into leadership routines (see Figure 14.5).

14.8 From Structural Navigation to Somatic Regulation

Links nervous system state directly to strategic functioning.

The preceding chapter has outlined the systemic, cognitive, and relational dimensions of neurodivergent leadership. Yet these external navigations are intrinsically tied to internal physiological states. Leadership presence—particularly when enacted from a neurodivergent positionality—is not merely a matter of strategy or intellect. It is embodied.

As research in affective neuroscience and organizational psychology increasingly suggests, the ability to regulate one's nervous system is foundational to sustained executive function, emotional availability, and adaptive decision-making (Porges, 2011; Boyatzis et al., 2012). This is especially true for individuals whose sensory thresholds, cognitive rhythms, or trauma histories may diverge from dominant norms.

Rather than extending the structural lens, the next chapter shifts focus to internal regulation. Nervous system dynamics are examined not as

Leadership in Action: Restorative Rhythm Design

- Prioritize micro-recovery as a core leadership resource.
- Use rhythms of retreat, regulation, reflection, and routine to support resilience.
- Establish a leadership buffer zone to protect decision-making capacity.
- Monitor nervous system load and adjust proactively.
- Align tasks with focus cycles—treat rest as part of operational design.

Figure 14.5 Strategies for integrating recovery and regulation into leadership practice to support sustainable performance and cognitive resilience.

peripheral, but as central to effective, sustainable leadership—particularly under prolonged cognitive and relational load.

References

Botha, M., Hanlon, J., & Williams, G. L. (2021). Does language matter? Identity-first versus person-first language use in autism research: A response to Vivanti. *Journal of Autism and Developmental Disorders*, *53*(2), 870–878. https://doi.org/10.1007/s10803-020-04858-w

Bottema-Beutel, K., Kapp, S. K., Lester, J. N., Sasson, N. J., & Hand, B. N. (2021). Avoiding ableist language: Suggestions for autism researchers. *Autism in Adulthood*, *3*(1), 18–29. https://doi.org/10.1089/aut.2020.0014

Boyatzis, R. E., Rochford, K., & Taylor, S. N. (2012). The role of the positive emotional attractor in vision and shared vision: Toward effective leadership, relationships, and engagement. *Journal of Management Development*, *31*(9), 721–739. https://doi.org/10.1108/02621711211253240

Dinkler, L., Lundström, S., Gajwani, R., Lichtenstein, P., & Gillberg, C. (2022). Rejection sensitivity and internalizing symptoms in young adults with neurodevelopmental disorders. *European Child & Adolescent Psychiatry*, *31*(10), 1569–1580. https://doi.org/10.1007/s00787-021-01814-6

Eagly, A. H., & Chin, J. L. (2010). Diversity and leadership in a changing world. *American Psychologist*, *65*(3), 216–224. https://doi.org/10.1037/a0018957

Evers, A., Rasche, L., & Schulte-Rüther, M. (2020). The costs of camouflaging in autism: A review. *Autismus-Spektrum-Störung – Forschung & Praxis*, *10*(2), 58–66.

Hofstede, G. (2001). *Culture's consequences: Comparing values, behaviors, institutions, and organizations across nations* (2nd ed.). SAGE Publications.

Meyer, E. (2014). *The culture map: Breaking through the invisible boundaries of global business*. PublicAffairs.

Porges, S. W. (2011). *The polyvagal theory: Neurophysiological foundations of emotions, attachment, communication, and self-regulation*. W. W. Norton.

Wood, J. D., Petriglieri, G., & Petriglieri, J. L. (2012). Up close and personal: Building foundations for leaders' development through the personalization of management learning. *Academy of Management Learning & Education*, *11*(3), 432–451. https://doi.org/10.5465/amle.2010.0032

Chapter 15

Regulating the Nervous System in Leadership

Leadership as an Embodied State and the Autonomic Nervous System in Action

15.1 The Biology behind the Behavior

Understanding leadership through the nervous system.

Effective leadership is often framed as a matter of strategy, communication, or decision-making. Yet beneath these visible behaviors lies a biological infrastructure that fundamentally shapes how leaders perceive, relate, and act: the nervous system. Without awareness of its regulatory patterns, even the most well-intentioned leadership interventions risk being reactive, disconnected, or unsustainable.

This chapter explores the relevance of autonomic nervous system regulation as a critical, yet frequently overlooked, foundation for leadership performance, interpersonal functioning, and team dynamics. Grounded in contemporary neurophysiological theory, particularly the Polyvagal Theory developed by Stephen Porges (2011), the discussion emphasizes that leadership is not merely a cognitive process—but a deeply embodied one.

15.2 Why Nervous System Regulation Is Foundational to Leadership

The silent driver of leadership presence.

The autonomic nervous system (ANS) governs our internal states of arousal, safety, and social engagement. These states are biologically grounded and take shape within relational contexts. That is, the state of a person's nervous system has measurable effects on the behavior, stress regulation, and communication patterns of those around them (Dana, 2018). When regulation breaks down in leadership, reactivity tends to escalate, psychological safety declines, and executive functioning is compromised—both individually and collectively.

DOI: 10.4324/9781003681540-18

Key capacities are directly shaped by the regulatory status of the nervous system, including:

- Emotional self-regulation and impulse control.
- Social perception and interpersonal attunement.
- Tolerance for uncertainty, complexity, and ambiguity.
- Cognitive flexibility and access to executive functions.
- Capacity for reflective decision-making under pressure.

While stress itself is not inherently detrimental, chronic dysregulation—manifesting as persistent sympathetic activation (fight/flight) or parasympathetic collapse (shutdown/freeze)—can lead to burnout, poor judgment, conflict escalation, and reduced relational bandwidth.

15.3 Is This Only Relevant for Neurodivergent Leaders?

Why nervous system literacy benefits everybody?

While neurodivergent individuals may experience dysregulation more frequently or intensely, the principles of nervous system regulation are universally applicable. All human beings are subject to neurophysiological shifts in response to environmental stimuli, social threat cues, and internal states.

Neurodivergent professionals often have reduced access to recovery conditions in traditional work environments. For this reason, a nervous-system-informed leadership model is structurally more adaptive. When leaders develop the capacity to regulate themselves and recognize patterns of dysregulation in others, they create a steadier ground for working and relating—across neurotypes.

Cultivating somatic awareness and self-regulation allows leaders to perceive subtle team dynamics, respond to unspoken needs, and design environments that align with human neurobiology rather than performance pressure.

> You can't think your way out of a dysregulated state.
>
> Deb Dana (2018)

This is why effective leadership cannot be reduced to strategy alone. It begins with presence—the ability to stay attuned and choice-oriented under pressure.

15.4 From Emotion to Regulation: How It Feels before You Know What It Is

Leadership starts in sensation: When the body speaks before the brain.

Before examining specific nervous system states in leadership, it is important to acknowledge that they are first experienced as feelings rather than theories or labels. Leaders may not identify themselves as "dysregulated," but they often notice irritability, fatigue, restlessness, or numbness. These emotional signals are not random—they are early indicators of underlying shifts in the autonomic nervous system (ANS), which operates largely below conscious awareness (Siegel, 2020).

Emotional correlates offer a gateway to internal literacy—translating vague sensations into actionable insight. The following table bridges subjective experience and physiological patterns, providing a practical entry point for self-awareness and co-regulation in real-time leadership contexts.

15.5 Felt before Known: Affective Correlates of Autonomic States

Emotional cues as early signals of nervous system activation.

Emotions often surface before cognition catches up. In leadership contexts, these affective cues serve as early indicators of underlying autonomic states—signals that can foreshadow clarity, urgency, avoidance, or collapse. Recognizing these patterns provides a practical lens for interpreting both one's own responses and the dynamics unfolding within teams, anchoring nervous system literacy in observable experience (Table 15.1).

Understanding how these emotional states correlate with autonomic patterns is only the first step. The next is recognizing that while our nervous system state shifts dynamically in response to stimuli, we each tend to follow a consistent stress trajectory—a pattern we return to under pressure, often without noticing.

15.6 From State to Signature

Understanding your dominant stress response.

While nervous system states fluctuate based on situational load, most individuals exhibit a dominant stress signature: a recurring pattern of emotional, cognitive, and behavioral responses under pressure. This signature acts as a default pathway—shaped by temperament, reinforcement history, and neurocognitive style (Buss & Plomin, 1984; Carver et al., 1989; Porges, 2011).

Table 15.1 Illustrates the relationship between subjective emotional cues and specific patterns of autonomic activation to support applied nervous system literacy in leadership.

Autonomic state	*Felt emotional cues*	*Indicative leadership implications*
Ventral vagal (safety/engagement)	"I feel present and flexible." "I'm able to pause and reflect." "I can hold complexity without shutting down."	Regulated cognition, open perspective, relational responsiveness, sustainable decision-making
Sympathetic (fight/flight)	"I need to act now." "I feel cornered/under pressure." "Everything feels urgent or high-stakes."	Action urgency, narrowed perception, reduced empathy, overcontrol, risk of micromanagement
Fawn/appease (mixed state)	"I'm saying yes, but feel depleted." "I'm performing calm, but I'm fraying." "I just want harmony, no conflict."	Suppression of dissent, masking, boundary avoidance, people-pleasing at personal cost
Dorsal vagal (shutdown/collapse)	"I feel numb or detached." "Nothing matters right now." "I want to disappear or shut everything out."	Disengagement, withdrawal, slowed cognition, decreased relational presence, risk of burnout or learned helplessness

Stress within each signature unfolds along a spectrum—from functional tension to functional collapse—rather than as a binary state. These internal escalations reflect the interplay of task load, recovery capacity, and perceived psychological safety.

Mapping one's thresholds—such as when a fast-moving problem-solver turns compulsive or a reflective team member begins to withdraw—enables earlier recognition and intentional course correction. Stress responses often manifest counterintuitively: an assertive leader may shift into detachment, while a quiet thinker may default to overdrive.

The following stress signatures serve as reflective heuristics—orienting without reducing. Each describes a recognizable choreography of how stress emerges and escalates. Leaders may blend elements of several patterns or express them differently depending on context, relational dynamics, and regulation strategies.

This model supports a shift from reactive self-management to strategic nervous system ownership—a core capacity for sustainable leadership. Especially for neurodivergent professionals, distinguishing between one's functional edge and the point of depletion is essential for preserving both performance and psychological integrity.

The goal is self-mapping: to better understand habitual stress rhythms, spot early signs of overload, and enable timely recovery. Clarity enables agency. Recognition invites regulation. Knowing it makes owning it.

Importantly, neurodivergent stress responses—such as masking, delayed collapse, or shutdown—are often overlooked or misinterpreted in conventional leadership settings. Such misrecognition distorts interpersonal readings and may reinforce inaccurate assumptions about engagement or capability.

Intentional dialogue, shared vocabulary, and inclusive training help teams read these patterns more accurately—strengthening individual resilience and collective psychological safety.

15.7 Stress Signature Spectrum—Functional Zones Overview

From signal to shutdown: Recognizing stress persona across functional states.

Stress signatures represent patterned ways individuals respond under pressure, linking cognition, behavior, and emotional tone. Identifying how these patterns unfold across functional zones offers leaders a diagnostic lens for anticipating breakdown points and activating timely regulation strategies (Table 15.2).

- the **Green Zone**, this default mode reflects one's baseline coping choreography before dysregulation emerges;
- the **Yellow Zone**, indicating early signs of dysregulation and behavioral shifts; and
- the **Red Zone**, marking full stress activation, loss of strategic clarity, and diminished relational or task engagement.

To contextualize these individualized stress signatures within a broader physiological framework, the following model outlines four core autonomic states that shape leadership behavior and team climate.

Table 15.2 This table outlines nine distinct stress signatures—individualized patterns of cognitive, emotional, and behavioral response under pressure. Each signature is presented along a three-tiered functional continuum.

Stress signature	*Green zone*	*Yellow zone*	*Red zone*
Frantic fixer	F	Overfunctions, multitasks, micromanages	Hyperactive, chaotic, burns out
Frozen thinker	L	Overthinks, hesitates, avoids action	Frozen, paralyzed, mentally offline
Pleasing overloader	O	Says yes too often, skips self-care	Collapsed, overwhelmed, resentful
Silent resigner	W	Withdraws, silent, low initiative	Checked out, emotionally numb
Controller	S	Controls details, defensive, rigid	Explosive, micromanages everything
Reactor	T	Reactive tone, mood swings emerge	Volatile, unpredictable, conflict-prone
Ghost	A	Starts ghosting, avoids meetings	Disappears completely, unreachable
Juggler	T	Overbooks, forgets tasks	Disorganized, shuts down silently
Lone wolf	E	Refuses help, isolates emotionally	Quits, breaks down, full shutdown

15.8 Recognizing and Responding to Nervous System States in Leadership

The model outlines how physiological regulation patterns inform leadership behavior and relational dynamics within teams.

Leadership states are not abstract categories but embodied modes of regulation that influence perception, interaction, and decision-making. Mapping these autonomic states provides leaders with a framework to recognize how physiological activation translates into relational climate and organizational impact (Figure 15.1).

What follows is a structured typology of how these states shape leadership in practice. Each includes intrapersonal and interpersonal indicators, alongside evidence-informed strategies for self-regulation. The goal is to strengthen what Siegel (2020) terms *mindsight*—the capacity to track internal shifts and lead with physiological clarity rather than reactivity.

15.9 Autonomic Leadership States: A Typology of Nervous System-Driven Behavior and Regulation

This typology maps how nervous system dynamics shape behavior and self-regulation.

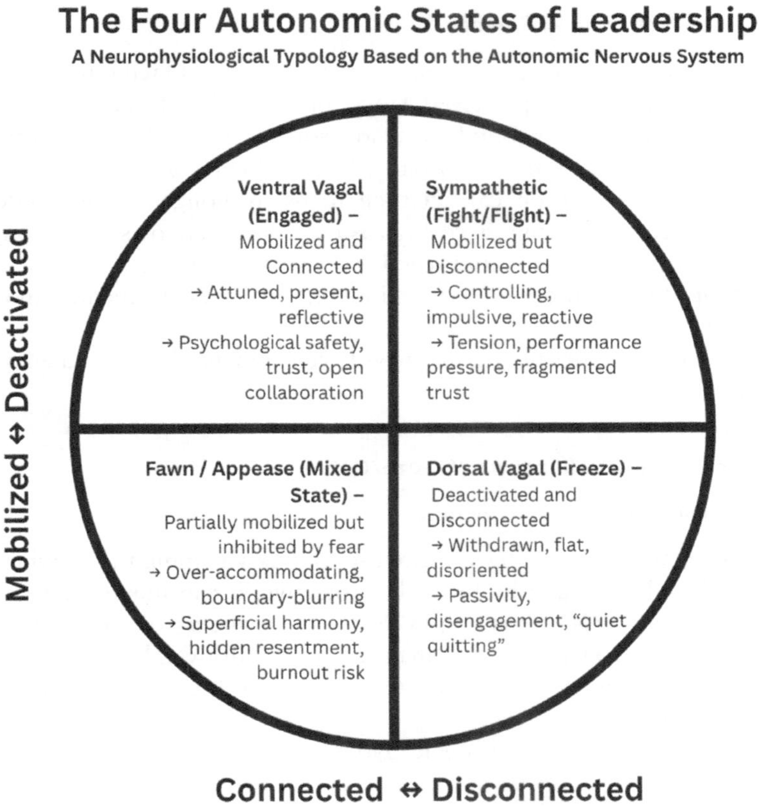

Figure 15.1 The four autonomic states of leadership: This figure maps four core autonomic states—ventral vagal, sympathetic, dorsal vagal, and fawn—along the axes of activation and relational openness. Each quadrant reflects typical leadership behaviors and corresponding team climate patterns, drawing on Polyvagal Theory (Porges, 2011).

Leadership unfolds through the body as much as the mind. This framework outlines four autonomic states, each with distinct implications for executive functioning, relational behavior, and group dynamics.

For each state, the model highlights:

- Functional Definition
- Leadership Presentation
- Collective Impact

A corresponding regulation compendium follows, offering practical tools to support adaptive leadership across physiological states.

15.9.1 *Sympathetic Activation (Fight/Flight)*

15.9.1.1 *Mobilization under Threat*

The sympathetic branch of the autonomic nervous system facilitates rapid mobilization in response to perceived danger or demand. In leadership, this state is often triggered by psychological stressors—e.g., deadline pressure, interpersonal conflict, or role overload (Porges, 2011; McEwen, 2007). While short-term activation can sharpen focus, prolonged sympathetic dominance reduces prefrontal access (Arnsten, 2009), narrows cognition, and elevates urgency, control, and reactivity (Dana, 2018).

Leadership Presentation: Overfunctioning, micromanagement, emotional volatility.

Team Impact: Conflict-prone, urgency-driven climate, diminished emotional availability.

15.9.2 *Dorsal Vagal Shutdown (Freeze/Collapse)*

15.9.2.1 *Immobilization and Withdrawal*

The dorsal vagal state activates in response to overwhelming threat when active coping fails. Though biologically protective, it can impair engagement, clarity, and decision-making in leadership contexts (Porges, 2011; Ogden et al., 2006). This state may manifest as withdrawal, low affect, or cognitive disengagement—often misinterpreted as disinterest rather than adaptive shutdown.

Leadership Presentation: Strategic avoidance, flat presence, decision paralysis.

Team Impact: Passive dynamics, psychological disengagement, low cohesion.

15.9.3 *Fawn/Appease State (Mixed Activation)*

15.9.3.1 *Social Overfunctioning with Boundary Suppression*

The appease or "fawn" response blends sympathetic arousal with dorsal inhibition and reflects relational threat adaptation (van der Kolk, 2014). Leaders in this state may over-accommodate, avoid conflict, or prioritize harmony over clarity. Though seemingly collaborative, this mode suppresses authentic leadership expression and increases long-term fatigue.

Leadership Presentation: Excessive agreeableness, blurred boundaries, conflict avoidance

Team Impact: Surface consensus, suppressed dissent, anxiety-driven performance

15.9.4 *Ventral Vagal Regulation (Safety/Engagement)*

15.9.4.1 Presence and Integration

The ventral vagal state supports calm engagement, emotional regulation, and cognitive flexibility (Porges, 2011; Dana, 2018). In leadership, this state enables grounded decision-making, complexity tolerance, and relational clarity. Unlike survival-driven states, it fosters integration across self-awareness, ethical reasoning, and social responsiveness.

Leadership Presentation: Grounded presence, reflective responsiveness, healthy boundaries.

Team Impact: Psychological safety, collaborative creativity, resilience under pressure.

While the ventral vagal state reflects an individual's capacity for regulated leadership, its cultivation and sustainability depend heavily on the surrounding social and systemic context (Table 15.3).

Table 15.3 Regulation by nervous system state—This matrix maps arousal states to social strategies, highlighting Appease/Fawn as a mixed adaptive response. Recognizing its pattern is key to relational clarity in neurodivergent leadership.

Nervous system state	*Regulation focus*	*Targeted micro-interventions*
Sympathetic activation (fight/flight)	Interrupt urgency and hyperactivation	Movement burst, rapid bilateral tapping, 90-sec pause, color scan
Dorsal immobilization (shutdown)	Restore energy, engagement, agency	Vocal activation (humming), spatial shift, upright posture
Appease/fawn (social overfunctioning)	Reclaim boundaries and self-reference	Refusal scripting, somatic self-affirmation, boundary visualization
Ventral vagal regulation (Ssafe/engaged)	Sustain clarity and relational presence	Co-regulation, open gaze, breath sync, deliberate pacing

15.10 From Individual Regulation to Cultural Practice: Co-Regulation as a Leadership Function

Leadership is never a solo nervous system event.

While individual nervous system regulation is foundational, it is insufficient when isolated from the broader relational and structural context in which leadership operates. Leaders do not regulate in a vacuum; they shape the very environments that influence how others engage, respond, and recover. Current research highlights that core relational dynamics in organizations emerge from individual empathy and the systemic design of interactional environments (Boyatzis, Rochford, & Taylor, 2015; Edmondson, 2019). Meeting formats, communication rhythms, feedback systems, and even the pace of decision-making act as implicit regulators of team nervous systems. For example, integrating micro-pauses into high-stimulation meetings, allowing asynchronous input to reduce cognitive overload, or pacing strategic decisions to align with energy cycles can all serve as systemic buffers. In this way, regulation becomes a personal competence and a cultural technology—one that determines whether a leadership system fosters resilience or reactivity. As such, co-regulation may be recognized as a core leadership function, bridging individual physiology with collective functionality (Dana, 2018; Siegel, 2020).

The following cross-state tools translate the concept of co-regulation into concrete practices that support individual and collective reset.

15.11 State-Specific Regulation Tools

The strategies help maintain nervous system balance during both heightened and depleted states.

These interventions support vagal tone and executive functioning (Dana, 2018; Porges, 2011). Practiced regularly, such micro-resets reduce reactivity and foster embodied presence. The following visual guide expands on these strategies with a broader set of state-specific tools—organized by affective need and designed for rapid nervous system recalibration. They can be used individually or integrated into daily leadership routines as part of nervous system hygiene.

Building on this awareness, effective self-regulation in leadership requires the ability to recognize, tolerate, interpret, and shift that state with intention. A helpful sequence involves noticing the dysregulation (*spot it*), allowing its physical and emotional presence (*feel it*), discerning its root cause or message (*decode it*), applying an appropriate intervention (*reset it*), and re-engaging with situational clarity (*re-enter with choice*). This process reframes regulation as a responsive relational access—anchored in somatic literacy and aligned with neurodivergent variation.

While the sequence of regulation is consistent, the pathways into it differ. The following Reset Languages™ outline five core modalities through which individuals access regulation based on sensory and cognitive preferences (Figure 15.3).

Nervous System Reset Guide

Quick resets to shift in under 2 minutes.

RESISTANCE → Start

- ☐ Break task into micro-actions
- ☐ 2-min timer → "just begin"
- ☐ Say: "I can do this imperfectly."
- ☐ Write down why this task matters
- ☐ Splash water / hold ice

ANGER → Cool

- ☐ Exhale longer than you inhale
- ☐ Walk out of the room
- ☐ Ice or cold water on neck or wrists
- ☐ Put your hand on something solid
- ☐ Instrumental playlist → low BPM

FEAR → Anchor

- ☐ 5-4-3-2-1 grounding scan
- ☐ Feet flat, name the sensation
- ☐ Sing! Fear & singing can't coexist
- ☐ One hand on heart, one on forehead
- ☐ Re-read purpose or "why"

OVERSTIMULATION → Pause

- ☐ Mute notifications + phone
- ☐ Close your eyes 30 sec. & breathe
- ☐ Stretch or do 5 jumping jacks
- ☐ Gratitude: write 3 things going right
- ☐ Brown noise, rain or silence (noise cancelling headphones)

RELAXATION → Protect

- ☐ Block out 90 minutes for deep work
- ☐ Turn down noise—ambient or silence
- ☐ Box breathing (4-4-4-4)
- ☐ Warm drink = parasympathetic
- ☐ Touch a grounding object

GRATITUDE → Rewire

- ☐ Gratitude: write 3 things going right
- ☐ Send a thank-you to someone
- ☐ Touch natural things: wood, stone..
- ☐ Hum or sing a bit
- ☐ Step outside—reset in sunlight

Figure 15.2 Nervous System Reset Guide: Quick Interventions to Shift State in Under Two Minutes.

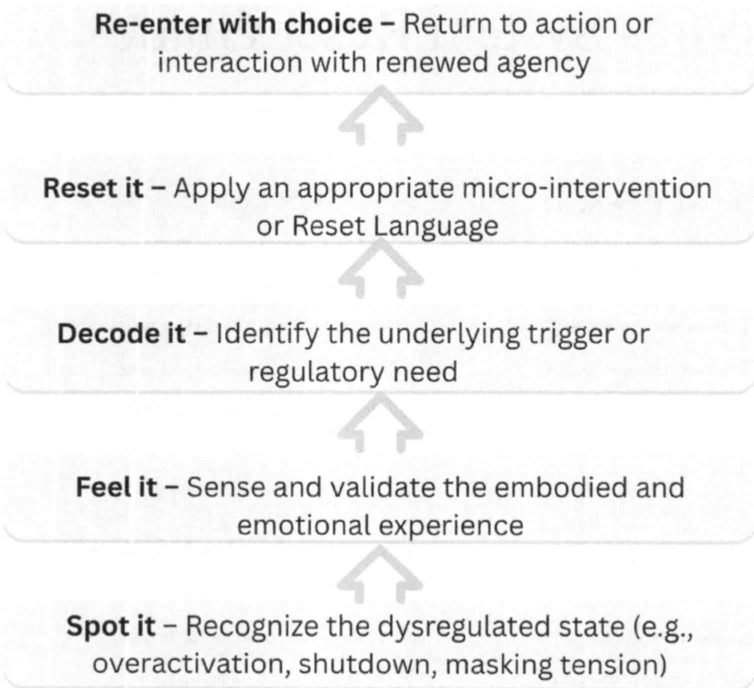

Figure 15.3 The Five-Step Reset Sequence. A concise framework for real-time self-regulation in leadership: spot dysregulation, feel it somatically, decode its trigger, reset through intervention, and re-enter with choice.

15.12 Reset Languages—Individualizing Somatic Regulation in Leadership

Understanding your re-entry path: The 5 Reset Languages of self-regulation.

While autonomic states follow shared patterns, the path back to regulation varies widely. Leaders differ in their stress responses but also in the sensory and cognitive modalities that best support re-regulation. These modalities often align with the five foundational sensory systems—touch, sound, movement, visual-spatial orientation, and verbal processing—each offering a unique access point into nervous system recovery. This diversity becomes particularly salient in neurodivergent contexts, where conventional tools like breathwork or mindfulness may be ineffective—or even counterproductive (Porges, 2011; Dana, 2018).

The 5 Reset Languages™ model offers a heuristic strategy for identifying one's dominant regulatory pathways—practical entry points for restoring internal safety and executive function.

1. **Cognitive Reset**—Reframing, scripting, structured decision trees, or affirmations. Especially effective for individuals with high metacognitive awareness or a preference for verbal processing (Siegel, 2020).
2. **Movement-Based Reset**—Physical action ranging from subtle gestures (toe tapping) to full-body engagement (walking, dancing). Beneficial for kinetic thinkers or those prone to dorsal collapse.
3. **Tactile Reset**—Regulation through touch: grounding objects, pressure, or self-contact. Particularly helpful for sensory-sensitive individuals or those recovering from dissociative patterns (Ogden et al., 2006).
4. **Auditory Reset**—Use of soundscapes, humming, music, or rhythmic stimuli to restore ventral vagal tone. Often underutilized yet potent, especially for auditory-dominant processors (Porges, 2011).
5. **Spatial/Orientation-Based Reset**—Shifting physical location, changing visual focus, or reestablishing spatial boundaries. This reset mode is critical for those sensitive to environmental cues or visual overstimulation (Kranowitz, 2005).

Understanding personal Reset Languages enables more effective self-regulation. When shared within teams, this awareness enhances mutual coordination and stress resilience under pressure (Figure 15.4).

The diagram illustrates five distinct, overlapping modalities of nervous system regulation: Cognitive, Movement, Tactile, Auditory, and Spatial. Each represents a biologically grounded entry point for re-regulation, underscoring that effective stress recovery is not one-size-fits-all, but modality-specific. The model invites leaders and teams to normalize their preferred "reset language" as part of an inclusive regulation toolkit.

15.12.1 Productive Activation: Reframing Arousal in Leadership Regulation

High activation remains functional when connection is intact.

Discourse on nervous system regulation often centers on calming practices designed to restore a parasympathetic baseline. While essential for recovery, this focus can inadvertently pathologize high-energy states that are, when directed, adaptive and empowering.

Neurobiologically, sympathetic arousal is not inherently dysregulating—it becomes problematic when chronic, unmanaged, or disconnected from intentional purpose. Leaders frequently need access to mobilized states such as focused urgency, assertiveness, or boundary setting—forms

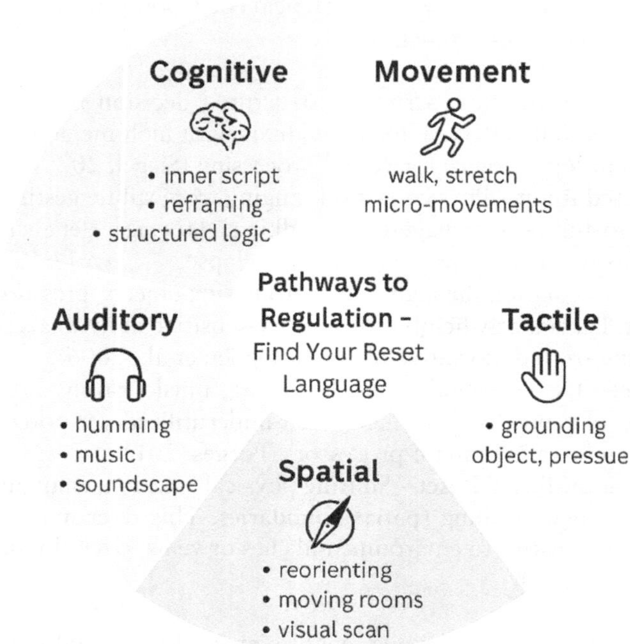

Figure 15.4 The 5 Reset Languages™

Developed by the author, this model draws on neuroscience and somatic regulation research (Porges, 2011; Dana, 2018; Siegel, 2020) but introduces an original typology.

of heightened arousal that are regulated, goal-aligned, and socially attuned (Boyatzis et al., 2012).

Emotions like anger or agitation, when metabolized rather than suppressed or discharged, can catalyze strategic clarity and principled action. Regulation, in this sense, is not about minimizing intensity, but integrating it while maintaining executive and relational coherence.

This reframing is particularly vital for neurodivergent professionals, many of whom have been conditioned to suppress affect as a prerequisite for workplace acceptance. Reclaiming "productive activation" thus becomes both a somatic and political act—affirming agency without erasing emotional expression.

15.12.2 Leadership Implication

Effective leaders distinguish between intensity and dysregulation. Rather than equating calm with competence, they develop the capacity to discern when heightened states carry signal—and when they require recalibration.

Regulation, ultimately, is the capacity to remain relationally present across the full spectrum of human affect.

While productive activation can support clarity and assertiveness, not all forms of high engagement are intentional or adaptive. In neurodivergent professionals especially, sustained overactivation may signal a deeper regulatory challenge—where work, perfectionism, or hyper-functioning operate less as performance strategies and more as unrecognized self-medication.

15.13 Beyond the Usual Suspects: Addiction, Self-Medication, and Functional Dysregulation in Neurodivergent Leadership

Why neurodivergent professionals are more prone to invisible addictions—and what that means for leadership culture.

Due to differences in nervous system regulation, interoception, sensory sensitivity, and emotional processing, neurodivergent professionals are statistically more vulnerable to both substance-based and behavioral forms of addiction (Maté, 2022; Sussman & Sussman, 2011). While addiction is typically associated with alcohol, stimulants, or opioids, the pathways into dependency are often more diffuse and socially masked in neurodivergent individuals.

While substances remain a concern, they are not the only domain where dependency forms. Hidden in plain sight are "functional" addictions: excessive work, compulsive exercise, doomscrolling, perfectionism, or relentless emotional caretaking. These behaviors are not merely bad habits or lifestyle choices. They often function as biologically driven self-regulation strategies in the absence of more adaptive alternatives—especially for individuals navigating executive dysfunction, trauma adaptation, or chronic masking demands (Porges, 2011; Kapp, 2020).

These patterns can have systemic ripple effects. Leaders who self-medicate through excessive productivity, hyperavailability, or perfectionism inadvertently model dysregulation as the norm. Teams mirror these rhythms, interpreting overextension as excellence. Over time, organizations internalize emotional suppression, urgency, and exhaustion as cultural values and not as red flags (Dana, 2018; Van der Kolk, 2014).

In high-performing individuals, early signs of behavioral self-medication—such as guilt-laden rest, emotional rigidity, post-effort crashes, or compulsive helpfulness—are often misread as dedication. Yet these patterns indicate systemic dysregulation. Leadership becomes sustainable when regulation is treated as a design principle embedded in daily practice.

To understand the roots of these patterns—and identify meaningful points of intervention—it is necessary to look beyond observable behavior.

Leadership emerges not solely from intention or action, but from underlying biochemical states. The following chapter examines how neurochemical messengers such as dopamine, serotonin, oxytocin, and cortisol influence clarity, motivation, emotional accessibility, and relational presence. Regulation, in this view, is as much a neurobiological condition as it is a behavioral practice.

References

Arnsten, A. F. T. (2009). Stress signalling pathways that impair prefrontal cortex structure and function. *Nature Reviews Neuroscience, 10*(6), 410–422. https://doi.org/10.1038/nrn2648

Boyatzis, R. E., Rochford, K., & Taylor, S. N. (2015). The role of the positive emotional attractor in vision and shared vision: Toward effective leadership, relationships, and engagement. *Frontiers in Psychology, 6*, 670. https://doi.org/10.3389/fpsyg.2015.00670

Boyatzis, R. E., Smith, M. L., & Beveridge, A. J. (2012). Coaching with compassion: Inspiring health, well-being, and development in organizations. *The Journal of Applied Behavioral Science*, *49*(2), 153–178. https://doi.org/10.1177/0021886312462236

Buss, A. H., & Plomin, R. (1984). *Temperament: Early developing personality traits*. Lawrence Erlbaum Associates.

Carver, C. S., Scheier, M. F., & Weintraub, J. K. (1989). Assessing coping strategies: A theoretically based approach. *Journal of Personality and Social Psychology, 56*(2), 267–283. https://doi.org/10.1037/0022-3514.56.2.267

Dana, D. (2018). *The Polyvagal Theory in therapy: Engaging the rhythm of regulation*. W. W. Norton & Company.

Edmondson, A. C. (2019). *The fearless organization: Creating psychological safety in the workplace for learning, innovation, and growth*. Wiley.

Kapp, S. K. (Ed.). (2020). *Autistic community and the neurodiversity movement: Stories from the frontline*. Springer. https://doi.org/10.1007/978-981-13-8437-0

Kranowitz, C. S. (2005). *The out-of-sync child: Recognizing and coping with sensory processing disorder* (Rev. ed.). Perigee.

Maté, G. (2022). *The myth of normal: Trauma, illness, and healing in a toxic culture*. Avery.

McEwen, B. S. (2007). Physiology and neurobiology of stress and adaptation: Central role of the brain. *Physiological Reviews, 87*(3), 873–904. https://doi.org/10.1152/physrev.00041.2006

Ogden, P., Minton, K., & Pain, C. (2006). *Trauma and the body: A sensorimotor approach to psychotherapy*. W. W. Norton & Company.

Porges, S. W. (2011). *The polyvagal theory: Neurophysiological foundations of emotions, attachment, communication, and self-regulation*. W. W. Norton & Company.

Siegel, D. J. (2020). *The developing mind: How relationships and the brain interact to shape who we are* (3rd ed.). Guilford Press.

Sussman, S., & Sussman, A. N. (2011). Considering the definition of addiction. *International Journal of Environmental Research and Public Health, 8*(10), 4025–4038. https://doi.org/10.3390/ijerph8104025

van der Kolk, B. A. (2014). *The body keeps the score: Brain, mind, and body in the healing of trauma*. Viking.

Chapter 16

The Neuroscience of Gentle Leadership

The Neurochemical Basis of Leadership

16.1 Leadership Is Biochemical before It Is Behavioral

Before the mindset shifts, the molecules move.

While this chapter is embedded within a broader neuroinclusive leadership framework, its insights extend far beyond neurodivergent profiles. Neurotransmitter regulation shapes all human behavior—and in leadership, it directly impacts focus, resilience, emotional presence, and decision-making.

Understanding how dopamine, serotonin, and other neurochemicals function is not a theoretical detour. While dysregulation in these systems often plays a role in neurodivergent experience, every leader benefits from knowing the biological drivers behind clarity, motivation, and regulation. This chapter offers a shared vocabulary to detect inner shifts, interpret overload, and regain coherence when things feel out of sync.

Think of it as a biochemical toolkit: part self-leadership primer, part re-entry companion—for moments when your internal signals feel scrambled and you need a physiological compass.

Leadership is not only a matter of mindset—it is fundamentally embodied. Every act of courage, every emotionally intelligent response, every complex decision is shaped by the real-time interplay of neurochemicals in the brain (McEwen, 1998; Palmiter, 2008). These molecules aren't background noise—they're the backstage crew running the show.

Neuroleadership, at the intersection of neuroscience and leadership practice, demands more than cognitive strategies. It calls for physiological awareness: an attunement to the biological levers behind presence, pacing, and relational intelligence (Rock & Ringleb, 2013). Leaders who understand these rhythms are better equipped to build resilient teams and foster psychological safety.

This chapter explores key neurotransmitters that shape how we lead. From dopamine's drive and serotonin's stability to oxytocin's bonding and

DOI: 10.4324/9781003681540-19

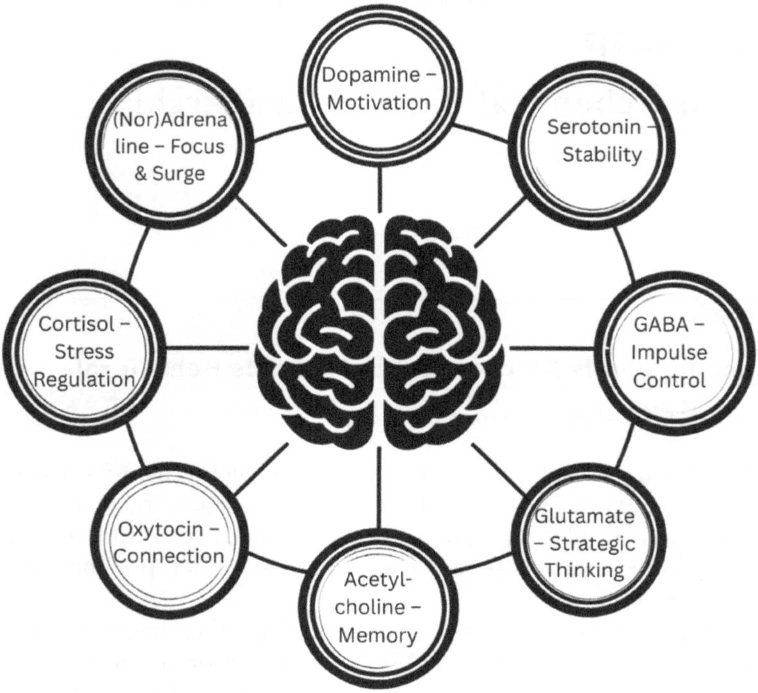

Figure 16.1 Core neurotransmitters relevant to leadership behavior and regulation.

cortisol's pressure response, these chemical messengers offer a powerful new lens for sustainable, embodied leadership (Figure 16.1).

16.2 Core Neurotransmitters and Their Leadership Functions

Neurochemical Foundations of Leadership Behavior and Decision-Making.

16.2.1 Dopamine and Leadership: Reward, Momentum, and Strategic Drive

Dopamine is a catecholamine neurotransmitter essential to the brain's mesolimbic reward system. It facilitates motivation, novelty-seeking, reinforcement learning, and goal-directed behavior by modulating prefrontal cortical activity (Schultz, 2007; Palmiter, 2008; Berridge & Robinson, 1998). In leadership contexts, well-regulated dopaminergic functioning enables strategic visioning, scenario planning, and high motivational drive.

This is particularly the case in uncertain or exploratory environments. Leaders with balanced dopamine cycles often act as momentum generators, sustaining team energy through enthusiasm, persistence, and a clear sense of directional progress.

Dopamine is activated by stimuli such as task completion, learning challenges, and social recognition (Schultz, 2015; Lisman & Grace, 2005; Kampe et al., 2001). These experiences reinforce adaptive leadership behaviors through dopaminergic feedback loops, increasing engagement and goal pursuit. However, under chronic stress or environmental monotony, dopamine regulation may be disrupted. Downregulation is associated with disengagement, decision inertia, and strategic fatigue (Pizzagalli, 2014), while overstimulation can result in impulsivity, tunnel vision, or reward-chasing behaviors disconnected from long-term reasoning (Volkow et al., 2011).

Sustainable leadership does not require perpetual activation; rather, it requires intelligent pacing. Designing work environments that offer cognitive reward—through novelty, feedback, and milestone structuring—helps maintain dopaminergic momentum without tipping into hyperarousal. In this sense, dopamine is not simply fuel for drive and should be understood as a regulator of meaningful progress.

16.2.2 Serotonin: The Neurochemical Anchor of Social Stability

Serotonin (5-HT) is a monoamine neurotransmitter that modulates mood, behavioral inhibition, and social cohesion by integrating cognitive, emotional, and somatic signals (Carver et al., 2008; Young, 2007). Functioning across both brain and gut, it serves as a neurobiological stabilizer—dampening reactivity, supporting impulse control, and fostering relational safety. In leadership contexts, balanced serotonergic tone enables emotional steadiness under pressure, subtle recalibration of group affect, and a calming presence that de-escalates interpersonal tension.

Unlike charisma-driven leadership, serotonin-supported leaders rarely dominate the room. Their influence is regulatory: they model emotional self-containment, maintain connection without overflow, and cultivate climates of psychological safety. These stabilizing behaviors become especially critical during periods of volatility or transition.

Serotonin levels can be supported by predictable rhythms, rhythmic movement, natural light exposure, and acts of social reciprocity (Lambert et al., 2002; Kringelbach & Berridge, 2009). Though often overlooked in performance cultures, such inputs are not indulgent. Healthy serotonin levels regulate processes that can that sustain team coherence and executive presence in professional contexts.

Conversely, serotonin depletion—caused by chronic stress, circadian disruption, or gut-brain imbalance—can lead to rigidity, irritability, or emotional withdrawal (Maes et al., 2011; Gershon, 1998).

16.2.3 Oxytocin: The Neurochemical Glue of Trust and Belonging

Oxytocin is a hypothalamically produced neuropeptide that facilitates social bonding, empathy, and prosocial behavior by modulating affective attunement and interpersonal safety (Heinrichs et al., 2009). Often dubbed the "bonding hormone," it strengthens relational coherence by synchronizing emotional cues, fostering group identification, and reinforcing affiliative behavior. In leadership contexts, oxytocin supports calm authority, mutual trust, and psychological safety, particularly during collective stress or interpersonal friction.

Oxytocin-rich leaders exhibit presence-based influence: they regulate not by exertion, but through attunement. Their leadership is characterized by emotional availability, subtle affective mirroring, and a capacity to stabilize team climate without overcontrol. This fosters durable commitment, interpersonal loyalty, and a sense of belonging that anchors teams through complexity.

Moreover, oxytocin can be supported through co-regulative practices such as relational rituals (e.g., check-ins, appreciation), physical proximity, shared laughter, or acts of mutual aid. These are not sentimental gestures; instead, they are biologically grounded mechanisms that strengthen trust building and cohesion (Coan & Sbarra, 2015).

Often due to chronic stress, social isolation, or emotionally dissonant environments, diminished oxytocin may manifest not as overt dysfunction but relational distance, over-intellectualization, or flattened emotional tone. In teams, this erodes trust and undermines psychological resilience, even when performance remains superficially intact.

16.2.4 GABA: The Neurochemical Brake behind Impulse Control and Composure

Gamma-aminobutyric acid (GABA) is the brain's primary inhibitory neurotransmitter. It is responsible for dampening excessive neural excitation and facilitating attentional regulation, mood stabilization, and impulse control (Nemeroff, 2003; Tanaka et al., 2013). Unlike excitatory transmitters that mobilize action, GABA enables strategic inhibition and provides the neurobiological basis for pausing, reflecting, and responding with intention.

In leadership contexts, sufficient GABA tone manifests as composed presence, emotional containment, and reduced cognitive reactivity under pressure. These leaders demonstrate regulated responses in conflict, clarity without urgency, and the capacity to create psychological space in high-demand moments. Rather than suppressing emotion, they metabolize it and manage to offer their teams a buffer against collective escalation.

GABA is supported by parasympathetic-aligned practices such as breathwork, rhythmic movement, adequate sleep, and specific micronutrients (e.g., magnesium, B6, L-theanine). Its regulatory effects are subtle yet essential: not dramatic like adrenaline, but stabilizing in complex, ambiguity-laden environments.

When downregulated through chronic overstimulation, multitasking, sleep deficits, or stimulant overuse—GABA loss may present as irritability, impulsivity, or diminished executive control. Such patterns can mimic high energy but undermine sustainable leadership clarity.

16.2.5 Glutamate: The Cognitive Catalyst behind Strategic Leadership

Glutamate is the brain's principal excitatory neurotransmitter, facilitating over 90% of synaptic signaling within the central nervous system (Platt, 2007). It underpins neuroplasticity, working memory, attention regulation, and higher-order executive function, particularly within the prefrontal cortex (Schousboe & Waagepetersen, 2005). In leadership contexts, glutamate fuels strategic synthesis: the capacity to integrate complexity, maintain cognitive endurance, and convert abstract insight into operational clarity.

Leaders with well-regulated glutamatergic tone exhibit sustained focus under pressure, adaptive problem-solving, and the ability to navigate ambiguity without fragmentation. Their cognition remains agile and cohesive, allowing for rapid scenario-shifting, systems thinking, and creative convergence of competing inputs.

Optimal activation occurs under meaningful cognitive challenge through deep work, novel learning, and purposeful complexity—not through overstimulation or multitasking. However, excessive glutamatergic activity can lead to excitotoxicity, characterized by hypervigilance, cognitive rigidity, and eventual depletion (Popoli et al., 2011). Without sufficient inhibitory balance (e.g., GABA), leaders risk slipping into overfunctioning states like tunnel vision, reactivity, and burnout.

16.2.6 Acetylcholine: The Strategic Memory Engine of Leadership

Acetylcholine is a key neuromodulator involved in attention, working memory, and neuroplasticity, particularly within the hippocampus and prefrontal cortex (Hasselmo, 2006; Ballinger et al., 2016). Unlike neurotransmitters that trigger arousal or reactivity, acetylcholine facilitates sustained cognitive precision. This allows leaders to retain context, navigate complexity, and synthesize information across multiple time frames.

Leaders with robust cholinergic tone often display high informational recall, strategic focus, and fluid integration of nuance and vision. Their leadership style is not an intense one but composed under cognitive load, which connects details to larger systems while maintaining clarity and deliberation.

Activation is supported through deep learning, undistracted focus, REM-rich sleep, and choline-rich nutrition (Zeisel & da Costa, 2009). Conversely, depletion via chronic multitasking, poor diet, or disrupted sleep cycles may erode cognitive sharpness and decision fluidity. Not, however, from a lack of competence, but from biochemical exhaustion.

In data-saturated or ambiguity-rich environments, acetylcholine enables leaders to pause, reflect, and respond with strategic precision. The neuromodulator underwrites leadership intelligence not by speed, but by synthesis.

16.2.7 Cortisol: The Biochemical Architecture of Acute Leadership Stress

Cortisol, a glucocorticoid released via the HPA axis, is the body's primary hormonal responder to acute stress. It enhances glucose mobilization, suppresses non-essential functions, and primes attentional resources for threat-related stimuli (McEwen, 2007). In leadership, this allows for rapid triage, strategic triaging, and emotional containment under pressure.

Temporarily elevated cortisol can sharpen executive focus and boost crisis performance. Leaders in this state often show heightened vigilance, decisiveness under uncertainty, and the ability to manage team affect in high-stakes contexts.

However, prolonged cortisol exposure disrupts neurocognitive function: it amplifies amygdala reactivity, dampens prefrontal reasoning, and erodes physiological resilience (McEwen & Gianaros, 2011; Arnsten, 2009). This may present as micromanagement, emotional detachment, or reduced empathy in work environments. These should not, however, be understood as character flaws, rather as physiological adaptations to unrelieved stress.

Sustainable leadership depends on recovery, not just endurance. Practices that downshift the nervous system are vagal-toning breathwork, post-stress decompression, and somatic awareness. They help complete the stress cycle and restore neurobiological integrity (Nagoski & Nagoski, 2019; Porges, 2011).

16.2.8 *Adrenaline and Noradrenaline: The Surge and the Filter of Acute Leadership*

Adrenaline (epinephrine) and noradrenaline (norepinephrine) are fast-acting catecholamines central to the body's acute stress response. Adrenaline drives physiological activation like elevated heart rate, respiration, and energy mobilization, while noradrenaline modulates attentional focus, signal filtering, and executive clarity (Berridge & Waterhouse, 2003; Goldstein, 2010).

In leadership, adrenaline supports bold, visible engagement in high-pressure moments, whereas noradrenaline enables cognitive precision under complexity. Optimal function allows leaders to act swiftly while maintaining discernment, reducing reactivity, and filtering distraction from priority.

However, prolonged activation leads to depletion: adrenaline overuse fosters urgency addiction and burnout; noradrenaline dysregulation can result in anxiety, rigidity, or executive shutdown. Leaders caught in chronic "surge mode" may conflate intensity with clarity, eroding both personal sustainability and team safety.

Strategic modulation of these systems by stimulus pacing, deep work, physical resets, and recovery rituals—enables leaders to shift from reaction to regulation. The goal should not be perpetual readiness, but responsive presence.

16.3 A Compact Overview of Eight Core Neurochemical Systems

Exploring their relevance for executive function, regulation, and relational leadership.

The following overview consolidates the eight most influential neurochemical systems for leadership practice, highlighting how each shapes drive, regulation, and relational capacity. By linking triggers and inhibitors to functional outcomes, the table provides a practical reference for understanding how biochemical dynamics underpin executive clarity and team presence (Table 16.1).

As a synthesis of the preceding neurochemical profiles, the following visual outlines simple, workplace-adapted micro-interventions that activate each of the four core neurotransmitters—dopamine, oxytocin, serotonin, and endorphins. While not exhaustive, this "Daily D.O.S.E." framework offers a practical entry point for leaders and teams to engage in intentional self-regulation and neurochemical resilience throughout the workday (Figure 16.2).

Table 16.1 Key biochemical systems influencing motivation, regulation, and relational leadership dynamics.

Neurotransmitter	*Role*	*Activates via…*	*Suppressed by…*
Dopamine	Drive and Motivation	Goals, novelty, recognition	Stress, monotony, overdrive
Serotonin	Stability and Belonging	Rhythm, sunlight, connection	Sleep loss, inflammation
GABA	Impulse Control	Breath, stillness, deep sleep	Overstimulation, poor recovery
Adrenaline	Acute Action	Crisis, visibility, urgency	Chronic stress, burnout
Noradrenaline	Focus and Filtering	Challenge, cold, movement	Fatigue, stimulants, overload
Oxytocin	Trust and Connection	Eye contact, care, shared rituals	Isolation, fear-based culture
Glutamate	Strategic Thinking	Deep work, learning, synthesis	Exhaustion, overwhelm
Acetylcholine	Memory and Precision	Learning, REM sleep, choline	Multitasking, sleep disruption
Cortisol	Stress Regulation	Perceived threat, pressure, triage	Chronic elevation, no recovery phase

16.4 Nutritional Neurochemistry: Dietary Modulation of Neurotransmitter Function in Leadership

Fueling focus, stability, and resilience—one meal at a time.

Recent research in nutritional neuroscience suggests that dietary intake of specific macro- and micronutrients plays a critical role in regulating neurotransmitter synthesis, synaptic efficiency, and autonomic nervous system balance (Kennedy, 2016; Fernstrom, 2013). These biochemical mechanisms influence stress response, executive functioning, and affective regulation. Such factors are closely linked to leadership performance and resilience in complex environments.

For neurodivergent individuals, whose baseline arousal thresholds and sensory processing patterns may differ, nutritional interventions can provide important stabilization. Evidence-based approaches include nutritional support for GABAergic and serotonergic pathways to enhance regulatory capacity, or targeted modulation of stress-related systems such as the HPA axis via cortisol and noradrenaline regulation (Benton, 2002; Markus et al., 2000).

Daily D.O.S.E.-

Neurochemical Self-Support at Work

Dopamine → Accomplish

The "I did it" hormone.
Triggers: wins, progress, quick completion.

- Check off a micro-task
- Break big projects into tiny steps
- Set & cross off one clear goal
- Share a win (Slack counts)
- Use a 25-min focus sprint
- Take a coffee break after finishing

Oxytocin → Connect

The "we're in this together" hormone.
Triggers: kindness, emot. safety, real interaction.

- Compliment someone (or yourself)
- Play your go-to feel-good playlist
- Join co-working session or 1:1
- Massage your own hands
- Send a "thinking of you" message
- Pet your dog (Zoom or not)

Serotonin → Ground

The "I've got this" hormone.
Triggers: routine, light, calm, confidence.

- Step into daylight (even briefly)
- Add plants or scents to your space
- Take 3 deep breaths between tasks
- Do standing work for a block of time
- Buffer blocks ↓ context switching
- Write down 3 things that went well t

Endorphins → Move

The natural mood booster.
Triggers: motion, joy, rhythm.

- Stretch/ walk between tasks
- Laugh at something on purpose
- Have a square of dark chocolate
- Walk or pace during calls
- Music while doing admin
- Doodle, sketch, or scribble freely

Figure 16.2 Daily D.O.S.E.—Neurochemical Self-Support at Work. This visual outlines simple daily actions that activate dopamine, oxytocin, serotonin, and endorphins to support motivation, connection, calm, and mood in workplace settings.

The following table synthesizes current evidence on dietary influences across key neurotransmitters relevant to leadership performance and neurodivergent well-being.

Table 16.2 A concise summary of foods that support or hinder neurotransmitters relevant to leadership focus, regulation, and resilience.

Neurotransmitter	*Function*	*Boosting foods (positive effects)*	*Inhibiting foods (negative effects)*
Dopamine	Motivation, focus, reward anticipation	Bananas, lean proteins (chicken, turkey, fish), dark chocolate, avocados, green tea (L-theanine)	Ultra-processed foods, artificial sweeteners (e.g., aspartame), excess alcohol
Serotonin	Mood regulation, well-being, emotional stability	Bananas, nuts and seeds, fatty fish, whole grains, leafy greens (magnesium)	Refined sugars, trans fats, excess caffeine, diet sodas
Oxytocin	Social bonding, trust, connection	Strawberries, watermelon, dark chocolate, dairy	Fast food, high-fat diets, artificial sweeteners, social isolation
GABA	Calmness, emotional regulation, inhibition of overexcitation	Green tea, avocados, almonds, spinach, shellfish	Excess caffeine, sugar, alcohol
Glutamate	Cognitive processing, learning, excitation	Lean meats, eggs, nuts, broccoli	MSG, alcohol, high-sugar diets
Acetylcholine	Memory, attention, learning capacity	Eggs, peanuts, Brussels sprouts, fatty fish, cheese	Smoking, processed foods, preservatives
Cortisol	Stress response, energy mobilization	Dark chocolate, leafy greens, berries, nuts	Refined sugars, excess caffeine, energy drinks, processed foods
Adrenaline	Acute stress response, alertness	Protein, healthy fats, dark chocolate, herbal teas	Sugar, excess caffeine, processed junk food
Noradrenaline	Focus, vigilance, response to challenge	Green tea, avocados, lean meats	Excess caffeine, sugar crashes, alcohol

16.5 Nutritional Influences on Neurotransmitter Activity in Leadership Contexts

Nourishment functions as a lever for enhancing focus, mood stability, and executive functioning in leadership contexts.

Nutritional factors directly shape the balance of neurotransmitter systems, influencing attention, emotional regulation, and resilience in leadership practice. By connecting specific foods with their enhancing or inhibiting effects, the table below translates biochemical pathways into accessible choices that support sustainable executive functioning (Table 16.2).

16.5.1 From Chemistry to Coherence: Integrating the Layers of Leadership Regulation

While nutritional modulation offers a biochemical entry point into regulation, it represents just one layer of a much broader architecture. Sustainable leadership, particularly for neurodivergent individuals, requires an integrated approach. One that spans nervous system literacy, relational dynamics, structural elasticity, and physiological care.

What emerges is not a prescriptive formula, but a multilayered model of self-leadership in which internal regulation becomes both a personal strategy and a collective responsibility.

The following conclusion synthesizes these threads and outlines key implications for the future of inclusive, regulation-informed leadership.

References

Arnsten, A. F. T. (2009). Stress signalling pathways that impair prefrontal cortex structure and function. *Nature Reviews Neuroscience*, *10*(6), 410–422. https://doi.org/10.1038/nrn2648

Ballinger, E. C., Ananth, M., Talmage, D. A., & Role, L. W. (2016). Basal forebrain cholinergic circuits and signaling in cognition and cognitive decline. *Neuron*, *91*(6), 1199–1218. https://doi.org/10.1016/j.neuron.2016.09.006

Benton, D. (2002). Carbohydrate ingestion, blood glucose and mood. *Neuroscience & Biobehavioral Reviews*, *26*(3), 293–308. https://doi.org/10.1016/S0149-7634(02)00004-0

Berridge, K. C., & Robinson, T. E. (1998). What is the role of dopamine in reward: Hedonic impact, reward learning, or incentive salience? *Brain Research Reviews*, *28*(3), 309–369. https://doi.org/10.1016/S0165-0173(98)00019-8

Berridge, C. W., & Waterhouse, B. D. (2003). The locus coeruleus–noradrenergic system: Modulation of behavioral state and state-dependent cognitive processes. *Brain Research Reviews*, *42*(1), 33–84. https://doi.org/10.1016/S0165-0173(03)00143-7

Carver, C. S., Johnson, S. L., & Joormann, J. (2008). Serotonergic function, two-mode models of self-regulation, and vulnerability to depression: What depression has in common with impulsive aggression. *Psychological Bulletin*, *134*(6), 912–943. https://doi.org/10.1037/a0013740

Coan, J. A., & Sbarra, D. A. (2015). Social baseline theory: The role of social proximity in emotion and economy of action. *Social and Personality Psychology Compass*, *9*(10), 505–517. https://doi.org/10.1111/spc3.12205

Fernstrom, J. D. (2013). Large neutral amino acids: Dietary effects on brain neurochemistry and function. *Amino Acids*, *45*(3), 419–430. https://doi.org/10.1007/s00726-012-1330-y

Gershon, M. D. (1998). *The second brain: A groundbreaking new understanding of nervous disorders of the stomach and intestine*. HarperCollins.

Goldstein, D. S. (2010). Adrenal responses to stress. *Cellular and Molecular Neurobiology*, *30*(8), 1433–1440. https://doi.org/10.1007/s10571-010-9606-9

Hasselmo, M. E. (2006). The role of acetylcholine in learning and memory. *Current Opinion in Neurobiology*, *16*(6), 710–715. https://doi.org/10.1016/j.conb.2006.09.002

Heinrichs, M., von Dawans, B., & Domes, G. (2009). Oxytocin, vasopressin, and human social behavior. *Frontiers in Neuroendocrinology*, *30*(4), 548–557. https://doi.org/10.1016/j.yfrne.2009.05.005

Kampe, K. K. W., Frith, C. D., Dolan, R. J., & Frith, U. (2001). Reward value of attractiveness and gaze. *Nature*, *413*(6856), 589. https://doi.org/10.1038/35098149

Kennedy, D. O. (2016). B Vitamins and the brain: Mechanisms, dose and efficacy—A review. *Nutrients*, *8*(2), 68. https://doi.org/10.3390/nu8020068

Kringelbach, M. L., & Berridge, K. C. (2009). Towards a functional neuroanatomy of pleasure and happiness. *Trends in Cognitive Sciences*, *13*(11), 479–487. https://doi.org/10.1016/j.tics.2009.08.006

Lambert, G. W., Reid, C., Kaye, D. M., Jennings, G. L., & Esler, M. D. (2002). Effect of sunlight and season on serotonin turnover in the brain. *The Lancet*, *360*(9348), 1840–1842. https://doi.org/10.1016/S0140-6736(02)11737-5

Lisman, J. E., & Grace, A. A. (2005). The hippocampal-VTA loop: Controlling the entry of information into long-term memory. *Neuron*, *46*(5), 703–713. https://doi.org/10.1016/j.neuron.2005.05.002

Maes, M., Kubera, M., & Leunis, J. C. (2011). The gut-brain barrier in major depression: Intestinal mucosal dysfunction with an increased translocation of LPS from gram-negative enterobacteria (leaky gut) plays a role in the inflammatory pathophysiology of depression. *Neuro Endocrinology Letters*, *32*(1), 117–124.

Markus, C. R., Olivier, B., & de Haan, E. H. F. (2000). Whey protein rich in alpha-lactalbumin increases the ratio of plasma tryptophan to the sum of the other large neutral amino acids and improves cognitive performance in stress-vulnerable subjects. *The American Journal of Clinical Nutrition*, *71*(6), 1536–1544. https://doi.org/10.1093/ajcn/71.6.1536

McEwen, B. S. (1998). Stress, adaptation, and disease: Allostasis and allostatic load. *Annals of the New York Academy of Sciences*, *840*(1), 33–44. https://doi.org/10.1111/j.1749-6632.1998.tb09546.x

McEwen, B. S. (2007). Physiology and neurobiology of stress and adaptation: Central role of the brain. *Physiological Reviews*, *87*(3), 873–904. https://doi.org/10.1152/physrev.00041.2006

McEwen, B. S., & Gianaros, P. J. (2011). Stress- and allostasis-induced brain plasticity. *Annual Review of Medicine*, *62*, 431–445. https://doi.org/10.1146/annurev-med-052209-100430

Nagoski, E., & Nagoski, A. (2019). *Burnout: The secret to unlocking the stress cycle*. Ballantine Books.

Nemeroff, C. B. (2003). The role of GABA in the pathophysiology and treatment of anxiety disorders. *Psychopharmacology Bulletin*, *37*(4), 133–146.

Palmiter, R. D. (2008). Dopamine signaling in the dorsal striatum is essential for motivated behaviors: Lessons from dopamine-deficient mice. *Annals of the New York Academy of Sciences*, *1129*(1), 35–46. https://doi.org/10.1196/annals.1417.003

Platt, S. R. (2007). The role of glutamate in central nervous system health and disease—A review. *Veterinary Journal*, *173*(2), 278–286. https://doi.org/10.1016/j.tvjl.2005.11.008

Pizzagalli, D. A. (2014). Depression, stress, and anhedonia: Toward a synthesis and integrated model. *Annual Review of Clinical Psychology*, *10*, 393–423. https://doi.org/10.1146/annurev-clinpsy-050212-185606

Popoli, M., Yan, Z., McEwen, B. S., & Sanacora, G. (2011). The stressed synapse: The impact of stress and glucocorticoids on glutamate transmission. *Nature Reviews Neuroscience*, *13*(1), 22–37. https://doi.org/10.1038/nrn3138

Porges, S. W. (2011). *The polyvagal theory: Neurophysiological foundations of emotions, attachment, communication, and self-regulation*. W. W. Norton.

Rock, D., & Ringleb, A. (2013). *Handbook of neuroleadership*. NeuroLeadership Institute.

Schousboe, A., & Waagepetersen, H. S. (2005). Role of astrocytes in glutamate homeostasis: Implications for excitotoxicity. *Neurotoxicity Research*, *8*(3–4), 221–225. https://doi.org/10.1007/BF03033802

Schultz, W. (2007). Behavioral dopamine signals. *Trends in Neurosciences*, *30*(5), 203–210. https://doi.org/10.1016/j.tins.2007.03.007

Schultz, W. (2015). Neuronal reward and decision signals: From theories to data. *Physiological Reviews*, *95*(3), 853–951. https://doi.org/10.1152/physrev.00023.2014

Tanaka, M., Yoshida, M., Emoto, H., & Ishii, H. (2013). Noradrenaline and serotonin involvement in the rat lateral habenula in the learned helplessness model of depression. *Behavioural Brain Research*, *256*, 472–478. https://doi.org/10.1016/j.bbr.2013.09.021

Volkow, N. D., Wang, G. J., Fowler, J. S., & Tomasi, D. (2011). Addiction circuitry in the human brain. *Annual Review of Pharmacology and Toxicology*, *52*, 321–336. https://doi.org/10.1146/annurev-pharmtox-010611-134625

Young, S. N. (2007). How to increase serotonin in the human brain without drugs. *Journal of Psychiatry & Neuroscience*, *32*(6), 394–399.

Zeisel, S. H., & da Costa, K. A. (2009). Choline: An essential nutrient for public health. *Nutrition Reviews*, *67*(11), 615–623. https://doi.org/10.1111/j.1753-4887.2009.00246.x

Conclusion

Rethinking Leadership, Rewriting the Norm

As outlined throughout this book, neurodivergence is no marginal concern. It shapes how people lead, decide, relate, and sustain performance across every sector and level of responsibility. Its significance has rarely been absent—only overlooked, misread, or structurally unacknowledged.

Quantifying its prevalence remains difficult. Many neurodivergent profiles overlap, shift across life stages, or remain masked under layers of coping. Mixed configurations defy diagnostic clarity, and recorded rates often reflect who has access to recognition—not who is affected. Far too often, insight arrives only late in life, if at all. Even figures with high visibility and specialist access—such as Sir Anthony Hopkins, who received an autism diagnosis in his later years—illustrate how long it can take to name what has always been present.

For many, the issue is not a lack of traits but a lack of language. Misalignment is experienced long before it is understood. And while categories offer structure, what leaders often need first is resonance—a way to map their experience without shame or reduction.

This book proposes a reframing of leadership: one that does not demand assimilation into legacy norms, but rethinks those norms through the lens of regulation, cognitive rhythm, and relational integrity.

Traits frequently pathologized in neurodivergent individuals—such as deep focus, pattern sensitivity, or ethical intensity—are often the same capacities that drive innovation, foresight, and trust. When these traits clash with systems, the fault lies less in the individual than in a lack of structural accommodation.

Cognitive strain, communicative misfires, or cycles of exhaustion are not signs of personal inadequacy. They are signals—indicating a need for redesign, not self-erasure.

Leadership cultures that prioritize conformity over clarity end up limiting both people and outcomes. To support sustained, inclusive leadership,

DOI: 10.4324/9781003681540-20

organizations must move from reactive accommodation toward proactive integration. This includes embedding psychological safety, embracing communicative diversity, and aligning responsibility with individual regulatory capacity.

Gentle Leading™ offers a framework for this shift—an approach to leadership that values coherence over compliance, and presence over performativity.

Ultimately, leadership is more than the execution of tasks.

It is a relationship we cultivate—with others, and with our own nervous systems.

I look forward to what awareness will unfold—personally, collectively, and systemically.

Index

For Product Safety Concerns and Information please contact our EU representative GPSR@taylorandfrancis.com Taylor & Francis Verlag GmbH, Kaufingerstraße 24, 80331 München, Germany